READINGS IN PHILOSOPHICAL AESTHETICS

Edited by

Barry Allen
McMaster University

© 2017

TABLE OF CONTENTS

PLATO
Symposium 1
Republic 10

ARISTOTLE
Poetics 28

PLOTINUS
Concerning the Beautiful . . . 35

DAVID HUME
The Standard of Taste 45

IMMANUEL KANT
Critique of Aesthetic Judgment 57

G. W. F. HEGEL
The Philosophy of Fine Art 107

ARTHUR SCHOPENHAUER
The Metaphysics of Fine Art 124

FRIEDRICH NIETZSCHE
The Birth of Tragedy 132

HENRI BERGSON
Laughter: An Essay on the Meaning of the Comic 181

MICHEL FOUCAULT
This Is Not A Pipe 267

PLATO
SYMPOSIUM

Translated by Benjamin Jowett

[Excerpt: Socrates recounts a speech he heard as a young man from Diotima, a priestess from Mantineia.]

And now I would rehearse a tale of love which I heard from Diotima of Mantineia, a woman wise in this and in many other kinds of knowledge, who in the days of old, when the Athenians offered sacrifice before the coming of the plague, delayed the disease ten years. She was my instructress in the art of love, and I shall repeat to you what she said to me, beginning with the admissions made by Agathon, which are nearly if not quite the same which I made to the wise woman when she questioned me: I think that this will be the easiest way, and I shall take both parts myself as well as I can.

As you, Agathon, suggested, I must speak first of the being and nature of Love, and then of his works. First I said to her in nearly the same words which he used to me, that Love was a mighty god, and likewise fair; and she proved to me as I proved to him that, by my own showing, Love was neither fair nor good. 'What do you mean, Diotima,' I said, 'is love then evil and foul?' 'Hush,' she cried; 'must that be foul which is not fair?' 'Certainly,' I said. 'And is that which is not wise, ignorant? do you not see that there is a mean between wisdom and ignorance?' 'And what may that be?' I said. 'Right opinion,' she replied; 'which, as you know, being incapable of giving a reason, is not knowledge (for how can knowledge be devoid of reason? nor again, ignorance, for neither can ignorance attain the truth), but is clearly something which is a mean between ignorance and wisdom.'

'Quite true,' I replied. 'Do not then insist,' she said, 'that what is not fair is of necessity foul, or what is not good evil; or infer that because love is not fair and good he is therefore foul and evil; for he is in a mean between them.' 'Well,' I said, 'Love is surely admitted by all to be a great god.' 'By those who know or by those who do not know?' 'By all.' 'And how, Socrates,' she said with a smile, 'can Love be acknowledged to be a great god by those who say that he is not a god at all?' 'And who are they?' I said. 'You and I are two of them,' she replied. 'How can that be?' I said. 'It is quite intelligible,' she replied; 'for you yourself would acknowledge that the gods are happy and fair—of course you would—would you dare to say that any god was not?' 'Certainly not,' I replied. 'And you mean by the happy, those who are the possessors of things good or fair?' 'Yes.' 'And you admitted that Love, because he was in want, desires those good and fair things of which he is in want?' 'Yes, I did.' 'But how can he be a god who has no portion in what is either good or fair?' 'Impossible.' 'Then you see that you also deny the divinity of Love.'

'What then is Love?' I asked; 'Is he mortal?' 'No.' 'What then?' 'As in the former instance, he is neither mortal nor immortal, but in a mean between the two.' 'What is he, Diotima?' 'He is a great spirit (daimon), and like all spirits he is intermediate between the divine and the mortal.' 'And what,' I said, 'is his power?' 'He interprets,' she replied, 'between gods and men, conveying and taking across to the gods the prayers and sacrifices of men, and to men the commands and replies of the gods; he is the mediator who spans the chasm which divides them, and therefore in him all is bound together, and through him the arts of the prophet and the priest, their sacrifices and mysteries and charms, and all prophecy and incantation, find their way. For God mingles not with man; but through Love all the intercourse and converse of God with man, whether awake or asleep, is carried on. The wisdom which understands this is spiritual; all other wisdom, such as that of arts and handicrafts, is mean and vulgar. Now these spirits or intermediate powers are many and diverse, and one of them is Love.'

'And who,' I said, 'was his father, and who his mother?' 'The tale,' she said, 'will take time; nevertheless I will tell you. On the birthday of Aphrodite there was a feast of the gods, at which the god Poros or Plenty, who is the son of Metis or Discretion, was one of the guests. When the feast was over, Penia or Poverty, as the manner is on such occasions, came about the doors to beg. Now Plenty who was the worse for nectar (there was no wine in those days), went into the garden of Zeus and fell into a heavy sleep, and Poverty considering her own straitened circumstances, plotted to have a child by him, and accordingly she lay down at his side and conceived Love, who partly because he is naturally a lover of the beautiful, and because Aphrodite is herself beautiful, and also because he was born on her birthday, is her follower and attendant.

'And as his parentage is, so also are his fortunes. In the first place he is always poor, and anything but tender and fair, as the many imagine him; and he is rough and squalid, and has no shoes, nor a house to dwell in; on the bare earth exposed he lies under the open heaven, in the streets, or at the doors of houses, taking his rest; and like his mother he is always in distress. Like his father too, whom he also partly resembles, he is always plotting against the fair and good; he is bold, enterprising, strong, a mighty hunter, always weaving some intrigue or other, keen in the pursuit of wisdom, fertile in resources; a philosopher at all times, terrible as an enchanter, sorcerer, sophist. He is by nature neither mortal nor immortal, but alive and flourishing at one moment when he is in plenty, and dead at another moment, and again alive by reason of his father's nature. But that which is always flowing in is always flowing out, and so he is never in want and never in wealth; and, further, he is in a mean between ignorance and knowledge. The truth of the matter is this: No god is a philosopher or seeker after wisdom, for he is wise already; nor does any man who is wise seek after wisdom. Neither do the ignorant seek after wisdom. For herein is the evil of ignorance, that he who is neither good nor wise is nevertheless satisfied with himself: he has no desire for that of which he feels no want.'

'But who then, Diotima,' I said, 'are the lovers of wisdom, if they are neither the wise nor the foolish?' 'A child may answer that question,' she replied; 'they are those who are in a mean between the two; Love is one of them. For wisdom is a most beautiful thing, and Love is of the beautiful; and therefore Love is also a philosopher or lover of wisdom, and being a lover of wisdom is in a mean between the wise and the ignorant. And of this too his birth is the cause; for his father is wealthy and wise, and his mother poor and foolish. Such, my dear Socrates, is the nature of the spirit Love. The error in your conception of him was very natural, and as I imagine from what you say, has arisen out of a confusion of love and the beloved, which made you think that love was all beautiful. For the beloved is the truly beautiful, and delicate, and perfect, and blessed; but the principle of love is of another nature, and is such as I have described.'

I said, 'O thou stranger woman, thou sayest well; but, assuming Love to be such as you say, what is the use of him to men?' 'That, Socrates,' she replied, 'I will attempt to unfold: of his nature and birth I have already spoken; and you acknowledge that love is of the beautiful. But some one will say: Of the beautiful in what, Socrates and Diotima?-or rather let me put the question more clearly, and ask: When a man loves the beautiful, what does he desire?' I answered her 'That the beautiful may be his.' 'Still,' she said, 'the answer suggests a further question: What is given by the possession of beauty?' 'To what you have asked,' I replied, 'I have no answer ready.' 'Then,' she said, 'let me put the word "good" in the place of the beautiful, and repeat the question once more: If he who loves loves the good, what is it then that he loves?' 'The possession of the good,' I said.

'And what does he gain who possesses the good?' '

Happiness,' I replied; 'there is less difficulty in answering that question.' 'Yes,' she said, 'the happy are made happy by the acquisition of good things. Nor is there any need to ask why a man desires happiness; the answer is already final.'

'You are right.' I said. 'And is this wish and this desire common to all? and do all men always desire their own good, or only some men?—what say you?' 'All men,' I replied; 'the desire is common to all.' 'Why, then,' she rejoined, 'are not all men, Socrates, said to love, but only some of them? whereas you say that all men are always loving the same things.' 'I myself wonder,' I said, 'why this is.' 'There is nothing to wonder at,' she replied; 'the reason is that one part of love is separated off and receives the name of the whole, but the other parts have other names.' 'Give an illustration,' I said. She answered me as follows:

'There is poetry, which, as you know, is complex and manifold. All creation or passage of non-being into being is poetry or making, and the processes of all art are creative; and the masters of arts are all poets or makers.' 'Very true.' 'Still,' she said, 'you know that they are not called poets, but have other names; only that portion of the art which is separated off from the rest, and is concerned with music and metre, is termed poetry, and they who possess poetry in this sense of the word are called poets.' 'Very true,' I said. 'And the same holds of love. For you may say generally that all desire of good and happiness is only the great and subtle power of love; but they who are drawn towards him by any other path, whether the path of money-making or gymnastics or philosophy, are not called lovers-the name of the whole is appropriated to those whose affection takes one form only-they alone are said to love, or to be lovers.' 'I dare say,' I replied, 'that you are right.' 'Yes,' she added, 'and you hear people say that lovers are seeking for their other half; but I say that they are seeking neither for the half of themselves, nor for the whole, unless the half or the whole be also a good. And they will cut off their own hands and feet and cast them away, if they are evil; for they love not what is their own, unless perchance there be some one who calls what belongs to him the good, and what belongs to another the evil. For there is nothing which men love but the good. Is there anything?'

'Certainly, I should say, that there is nothing.' 'Then,' she said, 'the simple truth is, that men love the good.' 'Yes,' I said. 'To which must be added that they love the possession of the good?' 'Yes, that must be added.' 'And not only the possession, but the everlasting possession of the good?' 'That must be added too.' 'Then love,' she said, 'may be described generally as the love of the everlasting possession of the good?' 'That is most true.' 'Then if this be the nature of love, can you tell me further,' she said, 'what is the manner of the pursuit? what are they doing who show all this eagerness and heat which is called love? and what is the object which they have in view? Answer me.'

'Nay, Diotima,' I replied, 'if I had known, I should not have wondered at your wisdom, neither should I have come to learn from you about this very matter.' 'Well,' she said, 'I will teach you: The object which they have in view is birth in beauty, whether of body or soul.' 'I do not understand you,' I said; 'the oracle requires an explanation.' 'I will make my meaning clearer,' she replied. 'I mean to say, that all men are bringing to the birth in their bodies and in their souls. There is a certain age at which human nature is desirous of procreation— procreation which must be in beauty and not in deformity; and this procreation is the union of man and woman, and is a divine thing; for conception and generation are an immortal principle in the mortal creature, and in the inharmonious they can never be. But the deformed is always inharmonious with the divine, and the beautiful harmonious. Beauty, then, is the destiny or goddess of parturition who presides at birth, and therefore, when approaching beauty, the conceiving power is propitious, and diffusive, and benign, and begets and bears fruit: at the sight of ugliness she frowns and contracts and has a sense of pain, and turns away, and shrivels up, and not without a pang refrains from conception. And this is the reason why, when the hour of conception arrives, and the teeming nature is full, there is such a flutter and ecstasy about beauty whose approach is the alleviation of the pain of travail. For love, Socrates, is not, as you imagine, the love of the beautiful only.'

'What then?' 'The love of generation and of birth in beauty.' 'Yes,' I said. 'Yes, indeed,' she replied. 'But why of generation?' 'Because to the mortal creature, generation is a sort of eternity and immortality,' she replied; 'and if, as has been already admitted, love is of the everlasting possession of the good, all men will necessarily desire immortality together with good: Wherefore love is of immortality.' All this she taught me at various times when she spoke of love. And I remember her once saying to me, 'What is the cause, Socrates, of love, and the attendant desire? See you not how all animals, birds, as well as beasts, in their desire of procreation, are in agony when they take the infection of love, which begins with the desire of union; whereto is added the care of offspring, on whose behalf the weakest are ready to battle against the strongest even to the uttermost, and to die for them, and will let themselves be tormented with hunger or suffer anything in order to maintain their young. Man may be supposed to act thus from reason; but why should animals have these passionate feelings? Can you tell me why?'

Again I replied that I did not know. She said to me: 'And do you expect ever to become a master in the art of love, if you do not know this?' 'But I have told you already, Diotima, that my ignorance is the reason why I come to you; for I am conscious that I want a teacher; tell me then the cause of this and of the other mysteries of love.' 'Marvel not,' she said, 'if you believe that love is of the immortal, as we have several times acknowledged; for here again, and on the same principle too, the mortal nature is seeking as far as is possible to be everlasting and immortal: and this is only to be attained by generation, because generation always leaves behind a new existence in the place of the old. Nay even in the life of the same individual there is succession and not absolute unity: a man is called the same, and yet in the short interval which elapses between youth and age, and in which every animal is said to have life and identity, he is undergoing a perpetual process of loss and reparation-hair, flesh, bones, blood, and the whole body are always changing.

'That is true not only of the body, but also of the soul, whose habits, tempers, opinions, desires, pleasures, pains, fears, never remain the same in any one of us, but are always coming and going; and equally true of knowledge, and what is still more surprising to us mortals, not only do the sciences in general spring up and decay, so that in respect of them we are never the same; but each of them individually experiences a like change. For what is implied in the word "recollection," but the departure of knowledge, which is ever being forgotten, and is renewed and preserved by recollection, and appears to be the same although in reality new, according to that law of succession by which all mortal things are preserved, not absolutely the same, but by substitution, the old worn-out mortality leaving another new and similar existence behind- unlike the divine, which is always the same and not another? And in this way, Socrates, the mortal body, or mortal anything, partakes of immortality; but the immortal in another way. Marvel not then at the love which all men have of their offspring; for that universal love and interest is for the sake of immortality.'

I was astonished at her words, and said: 'Is this really true, O thou wise Diotima?' And she answered with all the authority of an accomplished sophist: 'Of that, Socrates, you may be assured; think only of the ambition of men, and you will wonder at the senselessness of their ways, unless you consider how they are stirred by the love of an immortality of fame. They are ready to run all risks greater far than they would have run for their children, and to spend money and undergo any sort of toil, and even to die, for the sake of leaving behind them a name which shall be eternal. Do you imagine that Alcestis would have died to save Admetus, or Achilles to avenge Patroclus, or your own Codrus in order to preserve the kingdom for his sons, if they had not imagined that the memory of their virtues, which still survives among us, would be immortal? Nay,' she said, 'I am persuaded that all men do all things, and the better they are the more they do them, in hope of the glorious fame of immortal virtue; for they desire the immortal.

'Those who are pregnant in the body only, betake themselves to women and beget children—this is the character of their love; their offspring, as they hope, will preserve their memory and giving them the blessedness and immortality which they desire in the future. But souls which are pregnant—for there certainly are men who are more creative in their souls than in their bodies—conceive that which is proper for the soul to conceive or contain. And what are these conceptions? Wisdom and virtue in general. And such creators are poets and all artists who are deserving of the name inventor. But the greatest and fairest sort of wisdom by far is that which is concerned with the ordering of states and families, and which is called temperance and justice.

'And he who in youth has the seed of these implanted in him and is himself inspired, when he comes to maturity desires to beget and generate. He wanders about seeking beauty that he may beget offspring—for in deformity he will beget nothing, and naturally embraces the beautiful rather than the deformed body; above all when he finds a fair and noble and well-nurtured soul, he embraces the two in one person, and to such an one he is full of speech about virtue and the nature and pursuits of a good man; and he tries to educate him; and at the touch of the beautiful which is ever present to his memory, even when absent, he brings forth that which he had conceived long before, and in company with him tends that which he brings forth; and they are married by a far nearer tie and have a closer friendship than those who beget mortal children, for the children who are their common offspring are fairer and more immortal. Who, when he thinks of Homer and Hesiod and other great poets, would not rather have their children than ordinary human ones? Who would not emulate them in the creation of children such as theirs, which have preserved their memory and given them everlasting glory? Or who would not have such children as Lycurgus left behind him to be the saviours, not only of [Sparta], but of Hellas, as one may say? There is Solon, too, who is the revered father of Athenian laws; and many others there are in many other places, both among Hellenes and barbarians, who have given to the world many noble works, and have been the parents of virtue of every kind; and many temples have been raised in their honour for the sake of children such as theirs; which were never raised in honour of any one, for the sake of his mortal children.

'These are the lesser mysteries of love, into which even you, Socrates, may enter; to the greater and more hidden ones which are the crown of these, and to which, if you pursue them in a right spirit, they will lead, I know not whether you will be able to attain. But I will do my utmost to inform you, and do you follow if you can. For he who would proceed aright in this matter should begin in youth to visit beautiful forms; and first, if he be guided by his instructor aright, to love one such form only, out of that he should create fair thoughts; and soon he will of himself perceive that the beauty of one form is akin to the beauty of another; and then if beauty of form in general is his pursuit, how foolish would he be not to recognize that the beauty in every form is and the same! And when he perceives this he will abate his violent love of the one, which he will despise and deem a small thing, and will become a lover of all beautiful forms; in the next stage he will consider that the beauty of the mind is more honourable than the beauty of the outward form.

'So that if a virtuous soul have but a little comeliness, he will be content to love and tend him, and will search out and bring to the birth thoughts which may improve the young, until he is compelled to contemplate and see the beauty of institutions and laws, and to understand that the beauty of them all is of one family, and that personal beauty is a trifle; and after laws and institutions he will go on to the sciences, that he may see their beauty, being not like a servant in love with the beauty of one youth or man or institution, himself a slave mean and narrow-minded, but drawing towards and contemplating the vast sea of beauty, he will create many fair and noble thoughts and notions in boundless love of wisdom; until on that shore he grows and waxes strong, and at last the vision is revealed to him of a single science, which is the science of beauty everywhere. To this I will proceed; please to give me your very best attention:

'He who has been instructed thus far in the things of love, and who has learned to see the beautiful in due order and succession, when he comes toward the end will suddenly perceive a nature of wondrous beauty (and this, Socrates, is the final cause of all our former toils), a nature which in the first place is everlasting, not growing and decaying, or waxing and waning; secondly, not fair in one point of view and foul in another, or at one time or in one relation or at one place fair, at another time or in another relation or at another place foul, as if fair to some and foul to others, or in the likeness of a face or hands or any other part of the bodily frame, or in any form of speech or knowledge, or existing in any other being, as for example, in an animal, or in heaven, or in earth, or in any other place; but beauty absolute, separate, simple, and everlasting, which without diminution and without increase, or any change, is imparted to the ever-growing and perishing beauties of all other things. He who from these ascending under the influence of true love, begins to perceive that beauty, is not far from the end. And the true order of going, or being led by another, to the things of love, is to begin from the beauties of earth and mount upwards for the sake of that other beauty, using these as steps only, and from one going on to two, and from two to all fair forms, and from fair forms to fair practices, and from fair practices to fair notions, until from fair notions he arrives at the notion of absolute beauty, and at last knows what the essence of beauty is.

'This, my dear Socrates,' said the stranger of Mantineia, 'is that life above all others which man should live, in the contemplation of beauty absolute; a beauty which if you once beheld, you would see not to be after the measure of gold, and garments, and fair boys and youths, whose presence now entrances you; and you and many a one would be content to live seeing them only and conversing with them without meat or drink, if that were possible—you only want to look at them and to be with them. But what if man had eyes to see the true beauty—the divine beauty, I mean, pure and clear and unalloyed, not clogged with the pollutions of mortality and all the colours and vanities of human life, thither looking, and holding converse with the true beauty simple and divine? Remember how in that communion only, beholding beauty with the eye of the mind, he will be enabled to bring forth, not images of beauty, but realities (for he has hold not of an image but of a reality), and bringing forth and nourishing true virtue to become the friend of God and be immortal, if mortal man may. Would that be an ignoble life?'

PLATO
REPUBLIC

Translated by Benjamin Jowett

Book 3

SOCRATES: We must come to an understanding about the mimetic art—whether the poets, in narrating their stories, are to be allowed by us to imitate, and if so, whether in whole or in part, and if the latter, in what parts; or should all imitation be prohibited?

ADEIMANTUS: You mean, I suspect, to ask whether tragedy and comedy shall be admitted into our State?

Yes, I said; but there may be more than this in question: I really do not know as yet, but whither the argument may blow, thither we go.

And go we will, he said.

Then, Adeimantus, let me ask you whether our guardians ought to be imitators; or rather, has not this question been decided by the rule already laid down that one man can only do one thing well, and not many; and that if he attempt many, he will altogether fail of gaining much reputation in any?

Certainly.

And this is equally true of imitation; no one man can imitate many things as well as he would imitate a single one?

He cannot.

Then the same person will hardly be able to play a serious part in life, and at the same time to be an imitator and imitate many other parts as well; for even when two species of imitation are nearly allied, the same persons cannot succeed in both, as, for example, the writers of tragedy and comedy—did you not just now call them imitations?

Yes, I did; and you are right in thinking that the same persons cannot succeed in both.

Any more than they can be rhapsodists and actors at once?

True.

Neither are comic and tragic actors the same; yet all these things are but imitations.

They are so.

And human nature, Adeimantus, appears to have been coined into yet smaller pieces, and to be as incapable of imitating many things well, as of performing well the actions of which the imitations are copies.

Quite true, he replied.

If then we adhere to our original notion and bear in mind that our guardians, setting aside every other business, are to dedicate themselves wholly to the maintenance of freedom in the State, making this their craft, and engaging in no work which does not bear on this end, they ought not to practise or imitate anything else; if they imitate at all, they should imitate from youth upward only those characters which are suitable to their profession—the courageous, temperate, holy, free, and the like; but they should not depict or be skilful at imitating any kind of illiberality or baseness, lest from imitation they should come to be what they imitate. Did you never observe how imitations, beginning in early youth and continuing far into life, at length grow into habits and become a second nature, affecting body, voice, and mind?

Yes, certainly, he said. . . .

I answered: Of the harmonies I know nothing, but I want to have one warlike, to sound the note or accent which a brave man utters in the hour of danger and stern resolve, or when his cause is failing, and he is going to wounds or death or is overtaken by some other evil, and at every such crisis meets the blows of fortune with firm step and a determination to endure; and another to be used by him in times of peace and freedom of action, when there is no pressure of necessity, and he is seeking to persuade God by prayer, or man by instruction and admonition, or on the other hand, when he is expressing his willingness to yield to persuasion or entreaty or admonition, and which represents him when by prudent conduct he has attained his end, not carried away by his success, but acting moderately and wisely under the circumstances, and acquiescing in the event. These two harmonies I ask you to leave; the strain of necessity and the strain of freedom, the strain of the unfortunate and the strain of the fortunate, the strain of courage, and the strain of temperance; these, I say, leave. . . .

Then let us now finish the purgation, I said. Next in order to harmonies, rhythms will naturally follow, and they should be subject to the same rules, for we ought not to seek out complex systems of metre, or metres of every kind, but rather to discover what rhythms are the expressions of a courageous and harmonious life; and when we have found them, we shall adapt the foot and the melody to words having a like spirit, not the words to the foot and melody. To say what these rhythms are will be your duty—you must teach me them, as you have already taught me the harmonies. But, indeed, he replied, I cannot tell you. I only know that there are some three principles of rhythm out of which metrical systems are framed, just as in sounds there are four notes out of which all the harmonies are composed; that is an observation which I have made. But of what sort of lives they are severally the imitations I am unable to say.

Then, I said, we must take Damon into our counsels; and he will tell us what rhythms are expressive of meanness, or insolence, or fury, or other unworthiness, and what are to be reserved for the expression of opposite feelings. . . .

There is no difficulty in seeing that grace or the absence of grace is an effect of good or bad rhythm.

None at all.

And also that good and bad rhythm naturally assimilate to a good and bad style; and that harmony and discord in like manner follow style; for our principle is that rhythm and harmony are regulated by the words, and not the words by them.

Just so, he said, they should follow the words.

And will not the words and the character of the style depend on the temper of the soul?

Yes.

And everything else on the style?

Yes.

Then beauty of style and harmony and grace and good rhythm depend on simplicity —I mean the true simplicity of a rightly and nobly ordered mind and character, not that other simplicity which is only an euphemism for folly?

Very true, he replied.

And if our youth are to do their work in life, must they not make these graces and harmonies their perpetual aim?

They must.

And surely the art of the painter and every other creative and constructive art are full of them— weaving, embroidery, architecture, and every kind of manufacture; also nature, animal and vegetable—in all of them there is grace or the absence of grace. And ugliness and discord and inharmonious motion are nearly allied to ill-words and ill-nature, as grace and harmony are the twin sisters of goodness and virtue and bear their likeness.

That is quite true, he said.

But shall our superintendence go no further, and are the poets only to be required by us to express the image of the good in their works, on pain, if they do anything else, of expulsion from our State? Or is the same control to be extended to other artists, and are they also to be prohibited from exhibiting the opposite forms of vice and intemperance and meanness and indecency in sculpture and building and the other creative arts; and is he who cannot conform to this rule of ours to be prevented from practising his art in our State, lest the taste of our citizens be corrupted by him? We would not have our guardians grow up amid images of moral deformity, as in some noxious pasture, and there browse and feed upon many a baneful herb and flower day by day, little by little, until they silently gather a festering mass of corruption in their own soul. Let our artists rather be those who are gifted to discern the true nature of the beautiful and graceful; then will our youth dwell in a land of health, amid fair sights and sounds, and receive the good in everything; and beauty, the effluence of fair works, shall flow into the eye and ear, like a health-giving breeze from a purer region, and insensibly draw the soul from earliest years into likeness and sympathy with the beauty of reason.

There can be no nobler training than that, he replied.

And therefore musical training is a more potent instrument than any other, because rhythm and harmony find their way into the inward places of the soul, on which they mightily fasten, imparting grace, and making the soul of him who is rightly educated graceful, or of him who is ill-educated ungraceful; and also because he who has received this true education of the inner being will most shrewdly perceive omissions or faults in art and nature, and with a true taste, while he praises and rejoices over and receives into his soul the good, and becomes noble and good, he will justly blame and hate the bad, now in the days of his youth, even before he is able to know the reason why; and when reason comes he will recognize and salute the friend with whom his education has made him long familiar.

Yes, he said, I quite agree with you in thinking that our youth should be trained in music and on the grounds which you mention.

Just as in learning to read, I said, we were satisfied when we knew the letters of the alphabet, which are very few, in all their recurring sizes and combinations; not slighting them as unimportant whether they occupy a space large or small, but everywhere eager to make them out; and not thinking ourselves perfect in the art of reading until we recognize them wherever they are found:

True.

Or, as we recognize the reflection of letters in the water, or in a mirror, only when we know the letters themselves; the same art and study giving us the knowledge of both.

Exactly.

Even so, as I maintain, neither we nor our guardians, whom we have to educate, can ever become musical until we and they know the essential forms of temperance, courage, liberality, magnificence, and their kindred, as well as the contrary forms, in all their combinations, and can recognize them and their images wherever they are found, not slighting them either in small things or great, but believing them all to be within the sphere of one art and study.

Most assuredly.

And when a beautiful soul harmonizes with a beautiful form, and the two are cast in one mould, that will be the fairest of sights to him who has an eye to see it?

The fairest indeed.
And the fairest is also the loveliest?
That may be assumed.
And the man who has the spirit of harmony will be most in love with the loveliest; but he will not love him who is of an inharmonious soul?

Book 10

SOCRATES: Of the many excellences which I perceive in the order of our State, there is none which upon reflection pleases me better than the rule about poetry.

GLAUCON: To what do you refer?

To the rejection of imitative poetry, which certainly ought not to be received; as I see far more clearly now that the parts of the soul have been distinguished.

What do you mean?

Speaking in confidence, for I should not like to have my words repeated to the tragedians and the rest of the imitative tribe—but I do not mind saying to you, that all poetical imitations are ruinous to the understanding of the hearers, and that the knowledge of their true nature is the only antidote to them.

Explain the purport of your remark.

Well, I will tell you, although I have always from my earliest youth had an awe and love of Homer, which even now makes the words falter on my lips, for he is the great captain and teacher of the whole of that charming tragic company; but a man is not to be reverenced more than the truth, and therefore I will speak out.

Very good, he said.

Listen to me, then, or, rather, answer me.

Put your question.

Can you tell me what imitation is? for I really do not know.

A likely thing, then, that I should know.

Why not? for the duller eye may often see a thing sooner than the keener.

Very true, he said; but in your presence, even if I had any faint notion, I could not muster courage to utter it. Will you inquire yourself?

Well, then, shall we begin the inquiry in our usual manner: Whenever a number of individuals have a common name, we assume them to have also a corresponding idea or form; do you understand me?

I do.

Let us take any common instance; there are beds and tables in the world—plenty of them, are there not?

Yes.

But there are only two ideas or forms of them—one the idea of a bed, the other of a table.

True.

And the maker of either of them makes a bed or he makes a table for our use, in accordance with the idea—that is our way of speaking in this and similar instances—but no artificer makes the ideas themselves: how could he?

Impossible.

And there is another artist—I should like to know what you would say of him.

Who is he?

One who is the maker of all the works of all other workmen.

What an extraordinary man!

Wait a little, and there will be more reason for your saying so. For this is he who is able to make not only vessels of every kind, but plants and animals, himself and all other things—the earth and heaven, and the things which are in heaven or under the earth; he makes the gods also.

He must be a wizard and no mistake.

Oh! you are incredulous, are you? Do you mean that there is no such maker or creator, or that in one sense there might be a maker of all these things, but in another not? Do you see that there is a way in which you could make them all yourself?

What way?

An easy way enough; or rather, there are many ways in which the feat might be quickly and easily accomplished, none quicker than that of turning a mirror round and round —you would soon enough make the sun and the heavens, and the earth and yourself, and other animals and plants, and all the other things of which we were just now speaking, in the mirror.

Yes, he said; but they would be appearances only.

Very good, I said, you are coming to the point now. And the painter, too, is, as I conceive, just such another—a creator of appearances, is he not?

Of course.

But then I suppose you will say that what he creates is untrue. And yet there is a sense in which the painter also creates a bed?

Yes, he said, but not a real bed.

And what of the maker of the bed? were you not saying that he too makes, not the idea which, according to our view, is the essence of the bed, but only a particular bed?

Yes, I did.

Then if he does not make that which exists he cannot make true existence, but only some semblance of existence; and if anyone were to say that the work of the maker of the bed, or of any other workman, has real existence, he could hardly be supposed to be speaking the truth.

At any rate, he replied, philosophers would say that he was not speaking the truth.

No wonder, then, that his work, too, is an indistinct expression of truth.

No wonder.

Suppose now that by the light of the examples just offered we inquire who this imitator is?

If you please.

Well, then, here are three beds: one existing in nature, which is made by God, as I think that we may say—for no one else can be the maker?

No.

There is another which is the work of the carpenter?

Yes.

And the work of the painter is a third?

Yes.

Beds, then, are of three kinds, and there are three artists who superintend them: God, the maker of the bed, and the painter?

Yes, there are three of them.

God, whether from choice or from necessity, made one bed in nature and one only; two or more such ideal beds neither ever have been nor ever will be made by God.

Why is that?

Because even if He had made but two, a third would still appear behind them which both of them would have for their idea, and that would be the ideal bed and not the two others.

Very true, he said.

God knew this, and he desired to be the real maker of a real bed, not a particular maker of a particular bed, and therefore he created a bed which is essentially and by nature one only.

So we believe.

Shall we, then, speak of him as the natural author or maker of the bed?

Yes, he replied; inasmuch as by the natural process of creation he is the author of this and of all other things.

And what shall we say of the carpenter—is not he also the maker of the bed?

Yes.

But would you call the painter a creator and maker?

Certainly not.

Yet if he is not the maker, what is he in relation to the bed?

I think, he said, that we may fairly designate him as the imitator of that which the others make.

Good, I said; then you call him who is third in the descent from nature an imitator?

Certainly, he said.

And the tragic poet is an imitator, and, therefore, like all other imitators, he is thrice removed from the king and from the truth?

That appears to be so.

Then about the imitator we are agreed. And what about the painter? I would like to know whether he may be thought to imitate that which originally exists in nature, or only the creations of artists?

The latter.

As they are or as they appear? you have still to determine this.

What do you mean?

I mean, that you may look at a bed from different points of view, obliquely or directly or from any other point of view, and the bed will appear different, but there is no difference in reality. And the same of all things.

Yes, he said, the difference is only apparent.

Now let me ask you another question: Which is the art of painting designed to be— an imitation of things as they are, or as they appear—of appearance or of reality?

Of appearance.

Then the imitator, I said, is a long way off the truth, and can do all things because he lightly touches on a small part of them, and that part an image. For example: A painter will paint a cobbler, carpenter, or any other artist, though he knows nothing of their arts; and, if he is a good artist, he may deceive children or simple persons, when he shows them his picture of a carpenter from a distance, and they will fancy that they are looking at a real carpenter.

Certainly.

And whenever anyone informs us that he has found a man who knows all the arts, and all things else that anybody knows, and every single thing with a higher degree of accuracy than any other man— whoever tells us this, I think that we can only imagine him to be a simple creature who is likely to have been deceived by some wizard or actor whom he met, and whom he thought all-knowing, because he himself was unable to analyze the nature of knowledge and ignorance and imitation.

Most true.

And so, when we hear persons saying that the tragedians, and Homer, who is at their head, know all the arts and all things human, virtue as well as vice, and divine things too, for that the good poet cannot compose well unless he knows his subject, and that he who has not this knowledge can never be a poet, we ought to consider whether here also there may not be a similar illusion. Perhaps they may have come across imitators and been deceived by them; they may not have remembered when they saw their works that these were but imitations thrice removed from the truth, and could easily be made without any knowledge of the truth, because they are appearances only and not realities? Or, after all, they may be in the right, and poets do really know the things about which they seem to the many to speak so well?

The question should by all means be considered.

Now do you suppose that if a person were able to make the original as well as the image, he would seriously devote himself to the image-making branch? Would he allow imitation to be the ruling principle of his life, as if he had nothing higher in him?

I should say not.

The real artist, who knew what he was imitating, would be interested in realities and not in imitations; and would desire to leave as memorials of himself works many and fair; and, instead of being the author of encomiums, he would prefer to be the theme of them.

Yes, he said, that would be to him a source of much greater honor and profit.

Then, I said, we must put a question to Homer; not about medicine, or any of the arts to which his poems only incidentally refer: we are not going to ask him, or any other poet, whether he has cured patients like Asclepius, or left behind him a school of medicine such as the Asclepiads were, or whether he only talks about medicine and other arts at second-hand; but we have a right to know respecting military tactics, politics, education, which are the chiefest and noblest subjects of his poems, and we may fairly ask him about them. "Friend Homer," then we say to him, "if you are only in the second remove from truth in what you say of virtue, and not in the third—not an image maker or imitator—and if you are able to discern what pursuits make men better or worse in private or public life, tell us what State was ever better governed by your help? The good order of Lacedaemon is due to Lycurgus, and many other cities, great and small, have been similarly benefited by others; but who says that you have been a good legislator to them and have done them any good? Italy and Sicily boast of Charondas, and there is Solon who is renowned among us; but what city has anything to say about you?" Is there any city which he might name?

I think not; not even the Homerids themselves pretend that he was a legislator.

Well, but is there any war on record which was carried on successfully by him, or aided by his counsels, when he was alive?

There is not.

Or is there any invention of his, applicable to the arts or to human life, such as Thales the Milesian or Anacharsis the Scythian, and other ingenious men have conceived, which is attributed to him?

There is absolutely nothing of the kind.

But, if Homer never did any public service, was he privately a guide or teacher of any? Had he in his lifetime friends who loved to associate with him, and who handed down to posterity a Homeric way of life, such as was established by Pythagoras, who was so greatly beloved for his wisdom, and whose followers are to this day quite celebrated for the order which was named after him?

Nothing of the kind is recorded of him. For, surely, Socrates, Creophylus, the companion of Homer, that child of flesh, whose name always makes us laugh, might be more justly ridiculed for his stupidity, if, as is said, Homer was greatly neglected by him and others in his own day when he was alive?

Yes, that is the tradition. But can you imagine, Glaucon, that if Homer had really been able to educate and improve mankind—if he had possessed knowledge, and not been a mere imitator—can you imagine, I say, that he would not have had many followers, and been honored and loved by them? Protagoras of Abdera and Prodicus of Ceos and a host of others have only to whisper to their contemporaries: "You will never be able to manage either your own house or your own State until you appoint us to be your ministers of education"— and this ingenious device of theirs has such an effect in making men love them that their companions all but carry them about on their shoulders. And is it conceivable that the contemporaries of Homer, or again of Hesiod, would have allowed either of them to go about as rhapsodists, if they had really been able to make mankind virtuous? Would they not have been as unwilling to part with them as with gold, and have compelled them to stay at home with them? Or, if the master would not stay, then the disciples would have followed him about everywhere, until they had got education enough?

Yes, Socrates, that, I think, is quite true.

Then must we not infer that all these poetical individuals, beginning with Homer, are only imitators; they copy images of virtue and the like, but the truth they never reach? The poet is like a painter who, as we have already observed, will make a likeness of a cobbler though he understands nothing of cobbling; and his picture is good enough for those who know no more than he does, and judge only by colors and figures.

Quite so.

In like manner the poet with his words and phrases may be said to lay on the colors of the several arts, himself understanding their nature only enough to imitate them; and other people, who are as ignorant as he is, and judge only from his words, imagine that if he speaks of cobbling, or of military tactics, or of anything else, in metre and harmony and rhythm, he speaks very well—such is the sweet influence which melody and rhythm by nature have. And I think that you must have observed again and again what a poor appearance the tales of poets make when stripped of the colors which music puts upon them, and recited in simple prose.

Yes.

They are like faces which were never really beautiful, but only blooming; and now the bloom of youth has passed away from them?

Exactly.

Here is another point: The imitator or maker of the image knows nothing of true existence; he knows appearances only. Am I not right?

Yes.

Then let us have a clear understanding, and not be satisfied with half an explanation.

Proceed.

Of the painter we say that he will paint reins and a bit?

Yes.

And the worker in leather and brass will make them?

Certainly.

But does the painter know the right form of the bit and reins? Nay, hardly even the workers in brass and leather who make them; only the horseman who knows how to use them —he knows their right form.

Most true.

And may we not say the same of all things?

What?

That there are three arts which are concerned with all things: one which uses, another which makes, a third which imitates them?

Yes.

And the excellence or beauty or truth of every structure, animate or inanimate, and of every action of man, is relative to the use for which nature or the artist has intended them.

True.

Then the user of them must have the greatest experience of them, and he must indicate to the maker the good or bad qualities which develop themselves in use; for example, the flute-player will tell the flute-maker which of his flutes is satisfactory to the performer; he will tell him how he ought to make them, and the other will attend to his instructions?

Of course.

The one knows and therefore speaks with authority about the goodness and badness of flutes, while the other, confiding in him, will do what he is told by him?

True.

The instrument is the same, but about the excellence or badness of it the maker will only attain to a correct belief; and this he will gain from him who knows, by talking to him and being compelled to hear what he has to say, whereas the user will have knowledge?

True.

But will the imitator have either? Will he know from use whether or no his drawing is correct or beautiful? or will he have right opinion from being compelled to associate with another who knows and gives him instructions about what he should draw?

Neither.

Then he will no more have true opinion than he will have knowledge about the goodness or badness of his imitations?

I suppose not.

The imitative artist will be in a brilliant state of intelligence about his own creations?

Nay, very much the reverse.

And still he will go on imitating without knowing what makes a thing good or bad, and may be expected therefore to imitate only that which appears to be good to the ignorant multitude?

Just so.

Thus far, then, we are pretty well agreed that the imitator has no knowledge worth mentioning of what he imitates. Imitation is only a kind of play or sport, and the tragic poets, whether they write in iambic or in heroic verse, are imitators in the highest degree?

Very true.

And now tell me, I conjure you, has not imitation been shown by us to be concerned with that which is thrice removed from the truth?

Certainly.

And what is the faculty in man to which imitation is addressed?

What do you mean?

I will explain: The body which is large when seen near, appears small when seen at a distance?

True.

And the same objects appear straight when looked at out of the water, and crooked when in the water; and the concave becomes convex, owing to the illusion about colors to which the sight is liable. Thus every sort of confusion is revealed within us; and this is that weakness of the human mind on which the art of conjuring and of deceiving by light and shadow and other ingenious devices imposes, having an effect upon us like magic.

True.

And the arts of measuring and numbering and weighing come to the rescue of the human understanding—there is the beauty of them—and the apparent greater or less, or more or heavier, no longer have the mastery over us, but give way before calculation and measure and weight?

Most true.

And this, surely, must be the work of the calculating and rational principle in the soul?

To be sure.

And when this principle measures and certifies that some things are equal, or that some are greater or less than others, there occurs an apparent contradiction?

True.

But were we not saying that such a contradiction is impossible—the same faculty cannot have contrary opinions at the same time about the same thing?

Very true.

Then that part of the soul which has an opinion contrary to measure is not the same with that which has an opinion in accordance with measure?

True.

And the better part of the soul is likely to be that which trusts to measure and calculation?

Certainly.

And that which is opposed to them is one of the inferior principles of the soul?

No doubt.

This was the conclusion at which I was seeking to arrive when I said that painting or drawing, and imitation in general, when doing their own proper work, are far removed from truth, and the companions and friends and associates of a principle within us which is equally removed from reason, and that they have no true or healthy aim.

Exactly.

The imitative art is an inferior who marries an inferior, and has inferior offspring.

Very true.

And is this confined to the sight only, or does it extend to the hearing also, relating in fact to what we term poetry?

Probably the same would be true of poetry.

Do not rely, I said, on a probability derived from the analogy of painting; but let us examine further and see whether the faculty with which poetical imitation is concerned is good or bad.

By all means.

We may state the question thus: Imitation imitates the actions of men, whether voluntary or involuntary, on which, as they imagine, a good or bad result has ensued, and they rejoice or sorrow accordingly. Is there anything more?

No, there is nothing else.

But in all this variety of circumstances is the man at unity with himself—or, rather, as in the instance of sight there were confusion and opposition in his opinions about the same things, so here also are there not strife and inconsistency in his life? though I need hardly raise the question again, for I remember that all this has been already admitted; and the soul has been acknowledged by us to be full of these and ten thousand similar oppositions occurring at the same moment?

And we were right.

Yes, I said, thus far we were right; but there was an omission which must now be supplied.

What was the omission?

Were we not saying that a good man, who has the misfortune to lose his son or anything else which is most dear to him, will bear the loss with more equanimity than another?

Yes.

But will he have no sorrow, or shall we say that although he cannot help sorrowing, he will moderate his sorrow?

The latter, he said, is the truer statement.

Tell me: will he be more likely to struggle and hold out against his sorrow when he is seen by his equals, or when he is alone? It will make a great difference whether he is seen or not. When he is by himself he will not mind saying or doing many things which he would be ashamed of anyone hearing or seeing him do?

True.

There is a principle of law and reason in him which bids him resist, as well as a feeling of his misfortune which is forcing him to indulge his sorrow?

True.

But when a man is drawn in two opposite directions, to and from the same object, this, as we affirm, necessarily implies two distinct principles in him?

Certainly.

One of them is ready to follow the guidance of the law?

How do you mean?

The law would say that to be patient under suffering is best, and that we should not give way to impatience, as there is no knowing whether such things are good or evil; and nothing is gained by impatience; also, because no human thing is of serious importance, and grief stands in the way of that which at the moment is most required.

What is most required?

That we should take counsel about what has happened, and when the dice have been thrown order our affairs in the way which reason deems best; not, like children who have had a fall, keeping hold of the part struck and wasting time in setting up a howl, but always accustoming the soul forthwith to apply a remedy, raising up that which is sickly and fallen, banishing the cry of sorrow by the healing art.

Yes, that is the true way of meeting the attacks of fortune.

Yes; and the higher principle is ready to follow this suggestion of reason?

Clearly.

And the other principle, which inclines us to recollection of our troubles and to lamentation, and can never have enough of them, we may call irrational, useless, and cowardly?

Indeed, we may.

And does not the latter—I mean the rebellious principle— furnish a great variety of materials for imitation? Whereas the wise and calm temperament, being always nearly equable, is not easy to imitate or to appreciate when imitated, especially at a public festival when a promiscuous crowd is assembled in a theatre. For the feeling represented is one to which they are strangers.

Certainly.

Then the imitative poet who aims at being popular is not by nature made, nor is his art intended, to please or to affect the rational principle in the soul; but he will prefer the passionate and fitful temper, which is easily imitated?

Clearly.

And now we may fairly take him and place him by the side of the painter, for he is like him in two ways: first, inasmuch as his creations have an inferior degree of truth—in this, I say, he is like him; and he is also like him in being concerned with an inferior part of the soul; and therefore we shall be right in refusing to admit him into a well-ordered State, because he awakens and nourishes and strengthens the feelings and impairs the reason. As in a city when the evil are permitted to have authority and the good are put out of the way, so in the soul of man, as we maintain, the imitative poet implants an evil constitution, for he indulges the irrational nature which has no discernment of greater and less, but thinks the same thing at one time great and at another small—he is a manufacturer of images and is very far removed from the truth.

Exactly.

But we have not yet brought forward the heaviest count in our accusation: the power which poetry has of harming even the good (and there are very few who are not harmed), is surely an awful thing?

Yes, certainly, if the effect is what you say.

Hear and judge: The best of us, as I conceive, when we listen to a passage of Homer or one of the tragedians, in which he represents some pitiful hero who is drawling out his sorrows in a long oration, or weeping, and smiting his breast—the best of us, you know, delight in giving way to sympathy, and are in raptures at the excellence of the poet who stirs our feelings most.

Yes, of course, I know.

But when any sorrow of our own happens to us, then you may observe that we pride ourselves on the opposite quality—we would fain be quiet and patient; this is the manly part, and the other which delighted us in the recitation is now deemed to be the part of a woman.

Very true.

Now can we be right in praising and admiring another who is doing that which any one of us would abominate and be ashamed of in his own person?

No, that is certainly not reasonable.

Nay, quite reasonable from one point of view.

What point of view?

If you consider that when in misfortune we feel a natural hunger and desire to relieve our sorrow by weeping and lamentation, and that this feeling which is kept under control in our own calamities is satisfied and delighted by the poets; the better nature in each of us, not having been sufficiently trained by reason or habit, allows the sympathetic element to break loose because the sorrow is another's; and the spectator fancies that there can be no disgrace to himself in praising and pitying anyone who comes telling him what a good man he is, and making a fuss about his troubles; he thinks that the pleasure is a gain, and why should he be supercilious and lose this and the poem too? Few persons ever reflect, as I should imagine, that from the evil of other men something of evil is communicated to themselves. And so the feeling of sorrow which has gathered strength at the sight of the misfortunes of others is with difficulty repressed in our own.

How very true!

And does not the same hold also of the ridiculous? There are jests which you would be ashamed to make yourself, and yet on the comic stage, or indeed in private, when you hear them, you are greatly amused by them, and are not at all disgusted at their unseemliness; the case of pity is repeated; there is a principle in human nature which is disposed to raise a laugh, and this which you once restrained by reason, because you were afraid of being thought a buffoon, is now let out again; and having stimulated the risible faculty at the theatre, you are betrayed unconsciously to yourself into playing the comic poet at home.

Quite true.

And the same may be said of lust and anger and all the other affections, of desire, and pain, and pleasure, which are held to be inseparable from every action—in all of them poetry feeds and waters the passions instead of drying them up; she lets them rule, although they ought to be controlled, if mankind are ever to increase in happiness and virtue.

I cannot deny it.

Therefore, Glaucon, whenever you meet with any of the eulogists of Homer declaring that he has been the educator of Hellas, and that he is profitable for education and for the ordering of human things, and that you should take him up again and again and get to know him and regulate your whole life according to him, we may love and honor those who say these things—they are excellent people, as far as their lights extend; and we are ready to acknowledge that Homer is the greatest of poets and first of tragedy writers; but we must remain firm in our conviction that hymns to the gods and praises of famous men are the only poetry which ought to be admitted into our State. For if you go beyond this and allow the honeyed muse to enter, either in epic or lyric verse, not law and the reason of mankind, which by common consent have ever been deemed best, but pleasure and pain will be the rulers in our State.

That is most true.

And now since we have reverted to the subject of poetry, let this our defence serve to show the reasonableness of our former judgment in sending away out of our State an art having the tendencies which we have described; for reason constrained us. But that she may not impute to us any harshness or want of politeness, let us tell her that there is an ==ancient quarrel between philosophy and poetry==; of which there are many proofs, such as the saying of "the yelping hound howling at her lord," or of one "mighty in the vain talk of fools," and "the mob of sages circumventing Zeus," and the "subtle thinkers who are beggars after all"; and there are innumerable other signs of ancient enmity between them. Notwithstanding this, let us assure our sweet friend and the sister art of imitation, that if she will only prove her title to exist in a well-ordered State we shall be delighted to receive her—we are very conscious of her charms; but we may not on that account betray the truth. I dare say, Glaucon, that you are as much charmed by her as I am, especially when she appears in Homer?

Yes, indeed, I am greatly charmed.

Shall I propose, then, that she be allowed to return from exile, but upon this condition only—that she make a defence of herself in lyrical or some other metre?

Certainly.

And we may further grant to those of her defenders who are lovers of poetry and yet not poets the permission to speak in prose on her behalf: let them show not only that she is pleasant, but also useful to States and to human life, and we will listen in a kindly spirit; for if this can be proved we shall surely be the gainers—I mean, if there is a use in poetry as well as a delight?

Certainly we shall be the gainers.

If her defence fails, then, my dear friend, like other persons who are enamoured of something, but put a restraint upon themselves when they think their desires are opposed to their interests, so, too, must we after the manner of lovers give her up, though not without a struggle. We, too, are inspired by that love of poetry which the education of noble States has implanted in us, and therefore we would have her appear at her best and truest; but so long as she is unable to make good her defence, this argument of ours shall be a charm to us, which we will repeat to ourselves while we listen to her strains; that we may not fall away into the childish love of her which captivates the many. At all events we are well aware that poetry being such as we have described is not to be regarded seriously as attaining to the truth; and he who listens to her, fearing for the safety of the city which is within him, should be on his guard against her seductions and make our words his law.

Yes, I quite agree with you.

Yes, my dear Glaucon, for great is the issue at stake, greater than appears, whether a man is to be good or bad. And what will anyone be profited if under the influence of honor or money or power, aye, or under the excitement of poetry, he neglect justice and virtue?

ARISTOTLE
POETICS

Translated by S. H. Butcher

I

I propose to treat of Poetry in itself and of its various kinds, noting the essential quality of each, to inquire into the structure of the plot as requisite to a good poem; into the number and nature of the parts of which a poem is composed; and similarly into whatever else falls within the same inquiry. Following, then, the order of nature, let us begin with the principles which come first.

Epic poetry and Tragedy, Comedy also and Dithyrambic poetry, and the music of the flute and of the lyre in most of their forms, are all in their general conception modes of imitation. They differ, however, from one another in three respects—the medium, the objects, the manner or mode of imitation, being in each case distinct. For as there are persons who, by conscious art or mere habit, imitate and represent various objects through the medium of color and form, or again by the voice; so in the arts above mentioned, taken as a whole, the imitation is produced by rhythm, language, or 'harmony,' either singly or combined. Thus in the music of the flute and of the lyre, 'harmony' and rhythm alone are employed; also in other arts, such as that of the shepherd's pipe, which are essentially similar to these. In dancing, rhythm alone is used without 'harmony'; for even dancing imitates character, emotion, and action, by rhythmical movement.

There is another art which imitates by means of language alone, and that either in prose or verse— which verse, again, may either combine different meters or consist of but one kind—but this has hitherto been without a name. For there is no common term we could apply to the mimes of Sophron and Xenarchus and the Socratic dialogues on the one hand; and, on the other, to poetic imitations in iambic, elegiac, or any similar meter. People do, indeed, add the word 'maker' or 'poet' to the name of the meter, and speak of elegiac poets, or epic (that is, hexameter) poets, as if it were not the imitation that makes the poet, but the verse that entitles them all to the name. Even when a treatise on medicine or natural science is brought out in verse, the name of poet is by custom given to the author; and yet Homer and Empedocles have nothing in common but the meter, so that it would be right to call the one poet, the other physicist rather than poet. On the same principle, even if a writer in his poetic imitation were to combine all meters, as Chaeremon did in his Centaur, which is a medley composed of meters of all kinds, we should bring him too under the general term poet.

So much then for these distinctions. There are, again, some arts which employ all the means above mentioned—namely, rhythm, tune, and meter. Such are Dithyrambic and Nomic poetry, and also Tragedy and Comedy; but between them originally the difference is, that in the first two cases these means are all employed in combination, in the latter, now one means is employed, now another. Such, then, are the differences of the arts with respect to the medium of imitation

II

Since the objects of imitation are men in action, and these men must be either of a higher or a lower type (for moral character mainly answers to these divisions, goodness and badness being the distinguishing marks of moral differences), it follows that we must represent men either as better than in real life, or as worse, or as they are. It is the same in painting. Polygnotus depicted men as nobler than they are, Pauson as less noble, Dionysius drew them true to life. Now it is evident that each of the modes of imitation above mentioned will exhibit these differences, and become a distinct kind in imitating objects that are thus distinct. Such diversities may be found even in dancing, flute-playing, and lyre-playing. So again in language, whether prose or verse unaccompanied by music. . . . The same distinction marks off Tragedy from Comedy; for Comedy aims at representing men as worse, Tragedy as better than in actual life.

III

There is still a third difference—the manner in which each of these objects may be imitated. For the medium being the same, and the objects the same, the poet may imitate by narration—in which case he can either take another personality as Homer does, or speak in his own person, unchanged—or he may present all his characters as living and moving before us. These, then, as we said at the beginning, are the three differences which distinguish artistic imitation—the medium, the objects, and the manner. So that from one point of view, Sophocles is an imitator of the same kind as Homer—for both imitate higher types of character; from another point of view, of the same kind as Aristophanes—for both imitate persons acting and doing. Hence, some say, the name of 'drama' is given to such poems, as representing action. . . .

IV

Poetry in general seems to have sprung from two causes, each of them lying deep in our nature. First, the instinct of imitation is implanted in man from childhood, one difference between him and other animals being that he is the most imitative of living creatures, and through imitation learns his earliest lessons; and no less universal is the pleasure felt in things imitated. We have evidence of this in the facts of experience. Objects which in themselves we view with pain, we delight to contemplate when reproduced with minute fidelity: such as the forms of the most ignoble animals and of dead bodies. The cause of this again is, that to learn gives the liveliest pleasure, not only to philosophers but to men in general; whose capacity, however, of learning is more limited. Thus the reason why men enjoy seeing a likeness is, that in contemplating it they find themselves learning or inferring, and saying perhaps, 'Ah, that is he.' For if you happen not to have seen the original, the pleasure will be due not to the imitation as such, but to the execution, the coloring, or some such other cause.

Imitation, then, is one instinct of our nature. Next, there is the instinct for 'harmony' and rhythm, meters being manifestly sections of rhythm. Persons, therefore, starting with this natural gift developed by degrees their special aptitudes, till their rude improvisations gave birth to Poetry.

Poetry now diverged in two directions, according to the individual character of the writers. The graver spirits imitated noble actions, and the actions of good men. The more trivial sort imitated the actions of meaner persons, at first composing satires, as the former did hymns to the gods and the praises of famous men. A poem of the satirical kind cannot indeed be put down to any author earlier than Homer; though many such writers probably there were. But from Homer onward, instances can be cited—his own Margites, for example, and other similar compositions. The appropriate meter was also here introduced; hence the measure is still called the iambic or lampooning measure, being that in which people lampooned one another. Thus the older poets were distinguished as writers of heroic or of lampooning verse. As, in the serious style, Homer is preeminent among poets, for he alone combined dramatic form with excellence of imitation so he too first laid down the main lines of comedy, by dramatizing the ludicrous instead of writing personal satire. His Margites bears the same relation to comedy that the Iliad and Odyssey do to tragedy. But when Tragedy and Comedy came to light, the two classes of poets still followed their natural bent: the lampooners became writers of Comedy, and the Epic poets were succeeded by Tragedians, since the drama was a larger and higher form of art. . . .

V

Comedy is, as we have said, an imitation of characters of a lower type—not, however, in the full sense of the word bad, the ludicrous being merely a subdivision of the ugly. It consists in some defect or ugliness which is not painful or destructive. To take an obvious example, the comic mask is ugly and distorted, but does not imply pain. The successive changes through which Tragedy passed, and the authors of these changes, are well known, whereas Comedy has had no history, because it was not at first treated seriously. It was late before the Archon granted a comic chorus to a poet; the performers were till then voluntary. Comedy had already taken definite shape when comic poets, distinctively so called, are heard of. Who furnished it with masks, or prologues, or increased the number of actors— these and other similar details remain unknown. As for the plot, it came originally from Sicily; but of Athenian writers Crates was the first who abandoning the 'iambic' or lampooning form, generalized his themes and plots.

Epic poetry agrees with Tragedy in so far as it is an imitation in verse of characters of a higher type. They differ in that Epic poetry admits but one kind of meter and is narrative in form. They differ, again, in their length: for Tragedy endeavors, as far as possible, to confine itself to a single revolution of the sun, or but slightly to exceed this limit, whereas the Epic action has no limits of time. This, then, is a second point of difference; though at first the same freedom was admitted in Tragedy as in Epic poetry.

Of their constituent parts some are common to both, some peculiar to Tragedy: whoever, therefore knows what is good or bad Tragedy, knows also about Epic poetry. All the elements of an Epic poem are found in Tragedy, but the elements of a Tragedy are not all found in the Epic poem.

VI

Of the poetry which imitates in hexameter verse, and of Comedy, we will speak hereafter. Let us now discuss Tragedy, resuming its formal definition, as resulting from what has been already said.

Tragedy, then, is an imitation of an action that is serious, complete, and of a certain magnitude; in language embellished with each kind of artistic ornament, the several kinds being found in separate parts of the play; in the form of action, not of narrative; through pity and fear effecting the proper purgation of these emotions. By 'language embellished,' I mean language into which rhythm, 'harmony' and song enter. By 'the several kinds in separate parts,' I mean, that some parts are rendered through the medium of verse alone, others again with the aid of song. Now as tragic imitation implies persons acting, it necessarily follows in the first place, that Spectacular equipment will be a part of Tragedy. Next, Song and Diction, for these are the media of imitation. By 'Diction' I mean the mere metrical arrangement of the words: as for 'Song,' it is a term whose sense everyone understands.

Again, Tragedy is the imitation of an action; and an action implies personal agents, who necessarily possess certain distinctive qualities both of character and thought; for it is by these that we qualify actions themselves, and these—thought and character—are the two natural causes from which actions spring, and on actions again all success or failure depends. Hence, the Plot is the imitation of the action—for by plot I here mean the arrangement of the incidents. By Character I mean that in virtue of which we ascribe certain qualities to the agents. Thought is required wherever a statement is proved, or, it may be, a general truth enunciated. Every Tragedy, therefore, must have six parts, which parts determine its quality—namely, Plot, Character, Diction, Thought, Spectacle, Song. Two of the parts constitute the medium of imitation, one the manner, and three the objects of imitation. And these complete the first. These elements have been employed, we may say, by the poets to a man; in fact, every play contains Spectacular elements as well as Character, Plot, Diction, Song, and Thought.

But most important of all is the structure of the incidents. For Tragedy is an imitation, not of men, but of an action and of life, and life consists in action, and its end is a mode of action, not a quality. Now character determines men's qualities, but it is by their actions that they are happy or the reverse. Dramatic action, therefore, is not with a view to the representation of character: character comes in as subsidiary to the actions. Hence the incidents and the plot are the end of a tragedy; and the end is the chief thing of all. Again, without action there cannot be a tragedy; there may be without character. The tragedies of most of our modern poets fail in the rendering of character; and of poets in general this is often true. . . .

The plot, then, is the first principle, and, as it were, the soul of a tragedy; Character holds the second place. A similar fact is seen in painting. The most beautiful colors, laid on confusedly, will not give as much pleasure as the chalk outline of a portrait. Thus Tragedy is the imitation of an action, and of the agents mainly with a view to the action. Third in order is Thought—that is, the faculty of saying what is possible and pertinent in given circumstances. In the case of oratory, this is the function of the political art and of the art of rhetoric: and so indeed the older poets make their characters speak the language of civic life; the poets of our time, the language of the rhetoricians. Character is that which reveals moral purpose, showing what kind of things a man chooses or avoids.

Speeches, therefore, which do not make this manifest, or in which the speaker does not choose or avoid anything whatever, are not expressive of character. Thought, on the other hand, is found where something is proved to be or not to be, or a general maxim is enunciated.

Fourth among the elements enumerated comes Diction; by which I mean, as has been already said, the expression of the meaning in words; and its essence is the same both in verse and prose. Of the remaining elements Song holds the chief place among the embellishments. The Spectacle has, indeed, an emotional attraction of its own, but, of all the parts, it is the least artistic, and connected least with the art of poetry. For the power of Tragedy, we may be sure, is felt even apart from representation and actors. Besides, the production of spectacular effects depends more on the art of the stage machinist than on that of the poet.

VII

These principles being established, let us now discuss the proper structure of the Plot, since this is the first and most important thing in Tragedy. Now, according to our definition Tragedy is an imitation of an action that is complete, and whole, and of a certain magnitude; for there may be a whole that is wanting in magnitude. A whole is that which has a beginning, a middle, and an end. A beginning is that which does not itself follow anything by causal necessity, but after which something naturally is or comes to be. An end, on the contrary, is that which itself naturally follows some other thing, either by necessity, or as a rule, but has nothing following it. A middle is that which follows something as some other thing follows it. A well-constructed plot, therefore, must neither begin nor end at haphazard, but conform to these principles.

Again, a beautiful object, whether it be a living organism or any whole composed of parts, must not only have an orderly arrangement of parts, but must also be of a certain magnitude; for beauty depends on magnitude and order. Hence a very small animal organism cannot be beautiful; for the view of it is confused, the object being seen in an almost imperceptible moment of time. Nor, again, can one of vast size be beautiful; for as the eye cannot take it all in at once, the unity and sense of the whole is lost for the spectator; as for instance if there were one a thousand miles long. As, therefore, in the case of animate bodies and organisms a certain magnitude is necessary, and a magnitude which may be easily embraced in one view; so in the plot, a certain length is necessary, and a length which can be easily embraced by the memory.

The limit of length in relation to dramatic competition and sensuous presentment is no part of artistic theory. For had it been the rule for a hundred tragedies to compete together, the performance would have been regulated by the water-clock—as indeed we are told was formerly done. But the limit as fixed by the nature of the drama itself is this: the greater the length, the more beautiful will the piece be by reason of its size, provided that the whole be perspicuous. And to define the matter roughly, we may say that the proper magnitude is comprised within such limits, that the sequence of events, according to the law of probability or necessity, will admit of a change from bad fortune to good, or from good fortune to bad. . . .

IX

It is, moreover, evident from what has been said, that it is not the function of the poet to relate what has happened, but what may happen —what is possible according to the law of probability or necessity. The poet and the historian differ not by writing in verse or in prose. The work of Herodotus might be put into verse, and it would still be a species of history, with meter no less than without it. The true difference is that one relates what has happened, the other what may happen.

Poetry, therefore, is a more philosophical and a higher thing than history: for poetry tends to express the universal, history the particular. By the universal I mean how a person of a certain type on occasion speak or act, according to the law of probability or necessity; and it is this universality at which poetry aims in the names she attaches to the personages. The particular is—for example—what Alcibiades did or suffered. In Comedy this is already apparent: for here the poet first constructs the plot on the lines of probability, and then inserts characteristic names— unlike the lampooners who write about particular individuals. But tragedians still keep to real names, the reason being that what is possible is credible: what has not happened we do not at once feel sure to be possible; but what has happened is manifestly possible: otherwise it would not have happened. Still there are even some tragedies in which there are only one or two well-known names, the rest being fictitious. In others, none are well known-as in Agathon's *Antheus*, where incidents and names alike are fictitious, and yet they give none the less pleasure.

We must not, therefore, at all costs keep to the received legends, which are the usual subjects of Tragedy. Indeed, it would be absurd to attempt it; for even subjects that are known are known only to a few, and yet give pleasure to all. It clearly follows that the poet or 'maker' should be the maker of plots rather than of verses; since he is a poet because he imitates, and what he imitates are actions.. . . .

PLOTINUS
ENNEADS

Translated by Thomas Taylor

1.6 CONCERNING THE BEAUTIFUL

Beauty for the most part, consists in objects of sight; but it is also received through the ears, by the skilful composition of words, and the consonant proportion of sounds; for in every species of harmony, beauty is to be found. And if we rise from sense into the regions of soul, we shall there perceive studies and offices, actions and habits, sciences and virtues, invested with a much larger portion of beauty. But whether there is above these, a still higher beauty, will appear as we advance in its investigation. What is it then, which causes bodies to appear fair to the sight, sounds beautiful to the ear, and science and virtue lovely to the mind? May we not enquire after what manner they all partake of beauty? Whether beauty is one and the same in all? Or, whether the beauty of bodies is of one kind, and the beauty of souls of another? And again, what these are, if they are two? Or, what beauty is, if perfectly simple, and one? For some things, as bodies, are doubtless beautiful, not from the natures of the subjects in which they reside, but rather by some kind of participation; but others again appear to be essentially beautiful, or beauties themselves; and such is the nature of virtue. For, with respect, to the same bodies, they appear beautiful to one person, and the reverse of beauty to another; as if the essence of body were a thing different from the essence of beauty. In the first place then, what is that, which, by its presence, causes the beauty of bodies? Let us reflect, what most powerfully attracts the eyes of beholders, and seizes the spectator with rapturous delight; for if we can find what this is, we may perhaps use it as a ladder, enabling us to ascend into the region of beauty, and survey its immeasurable extent.

It is the general opinion that a certain commensuration of parts to each other, and to the whole, with the addition, of colour, generates that beauty which is the object of sight; and that in the commensurate and the moderate alone the beauty of everything consists. But from such an opinion the compound only, and not the simple, can be beautiful, the single parts will have no peculiar beauty; and will only merit that appellation by conferring to the beauty of the whole. But it is surely necessary that a lovely whole should consist of beautiful parts, for the fair can never rise out of the deformed. But from such a definition, it follows, that beautiful colours and the light of the sun, since they are simple and do not receive their beauty from commensuration, must be excluded the regions of beauty. Besides, how, from such an hypothesis can gold be beautiful? Or the glittering of night and the glorious spectacle of the stars? In like manner, the most simple musical sounds will be foreign from beauty, though in a song wholly beautiful every note must be beautiful, as necessary to the being of the whole.

Again, since the same proportion remaining, the same face is to one person beautiful and to another the reverse, is it not necessary to call the beauty of the commensurate one kind of beauty and the commensuration another kind, and that the commensurate is fair by means of something else? But if transferring themselves to beautiful studies and fair discourses, they shall assign as the cause of beauty in these the proportion of measure, what is that which in beautiful sciences, laws or disciplines, is called commensurate proportion? Or in what manner can speculations themselves be called mutually commensurate? If it be said because of the inherent concord, we reply that there is a certain concord and consent in evil souls, a conformity of sentiment, in believing (as it is said) that temperance is folly and justice generous ignorance. It appears, therefore, that the beauty of the soul is every virtue, and this species of the beautiful possesses far greater reality than any of the superior we have mentioned. But after what manner in this is commensuration to be found? For it is neither like the symmetry in magnitude nor in numbers. And since the parts of the soul are many, in what proportion and synthesis, in what temperament of parts or concord of speculations, does beauty consist? Lastly, of what kind is the beauty of intellect itself, abstracted from every corporeal concern, and intimately conversing with itself alone?

We still, therefore, repeat the question, What is the beauty of bodies? It is something which at first view presents itself to sense, and which the soul familiarly apprehends and eagerly embraces, as if it were allied to itself. But when it meets with the deformed, it hastily starts from the view and retires abhorrent from its discordant nature. For since the soul in its proper state ranks according to the most excellent essence in the order of things, when it perceives any object related to itself, or the mere vestige of a relation, it congratulates itself on the pleasing event, and astonished with the striking resemblance enters deep into its essence, and, by rousing its dormant powers, at length perfectly recollects its kindred and allies. What is the similitude then between the beauties of sense and that beauty which is divine? For if there be any similitude the respective objects must be similar. But after what manner are the two beautiful? For it is by participation of species that we call every sensible object beautiful. Thus, since everything void of form is by nature fitted for its reception, as far as it is destitute of reason and form it is base and separate from the divine reason, the great fountain of forms; and whatever is entirely remote from this immortal source is perfectly base and deformed.

Such is matter, which by its nature is ever averse from the supervening irradiations of form. Whenever, therefore, form accedes, it conciliates in amicable unity the parts which are about to compose a whole; for being itself one it is not wonderful that the subject of its power should tend to unity, as far as the nature of a compound will admit. Hence beauty is established in multitude when the many is reduced into one, and in this case it communicates itself both to the parts and to the whole. But when a particular one, composed from similar parts, is received it gives itself to the whole, without departing from the sameness and integrity of its nature. Thus at one and the same time it communicates itself to the whole building and its several parts; and at another time confines itself to a single stone, and then the first participation arises from the operations of art, but the second from the formation of nature. And hence body becomes beautiful through the communion supernally proceeding from divinity.

But the soul, by her innate power, than which nothing more powerful, in judging its proper concerns, when another soul concurs in the decision, acknowledges the beauty of forms. And, perhaps, its knowledge in this case arises from its accommodating its internal ray of beauty to form, and trusting to this in its judgment; in the same manner as a rule is employed in the decision of what is straight. But how can that which is inherent in body, accord with that which is above body? Let us reply by asking how the architect pronounces the building beautiful by accommodating the external structure the fabric of his soul? Perhaps, because the outward building, when entirely deprived of the stones, is no other than the intrinsic form, divided by the external mass of matter, but indivisibly existing, though appearing in the many. When, therefore, sense beholds the form in bodies, at strife with matter, binding and vanquishing its contrary nature, and sees form gracefully shining forth in other forms, it collects together the scattered whole, and introduces it to itself, and to the indivisible form within; and renders it consonant, congruous and friendly to its own intimate form.

Thus, to the good man, virtue shining forth in youth is lovely because consonant to the true virtue which lies deep in the soul. But the simple beauty of colour arises, when light, which is something incorporeal, and reason and form entering the obscure involutions of matter, irradiates and forms its dark and formless nature. It is on this account that fire surpasses other bodies in beauty, because, compared with the other elements, it obtains the order of form; for it is more eminent than the rest, and is the most subtle of all, bordering, as it were, on an incurporeal nature. And too, that though impervious itself it is intimately received by others, for it imparts heat, but admits no cold. Hence it is the first nature which is ornamented with colour, and is the source of it to others; and on this account it beams forth exalted like some immaterial form. But when it cannot vanquish its subject, as participating but a slender light, it is no longer beautiful, because it does not receive the whole form of colour. Again, the music of the voice rouses the harmony latent in the soul, and opens her eye to the perception of beauty, existing in many the same. But it is the property of the harmony perceived by sense, to be measured by numbers, yet not in every proportion of number or voice; but in that alone which is obedient to the production, and conquest of its species. And this much for the beauties of sense, which, like images and shadows flowing into matter, adorn with spectacles of beauty its formless being, and strike the respective senses with wonder and delight.

But it is now time, leaving every object of sense far behind, to contemplate, by a certain ascent, a beauty of a much higher order; a beauty not visible to the corporeal eye, but alone manifest to the brighter eye of the soul, independent of all corporeal aid. However, since, without some previous perception of beauty it is impossible to express by words the beauties of sense, but we must remain in the state of the blind, so neither can we ever speak of the beauty of offices and sciences, and whatever is allied to these, if deprived of their intimate possession. Thus we shall never be able to tell of virtue's brightness, unless by looking inward we perceive the fair countenance of justice and temperance, and are convinced that neither the evening nor morning star are half so beautiful and bright. But it is requisite to perceive objects of this kind by that eye by which the soul beholds such real beauties. Besides it is necessary that whoever perceives this species of beauty, should be seized with much greater delight, and more vehement admiration, than any corporeal beauty can excite; as now embracing beauty real and substantial. Such affections, I say, ought to be excited about true beauty, as admiration and sweet astonishment; desire also and love and a pleasant trepidation. For all souls, as I may say, are affected in this manner about invisible objects, but those the most who have the strongest propensity to their love; as it likewise happens about corporeal beauty; for all equally perceive beautiful corporeal forms, yet all are not equally excited, but lovers in the greatest degree.

But it may be allowable to interrogate those, who rise above sense, concerning the effects of love in this manner; of such we enquire, what do you suffer respecting fair studies, and beautiful manners, virtuous works, affections, and habits, and the beauty of souls? What do you experience on perceiving yourselves lovely within? After what manner are you roused as it were to a Bacchalian fury; striving to converse with yourselves, and collecting yourselves separate from the impediments of body? For thus are true lovers enraptured. But what is the cause of these wonderful effects? It is neither figure, nor colour, nor magnitude; but soul herself, fair through temperance, and not with the false gloss of colour, and bright with the splendors of virtue herself. And this you experience as often as you turn your eye inwards; or contemplate the amplitude of another soul; the just manners, the pure temperance; fortitude venerable by her noble countenance; and modesty and honesty walking with an intrepid step, and a tranquil and steady aspect; and what crowns the beauty of them all, constantly receiving the irradiations of a divine intellect.

In what respect then, shall we call these beautiful? For they are such as they appear, nor did ever anyone behold them, and not pronounce them realities. But as yet reason desires to know how they cause the loveliness of the soul; and what that grace is in every virtue which beams forth to view like light? Are you then willing we should assume the contrary part, and consider what in the soul appears deformed? For perhaps it will facilitate our search, if we can thus find what is base in the soul, and from whence it derives its original.

Let us suppose a soul deformed, to be one intemperate and unjust, filled with a multitude of desires, a prey to foolish hopes and vexed with idle fears; through its diminutive and avaricious nature the subject of envy; employed solely in thought of what is immoral and low, bound in the fetters of impure delights, living the life, whatever it may be, peculiar to the passion of body; and so totally merged in sensuality as to esteem the base pleasant, and the deformed beautiful and fair. But may we not say, that this baseness approaches the soul as an adventitious evil, under the pretext of adventitious beauty; which, with great detriment, renders it impure, and pollutes it with much depravity; so that it neither possesses true life, nor true sense, but is endued with a slender life through its mixture of evil, and this worn out by the continual depredations of death; no longer perceiving the objects of mental vision, nor permitted any more to dwell with itself, because ever hurried away to things obscure, external and low? Hence, becoming impure, and being on all sides snatched in the unceasing whirl of sensible forms, it is covered with corporeal stains, and wholly given to matter, contracts deeply its nature, loses all its original splendour, and almost changes its own species into that of another; just as the pristine beauty of the most lovely form would be destroyed by its total immersion in mire and clay. But the deformity of the first arises from inward filth, of its own contracting; of the second, from the accession of some foreign nature.

If such a one then desires to recover his former beauty, it is necessary to cleanse the infected parts, and thus by a thorough purgation to resume his original form. Hence, then if we assert that the soul, by her mixture, confusion and commerce with body and matter, becomes thus base, our assertion will, I think, be right. For the baseness of the soul consists in not being pure and sincere. And as the gold is deformed by the adherence of earthly clods, which are no sooner removed than on a sudden the gold shines forth with its native purity; and then becomes beautiful when separated from natures foreign from its own, and when it is content with its own purity for the possession of beauty; so the soul, when separated from the sordid desires engendered by its too great immersion in body, and liberated from the dominion of every perturbation, can thus and thus only, blot out the base stains imbibed from its union with body; and thus becoming alone, will doubtless expel all the turpitude contracted from a nature so opposite to its own.

Indeed, as the ancient oracle declares, temperance and fortitude, prudence and every virtue, are certain purgatives of the soul; and hence the sacred mysteries prophesy obscurely, yet with truth, that the soul not purified lies in Tartarus, immersed in filth. Since the impure is, from his depravity, the friend of filth, as swine, from their sordid body, delight in mire alone.

For what else is true temperance than not to indulge in corporeal delights, but to fly from their connection, as things which are neither pure, nor the offspring of purity? And true fortitude is not to fear death; for death is nothing more than a certain separation of soul from body, and this he will not fear, who desires to be alone. Again, magnanimity is the contempt of every mortal concern; it is the wing by which we fly into the regions of intellect. And lastly, prudence is no other than intelligence, declining subordinate objects; and directing the eye of the soul to that which is immortal and divine. The soul, thus defined, becomes form and reason, is altogether incorporeal and intellectual, and wholly participates of that divine nature, which is the fountain of loveliness, and of whatever is allied to the beautiful and fair. Hence the soul reduced to intellect becomes astonishingly beautiful; for as the lambent flame which appears detached from the burning wood, enlightens its dark and smoky parts, so intellect irradiates and adorns the inferior powers of the soul, which, without its aid, would be buried in the gloom of formless matter. But intellect, and whatever emanates from intellect, is not the foreign, but the proper ornament of the soul, for the being of the soul, when absorbed in intellect, is then alone real and true. It is, therefore, rightly said, that the beauty and good of the soul consists in her similitude to the Deity; for from hence flows all her beauty, and her allotment of a better being. But the beautiful itself is that which is called beings; and turpitude is of a different nature and participates more of non-entity than being.

But, perhaps, the good and the beautiful are the same, and must be investigated by one and the same process; and in like manner the base and the evil. And in the first rank we must place the beautiful, and consider it as the same with the good; from which immediately emanates intellect as beautiful. Next to this, we must consider the soul receiving its beauty from intellect, and every inferior beauty deriving its origin from the forming power of the soul, whether conversant in fair actions and offices, or sciences and arts. Lastly, bodies themselves participate of beauty from the soul, which, as something divine, and a portion of the beautiful itself, renders whatever it supervenes and subdues, beautiful as far as its natural capacity will admit.

Let us, therefore, re-ascend to the good itself, which every soul desires; and in which it can alone find perfect repose. For if anyone shall become acquainted with this source of beauty he will then know what I say, and after what manner he is beautiful. Indeed, whatever is desirable is a kind of good, since to this desire tends. But they alone pursue true good, who rise to intelligible beauty, and so far only tend to good itself; as far as they lay aside the deformed vestments of matter, with which they become connected in their descent. Just as those who penetrate into the holy retreats of sacred mysteries, are first purified and then divest themselves of their garments, until someone by such a process, having dismissed everything foreign from the God, by himself alone, beholds the solitary principle of the universe, sincere, simple and pure, from which all things depend, and to whose transcendent perfections the eyes of all intelligent natures are directed, as the proper cause of being, life and intelligence.

With what ardent love, with what strong desire will he who enjoys this transporting vision be inflamed while vehemently affecting to become one with this supreme beauty! For this it is ordained, that he who does not yet perceive him, yet desires him as good, but he who enjoys the vision is enraptured with his beauty, and is equally filled with admiration and delight. Hence, such a one is agitated with a salutary astonishment; is affected with the highest and truest love; derides vehement affections and inferior loves, and despises the beauty which he once approved. Such, too, is the condition of those who, on perceiving the forms of gods or daemons, no longer esteem the fairest of corporeal forms. What, then, must be the condition of that being, who beholds the beautiful itself?

In itself perfectly pure, not confined by any corporeal bond, neither existing in the heavens, nor in the earth, nor to be imaged by the most lovely form imagination can conceive; since these are all adventitious and mixed, and mere secondary beauties, proceeding from the beautiful itself. If, then, anyone should ever behold that which is the source of munificence to others, remaining in itself, while it communicates to all, and receiving nothing, because possessing an inexhaustible fullness; and should so abide in the intuition, as to become similar to his nature, what more of beauty can such a one desire? For such beauty, since it is supreme in dignity and excellence, cannot fail of rendering its votaries lovely and fair.

Add too, that since the object of contest to souls is the highest beauty, we should strive for its acquisition with unabated ardour, lest we should be deserted of that blissful contemplation, which, whoever pursues in the right way, becomes blessed from the happy vision; and which he who does not obtain is unavoidably unhappy. For the miserable man is not he who neglects to pursue fair colours, and beautiful corporeal forms; who is deprived of power, and falls from dominion and empire but he alone who is destitute of this divine possession, for which the ample dominion of the earth and sea and the still more extended empire of the heavens, must be relinquished and forgot, if, despising and leaving these far behind, we ever intend to arrive at substantial felicity, by beholding the beautiful itself.

What measures, then, shall we adopt? What machine employ, or what reason consult by means of which we may contemplate this ineffable beauty; a beauty abiding in the most divine sanctuary without ever proceeding from its sacred retreats lest it should be beheld by the profane and vulgar eye? We must enter deep into ourselves, and, leaving behind the objects of corporeal sight, no longer look back after any of the accustomed spectacles of sense. For, it is necessary that whoever beholds this beauty, should withdraw his view from the fairest corporeal forms; and, convinced that these are nothing more than images, vestiges and shadows of beauty, should eagerly soar to the fair original from which they are derived. For he who rushes to these lower beauties, as if grasping realities, when they are only like beautiful images appearing in water, will, doubtless, like him in the fable, by stretching after the shadow, sink into the lake and disappear. For, by thus embracing and adhering to corporeal forms, he is precipitated, not so much in his body as in his soul, into profound and horrid darkness; and thus blind, like those in the infernal regions, converses only with phantoms, deprived of the perception of what is real and true.

It is here, then, we may more truly exclaim, "Let us depart from hence, and fly to our father's delightful land." But, by what leading stars shall we direct our flight, and by what means avoid the magic power of Circe, and the detaining charms of Calypso? For thus the fable of Ulysses obscurely signifies, which feigns him abiding an unwilling exile, though pleasant spectacles were continually presented to his sight; and everything was promised to invite his stay which can delight the senses, and captivate the heart. But our true country, like that of Ulysses, is from whence we came, and where our father lives. But where is the ship to be found by which we can accomplish our flight? For our feet are unequal to the task since they only take us from one part of the earth to another. May we not each of us say,

> What ships have I, what sailors to convey,
> What oars to cut the long laborious way. (Homer, *Odyssey*, 5.182)

But it is in vain that we prepare horses to draw our ships to transport us to our native land. On the contrary, neglecting all these, as unequal to the task, and excluding them entirely from our view, having now closed the corporeal eye, we must stir up and assume a purer eye within, which all men possess, but which is alone used by a few. What is it, then, this inward eye beholds? Indeed, suddenly raised to intellectual vision, it cannot perceive an object exceeding bright. The soul must therefore be first accustomed to contemplate fair studies and then beautiful works, not such as arise from the operations of art, but such as are the offspring of worthy men; and next to this it is necessary to view the soul, which is the parent of this lovely race. But you will ask, after what manner is this beauty of a worthy soul to be perceived?

It is thus. Recall your thoughts inward, and if while contemplating yourself, you do not perceive yourself beautiful, imitate the statuary; who when he desires a beautiful statue cuts away what is superfluous, smooths and polishes what is rough, and never desists until he has given it all the beauty his art is able to effect. In this manner must you proceed, by lopping what is luxuriant, directing what is oblique, and, by purgation, illustrating what is obscure, and thus continue to polish and beautify your statue until the divine splendour of Virtue shines upon you, and Temperance seated in pure and holy majesty rises to your view. If you become thus purified residing in yourself, and having nothing any longer to impede this unity of mind, and no farther mixture to be found within, but perceiving your whole self to be a true light, and light alone; a light which though immense is not measured by any magnitude, nor limited by any circumscribing figure, but is everywhere immeasurable, as being greater than every measure, and more excellent than every quantity; if, perceiving yourself thus improved, and trusting solely to yourself, as no longer requiring a guide, fix now steadfastly your mental view, for with the intellectual eye alone can such immense beauty be perceived.

But if your eye is yet infected with any sordid concern, and not thoroughly refined, while it is on the stretch to behold this most shining spectacle, it will be immediately darkened and incapable of intuition, though someone should declare the spectacle present, which it might be otherwise able to discern. For, it is here necessary that the perceiver and the thing perceived should be similar to each other before true vision can exist. Thus the sensitive eye can never be able to survey, the orb of the sun, unless strongly endued with solar fire, and participating largely off the vivid ray.

    Everyone therefore must become divine, and of godlike beauty, before he can gaze upon a god and the beautiful itself. Thus proceeding in the right way of beauty he will first ascend into the region of intellect, contemplating every fair species, the beauty of which he will perceive to be no other than ideas themselves; for all things are beautiful by the supervening irradiations of these, because they are the offspring and essence of intellect. But that which is superior to these is no other than the fountain of good, everywhere widely diffusing around the streams of beauty, and hence in discourse called the beautiful itself because beauty is its immediate offspring. But if you accurately distinguish the intelligible objects you will call the beautiful the receptacle of ideas; but the good itself, which is superior, the fountain and principle of the beautiful; or, you may place the first beautiful and the good in the same principle, independent of the beauty which there subsists.

DAVID HUME
OF THE STANDARD OF TASTE

The great variety of taste as well as of opinion that prevails in the world is too obvious not to have come to everyone's attention. Men who never go far from home can see differences of taste within the narrow circle of people they are acquainted with—even when the people have been brought up under the same government and have early imbibed the same prejudices. Those who are in a position to take a broader view, in which they contemplate distant nations and remote ages, are even more surprised at how much difference and contrariety there is in people's tastes. We are apt to call 'barbarous' anything that departs widely from our own taste and viewpoint; but we soon find that others will condemn us in the same way. And even the most arrogant and self-satisfied people, when they find to their surprise that others with different tastes are equally sure of themselves, eventually become hesitant in this contest of sentiment to claim positively that they are right.

This variety of taste, which is obvious at a casual glance, turns out on examination to be even greater in reality than in appearance. Men often differ about beauty and ugliness of all kinds, even when they talk in the same way of what kinds of things are beautiful and what kinds are ugly. Every language contains some words that imply blame, others that imply praise; and all those who use that language must agree in how they apply them. All the voices are united in applauding elegance, propriety, simplicity, spirit in writing; and in blaming pomposity, affectation, coldness and spurious glitter. But when critics get down to particular details, this seeming unanimity vanishes and they turn out to have given very different meanings to their words. In all matters of opinion and knowledge it's the other way around: there the differences among men are more often found at the level of general propositions than in particular details, and really to be less than they appear to be. An explanation of the words usually ends the controversy, and the disputants are surprised to learn that basically they agreed in their judgment all the time when they were quarrelling. . . .

It is natural for us to seek a standard of taste—a rule by which the various sentiments of men can be reconciled, or at least a decision reached that confirms one sentiment and condemns another. One philosophical position cuts off all hopes of success in such an attempt, maintaining that it is impossible for there ever to be any standard of taste. There is a very wide difference between judgment and sentiment. All sentiment is right, because sentiment doesn't refer to anything beyond itself, and is always real whenever a man is conscious of it. But all not all states of the understanding are right, because they refer to something beyond themselves— namely, real matter of fact—and they don't always square with that. A thousand men may have a thousand different opinions about some one thing; but just exactly one of the opinions is true, and the only difficulty is to find out which one that is. As against that, a thousand different sentiments aroused by some one object are all right, because no sentiment represents what is really in the object, and so no sentiment runs any risk of being false. A sentiment does mark a certain conformity or relation between the object and the organs or faculties of the mind; but there is no chance of error there, because if that conformity didn't exist the sentiment wouldn't exist either. Beauty is not a quality in things themselves; it exists merely in the mind that contemplates them, and each mind perceives a different beauty. One person may even perceive ugliness where someone else senses beauty; and every individual ought to go along with his own sentiment, without trying to regulate those of others. . . .

But though this axiom, by turning into a proverb, seems to have gained the support of common sense, there is certainly a kind of common sense that opposes it, or at least serves to modify and restrain it. Someone who asserted an equality of genius and elegance between Ogilby and Milton, or between Bunyan and Addison, would be thought to defending something as extravagant as declaring a mole-hill to be as high as the Matterhorn or a pond as wide as the Atlantic. Perhaps there are people who prefer Ogilby and Bunyan, but no one pays any attention to such a taste, and we don't hesitate to say that the sentiment of these purported critics is absurd and ridiculous. In that context the principle of the natural equality of all tastes is totally forgotten; we admit it on some occasions, where the objects seem nearly equal, but it seems like an extravagant paradox—or rather an obvious absurdity—when it is applied to objects that are so disproportioned to one another.

Obviously, none of the rules of composition are fixed by a priori reasoning; they cannot be regarded as abstract conclusions that the understanding has arrived at by studying the relations between ideas that are eternal and unchanging. They are based on the same thing that all the practical sciences are based on— experience. All they are is general observations about what has been found—universally, in all countries and at all times—to please. Many of the beauties of poetry and even of eloquence are based on falsehood and fiction, on exaggerations, metaphors, and bending words from their natural meanings. To check the imagination's outbursts, and reduce every expression to geometrical truth and exactness, would be utterly contrary to the laws of criticism;

because it would produce a work of a kind that universal experience has shown to be the most insipid and disagreeable.

But though poetry can never submit to exact truth, it must be confined by rules of art that are revealed to the author either by his genius or by observation. If some negligent or irregular writers have given pleasure, they have done so in spite of their transgressions of rule or order, not because of them. Their work has had other beauties that would be approved by sound criticism; and the force of these beauties gives our minds a satisfaction that is greater than our distaste for the blemishes, and thus overpowers our censure. Ariosto pleases; but not by his monstrous and improbable fictions, or his bizarre mixture of the serious and comic styles, or the lack of coherence in his stories, or the continual interruptions of his narration. He charms by the force and clarity of his expression, by the readiness and variety of his inventions, and by his natural depiction of the emotions, especially those of the cheerful and amorous kind; and however greatly his faults may lessen our satisfaction, they can't entirely destroy it. And if our pleasure really did arise from the parts of his poem that we call faults, this would be no objection to criticism in general—i.e., it wouldn't be an objection to having some rules of criticism under which some things are judged to be faulty. It would be an objection only to the particular rules of criticism that imply that the passages in question are faulty, thus representing them as universally blamable. If the passages in question are found to please, they can't be faulty, however surprising and inexplicable is the pleasure they produce.

But though all the general rules of art are based purely on experience—on the observation of the common sentiments of human nature—we must not imagine that on every occasion the feelings of men will square with these rules. Those finer emotions of the mind are very tender and delicate, and they won't come smoothly and precisely into play according to their general and established principles unless many circumstances are in their favour. These finer emotions are like the small springs that drive a pocket-watch: the slightest interference from outside, or the slightest internal disorder, disturbs their motion and throws the operation of the whole machine out of balance. If we want to try this out, testing the power over our minds of some beauty or ugliness, we must carefully choose a suitable time and place, and get our imaginations into the right condition and attitude. If we are to judge concerning the universal beauty of some work of art, we need perfect serenity of mind, a gathering together of our thoughts, and proper attention to the work of art.

If any of these is lacking, our test won't be valid and we'll be unable to reach a conclusion. Or, anyway, the relation that nature has placed between the form of the work and the sentiment of the observer will be more obscure, and tracing it out and recognising it will require greater precision. Our best way of discovering its influence—i.e., discovering what works of art please the discriminating mind—will be not to investigate the operation of each particular beauty but rather to attend to which works of art have been admired through the centuries, surviving all the caprices of mode and fashion, all the mistakes of ignorance and envy. The same Homer who pleased people at Athens and Rome two thousand years ago is still admired today in Paris and in London. All the changes of climate, government, religion, and language haven't been able to obscure his glory.

Authority or prejudice may create a temporary fashion in favour of a bad poet or orator, but his reputation won't ever be lasting or general. When his compositions are examined by posterity or by foreigners, the enchantment disappears and his faults appear in their true colours. It is different with a real genius: the longer his works endure and the more widely they are spread, the more sincere is the admiration that he meets with. Envy and jealousy play too large a part in a narrow circle, and even being personally acquainted with the artist may cause one to give his work less applause than it deserves. But when these obstructions are removed by drawing the circle wider, the beauties that are naturally fitted to arouse pleasant sentiments immediately display their energy and maintain their power over the minds of men for as long as the world lasts.

So we find that amidst all the variety and caprice of taste there are certain general sources of approval or disapproval whose influence a careful eye can detect in all operations of the mind. Because of the original structure of the human constitution, some particular forms or qualities are apt to please and others to displease; and if they fail of their effect in any particular instance it is from some apparent defect or imperfection in the organ. A man in a fever wouldn't insist that his palate was a good judge of flavours; someone suffering from jaundice wouldn't claim to give a verdict regarding colours. For each creature there is a sound state and a defective state; and only the sound state can be supposed to give us a true standard of a taste and sentiment. If in the sound state of the organ there is a complete (or considerable) uniformity of sentiment among men, we can get from this an idea of perfect beauty; just as the appearance of objects in daylight to the eye of a healthy man is regarded as their true and real colour, although colour is agreed to be merely an image created by the senses.

Our internal organs are subject to defects—many occurrences of them, and of many kinds—that prevent or weaken the influence of the general sources that our sentiment of beauty or ugliness comes from. Though some objects are, because of the natural structure of the mind, naturally apt to give pleasure, it can't be expected that the pleasure will be equally felt in every individual. Particular incidents and situations occur that either throw a false light on the objects or block the true light from conveying to the imagination the appropriate sentiment and perception.

One obvious cause for many people's not feeling the appropriate sentiment of beauty is their lack of the delicacy of imagination that is needed to make someone capable of those finer emotions. Everyone claims to have this delicacy; everyone talks about it, and wants to reduce every kind of taste or sentiment to its standard. But my intention in this essay is to mingle some light of the understanding with the feelings of sentiment! So I should give a more accurate definition of delicacy than has previously been attempted. So as not to go too deep for my philosophical points, I shall have recourse to a noted story in Don Quixote. [The story is Sancho Panza's account of two of kinsmen who were invited to taste wine from a particular cask; one detected in it a taste of leather, the other a taste of iron; and they were both laughed at until the cask was emptied and found to have at the bottom an iron key with a leather thong attached to it.]

The mental taste that is the topic of this essay greatly resembles the bodily taste that is the subject of Sancho Panza's story, so it won't be hard for us to apply the story to our present topic. Sweet and bitter are not qualities in objects, but belong entirely to the external sentiments of the taster; it is even more certain that beauty and deformity are not qualities in objects, but belong entirely to the internal sentiments of readers, viewers, or hearers. Yet it has to be accepted that certain qualities that are in objects are fitted by nature to produce those particular feelings. Now, these qualities are sometimes (1) present in an object only to a small degree, so that one's taste is not affected with such tiny qualities; or they are (2) present all mixed up with other such qualities, so that one can't pick out all the particular flavours from the jumble in which they are presented. Where the organs are (1) so finely tuned that nothing escapes them, and at the same time (2) so exact that they perceive every ingredient in the mixture—that is what we call 'delicacy of taste', whether we use this phrase in its literal sense (as in tasting wine) or its metaphorical sense ('taste' in art).

Here, then, the general rules of beauty are useful, because they are based on established models and on the observation of what qualities please (or displease) when they are presented on their own (2), and in a high degree (1). If someone who encounters those qualities in a small degree (1), and as aspects of a complex composition (2), if his organs aren't affected with a sensible delight (or uneasiness), we regard him as having no claim to delicacy of taste. To produce these general rules, or well-tested patterns of composition, is like finding the key with the leather thong in Sancho Panza's story. The key with the thong justified the verdict of Sancho Panza's two kinsmen, and confounded the would-be judges of wine who had laughed at them. Even if the cask had never been emptied, it would still have been the case that the taste of the kinsmen was delicate and that of the others dull and sluggish; but it would have been harder to prove to every bystander that this was so.

Similarly, even if the beauties of writing had never been tackled methodically and reduced to general principles, and even if no works had ever been generally acknowledged to be excellent models, still the different degrees of taste would have existed, and one man's judgment would have been better than another's; but it would have been harder to silence the bad critic, who—in the absence of agreed rules and models—could always insist upon his particular sentiment and refuse to submit to his antagonist. But in the state of affairs that we actually have, where there are rules and models, we can confront the bad critic and show him an accepted principle of art, illustrate this principle by examples which his own particular taste tell him are cases of the principle, and prove that the same principle can be applied to the present case, where he didn't perceive or feel its influence; and when we do all that, he must conclude that basically the fault lies in himself and that he lacks the delicacy of taste that is required for him to be conscious of every beauty and every blemish in any work of art.

It is generally acknowledged that every sense or faculty shows itself to perfection when it perceives with exactness its tiniest objects, allowing nothing to escape its notice. The smaller the objects that an eye is sensitive to, the finer the eye and the more elaborate its structure. You don't test whether someone has a good palate by giving him food with strong flavours. Rather, you give him a mixture of small ingredients, where we are still aware of each part despite its smallness and its being mixed in with the rest. Similarly, our mental taste shows itself to perfection in a quick and acute perception of beauty and ugliness, and a man can't be satisfied with himself if he suspects that he has failed to notice some excellence (or some blemish) in a discourse. In this case the perfection of the sense or feeling is found to be united with the perfection of the man. A very delicate palate may often be a great inconvenience both to the man who has it and to his friends; but a delicate taste for wit or beauty must always be a desirable quality, because it is the source of all the finest and most innocent enjoyments of which human nature is capable.

In this matter the sentiments of all mankind are agreed. Whenever you can become sure of someone's delicacy of taste, it is sure to meet with approval; and the best way of being sure is to appeal to the models and principles that have been established by unanimous agreement across the world and down the centuries. People naturally differ widely in how much delicacy of taste they have, but such differences aren't set in stone: in this respect one can improve. The best way to increase and improve one's delicacy of taste is practice in a particular art, and often experiencing or thinking about a particular sort of beauty. When objects of any kind are first presented to the eye or imagination, the sentiment that comes with them is obscure and confused, and the mind is largely unable to pronounce concerning their merits or defects. One's taste can't perceive the various excellences of the work, much less distinguish the particular character of each excellence and ascertain its quality and degree.

If one pronounces the work to be, as a whole, beautiful (or ugly), that is the most that can be expected; and a person who is unpracticed in this art-form will be apt to express even this judgment with hesitation and caution. But when he gains experience with those objects, his feeling becomes more exact and fine-grained; he not only perceives the beauties and defects of each part, but also marks the distinguishing species of each quality and assigns it suitable praise or blame. A clear and distinct sentiment stays with him throughout his survey of the objects; and he notes exactly the amount and kind of approval or displeasure that each part is naturally fitted to produce. The mist that previously seemed to hang over the object dissipates; the internal organ becomes more perfect in its operations, and can offer judgments, without danger of mistake, concerning the merits of every work. In short, practice gives skill and dexterity in carrying out any work, and gives equal skill and dexterity in judging it.

Practice is so helpful to the discernment of beauty that before we can judge any work of importance we need to confront that very work more than once, carefully and deliberately surveying it in different lights. One's first experience of a work of art brings a flutter or hurry of thought, which gets in the way of the genuine sentiment of beauty. One doesn't notice how the parts of the work are interrelated; one does not pick out very well the features that give the work its style. The various perfections and defects seem to be wrapped up in a sort of confusion, and present themselves to the imagination in a jumble. Not to mention that there is a florid and superficial kind of beauty that pleases at first, but after being found incompatible with a true expression either of reason or emotion, soon becomes cloying and boring, and is then scornfully rejected or at least valued much less highly.

To continue in the practice of contemplating any kind of beauty, one often has to compare different sorts and degrees of excellence, and to estimate their proportion to each other. A man who has had no opportunity to compare the different kinds of beauty is indeed totally unquailfied to give an opinion about any object presented to him. It is only through comparisons that we develop a fixed, established terminology for expressing praise and blame, and learn how to make the intensity of our praise or blame appropriate. A slap-dash painting may contain a certain glow of colours and accuracy of imitation; these are beauties, as far as they go, and would affect the mind of a peasant or an Indian with the highest admiration. A very crude popular song may have a certain amount of harmony (in its music) or of nature (in its words), and its music would be found harsh or its lyrics uninteresting only by someone who is familiar with superior beauties. A great inferiority of beauty gives pain to someone who is familiar with the highest excellence of the kind in question, and for that reason is declared to be an ugliness. . . .

Only someone who is accustomed to seeing, examining, and evaluating various works that have been admired at different times and in different nations can rate the merits of a work exhibited to his view, and give it its proper rank among the productions of genius. If a critic is to do this thoroughly, he must keep his mind free from all prejudice, allowing nothing to enter into his consideration but the one particular work that he is examining. Every work of art, in order to produce its proper effect on the mind, must be surveyed from a certain point of view, and won't be fully appreciated by people whose situation—real or imaginary—doesn't fit with the one that the work requires. An orator addresses a particular audience, and must take account of their particular ways of thinking, interests, opinions, emotions and prejudices; otherwise he won't succeed in his aim of governing their decisions and inflaming their feelings. Suppose, even, that his intended audience are hostile to him—unreasonably hostile—he must not overlook this disadvantage; he must try to soothe their feelings and come to be in their good graces before he starts in on the subject of his speech.

A critic of a different time or nation, reading this speech, can't form a true judgment of the oration unless he has all these circumstances before his mind and places himself in the same situation as the audience. Similarly, when any work is offered to the public, even if I am a friend or an enemy of the author, as a critic I must set aside this friendship or enmity and, considering myself as a man in general, try to forget myself as an individual and my personal circumstances. A person influenced by prejudice doesn't comply with this condition, but obstinately maintains his natural position without getting himself into the point of view that the performance requires. If the work is aimed at people of a different age or nation from his own, he makes no allowance for their special views and prejudices. Instead, full of the customs of his own time and place, he rashly condemns what seemed admirable in the eyes of all the people for whom the discourse was intended. If the work was done for the public, he never sufficiently enlarges his grasp or forgets his bias as a friend or enemy, as a rival or friendly commentator. In this way his sentiments are perverted, and the beauties and blemishes of the work he is judging don't affect him in the way they would have done if he had forced his imagination to stay under control and had forgotten himself for a moment. So his taste evidently departs from the true standard, and consequently loses all credit and authority.

It's well known that when the understanding is at work, prejudice destroys sound judgment and perverts all operations of the intellectual faculties. Well, prejudice is just as contrary to good taste, and has just as much power to corrupt our sentiment of beauty as to distort our judgments on matters of fact. It is a matter of good sense to check the influence of prejudice in both cases; and in this respect, as well as in many others, reason is required for the operations of taste (if indeed it is not an essential part of taste). I now mention three of the ways in which understanding, intellect, comes into the exercise of taste.

(1) In all the most notable productions of genius, the parts of a work are inter-related in significant ways; and its beauties and blemishes can't be perceived by someone whose thought is not capacious enough to take in all those parts, holding them together in a single thought, in order to perceive the texture and uniformity of the whole.

(2) Every work of art has a certain end or purpose which it is designed to achieve, and is to be judged as more or less perfect depending on how much or little it is fitted to attain this end. Eloquence aims to persuade, history aims to instruct, poetry aims to please by means of the emotions and the imagination. We must keep these ends constantly in mind when we survey any performance, and we must be able to judge how suitable the means are for their respective purposes.

(3) Also, every kind of composition—even the most poetic—is nothing but a chain of propositions and reasonings; not always perfectly precise and valid, but still plausible, however much disguised by the colouring of the imagination. The personages in tragedy and epic poetry must be represented as reasoning, thinking, concluding, and acting suitably to their character and circumstances; and a poet cannot hope to succeed in such a delicate undertaking unless he employs judgment as well as taste and invention. And good judgment is not only needed in addition to good taste; it is needed for good taste. The

- excellence of faculties that contributes to the improvement of reason,
- clearness of conception,
- exactness in making distinctions, and
- liveliness of uptake

are all essential to the operations of true taste and always accompany it. If a man who has experience in some art-form also has good sense, he will almost certainly be a good judge of beauties in that art-form; and if a man does not have a sound understanding, he will almost certainly not have good taste.

Thus, though the principles of taste are universal and nearly if not entirely the same in all men, few are qualified to give judgment on any work of art or set up their own sentiment as the standard of beauty. The organs of internal sensation are seldom so perfect as to allow the general principles their full play and produce a feeling that corresponds to those principles. They either struggle with some defect, or are outright spoiled by some disorder, and so they arouse a sentiment that may be declared wrong. A critic who has no delicacy judges without attending to any fine details, and is affected only by the large-scale obvious qualities of the object; the finer touches pass unnoticed and disregarded. If he isn't aided by practice, his verdict is confused and hesitant. If he hasn't made relevant comparisons, he will admire the most frivolous beauties—ones that really ought to count as defects. When he is influenced by prejudice, all his natural sentiments are perverted. When good sense is lacking, he isn't qualified to discern the highest and most excellent beauties of design and reasoning. Virtually everyone labours under some of these imperfections; so there are very few true judges in the finer arts, even during the most civilized ages. For a critic to be entitled to the label 'true judge', he must have strong sense, united to delicate sentiment, improved by practice, perfected by comparison, and cleared of all prejudice.

The true standard of taste and beauty is the agreed verdict of people like that, wherever they are to be found. But where are such critics to be found? What signs can we know them by? How are we to distinguish them from fakes? These questions are troubling, and seem to throw us back into the same uncertainty that we have been trying to escape from in the course of this essay. But these are questions of fact, not of sentiment. Whether any particular person is endowed with good sense and a delicate imagination that is free from prejudice may often be the subject of dispute, and be liable to great discussion and enquiry. But all mankind will agree that such a character is valuable and admirable. When these doubts occur, men can only do what they do with other disputable questions that are submitted to the understanding: they must produce the best arguments that their ingenuity suggests to them; they must acknowledge that a true and decisive standard exists somewhere, namely real existence and matter of fact; and they must be patient with people who differ from them in their appeals to this standard. All I need for my present purpose is to have proved that the taste of all individuals is not on an equal footing, and that there are some men—however hard it may be to say which men—whom everyone will acknowledge to have a preference above others.

But the difficulty of finding the standard of taste, even in particular cases, isn't as great as it's said to be. In theory we may readily accept that there is a sure criterion in science and deny that there is one for sentiment, in practice we find that the criterion for science is harder to pin down than the one for sentiment. Theories of abstract philosophy, systems of profound theology, have held sway during one age and then later been universally exploded: their absurdity has been detected; other theories and systems have taken their place, and then they in turn were supplanted by their successors. We have never known anything more open to the revolutions of chance and fashion than these purported decisions of science.

The case is not the same with the beauties of eloquence and poetry. Well-done expressions of passion and nature are sure after a little time to earn public applause which they maintain for ever. Aristotle and Plato and Epicurus and Descartes may successively yield to each other; but Terence and Virgil maintain an undisputed sway over the minds of men in general. The abstract philosophy of Cicero isn't believed today; the power of his oratory still wins our admiration. Though men of delicate taste are rare, they can easily be picked out in society by the soundness of their understanding and how much abler they are than the rest of mankind. Because of the high status they have acquired, their lively approval of any work of art tends to become the general view. Many men when left to themselves have only a faint and hesitant perception of beauty, and yet they can enjoy any fine stroke that is pointed out to them. Every convert to the admiration of the real poet or orator is the cause of some new conversion. Prejudices may come out on top for a while, but they never unite in celebrating any rival to the true genius, and eventually they give way to the force of nature and sound sentiment. Thus, though a civilized nation may easily be mistaken in which philosopher they choose to admire, they have never been found to err for long in their affection for a favourite writer of epics or tragedies.

But despite all our attempts to fix a standard of taste, and to reconcile people's clashing intuitions, two sources of differences have been left standing; they are not enough to smudge all the boundaries of beauty and ugliness, but they often produce differences in how much a work is approved or disapproved. One is the different temperaments of particular men; the other the particular manners and opinions of our age and country. The general principles of taste are the same across mankind; when men vary in their judgments, there can often be seen to be some defect or malfunction in the faculties on one side or the other, arising from prejudice, from lack of practice, or from lack of delicacy; and in such cases we have good reason to approve one taste and condemn the other. But when the parties to the disagreement differ in their internal frame or external situation in a way that brings no discredit on either and provides no basis for preferring one above the other, then a certain degree of divergence in judgment is unavoidable, and it's no use out looking for a standard by which we can reconcile the conflicting sentiments.

Amorous and tender images will get through to the feelings of a young man whose emotions are warm more than they will to the feelings of an older man who takes pleasure in wise philosophical reflections concerning the conduct of life and moderation of the emotions. At twenty Ovid may be the favourite author, Horace at forty, and perhaps Tacitus at fifty. In such a case it would be useless for us to try to enter into the sentiments of others, divesting ourselves of the propensities that are natural to us. We choose favourite authors as we choose friends, from a conformity of mood and disposition. Gaiety or emotion, sentiment or reflection —whichever of these most predominates in our make-up gives us a special sympathy with the writer who resembles us.

One person is more pleased with the sublime, another with the tender, a third with light-hearted wit. One is acutely aware of blemishes and cares enormously about correctness; another has a more lively feeling for beauties, and pardons twenty absurdities and defects because of one little episode in the work that is inspiring or deeply touching. The ear of this man is entirely turned towards conciseness and energy, that man is delighted with a rich and harmonious expression. Simplicity draws one, ornament draws another. Comedy, tragedy, satire, odes—each has its partisans who prefer that particular type of writing to all others. It is plainly an error in a critic to give his approval to only one sort or style of writing and condemn all the rest. But it is almost impossible not to feel some inclination in favour of the sort or style that suits our particular temperament and character. Such preferences are harmless and unavoidable, and it is never reasonable to argue about them because there is no standard by which such an argument could be decided.

IMMANUEL KANT
THE CRITIQUE OF JUDGEMENT

Translated by James Creed Meredith

FIRST PART. CRITIQUE OF AESTHETIC JUDGEMENT

BOOK I. Analytic of the Beautiful
FIRST MOMENT. Of the Judgement of Taste: Moment of Quality

The definition of taste here relied upon is that it is the faculty of estimating the beautiful. But the discovery of what is required for calling an object beautiful must be reserved for the analysis of judgements of taste. In my search for the moments to which attention is paid by this judgement in its reflection, I have followed the guidance of the logical functions of judging (for a judgement of taste always involves a reference to understanding). I have brought the moment of quality first under review, because this is what the aesthetic judgement on the beautiful looks to in the first instance.

§1. The judgement of taste is aesthetic

If we wish to discern whether anything is beautiful or not, we do not refer the representation of it to the object by means of understanding with a view to cognition, but by means of the imagination (acting perhaps in conjunction with understanding) we refer the representation to the subject and its feeling of pleasure or displeasure. The judgement of taste, therefore, is not a cognitive judgement, and so not logical, but is aesthetic —which means that it is one whose determining ground cannot be other than subjective. Every reference of representations is capable of being objective, even that of sensations (in which case it signifies the real in an empirical representation). The one exception to this is the feeling of pleasure or displeasure. This denotes nothing in the object, but is a feeling which the subject has of itself and of the manner in which it is affectted by the representation.

To apprehend a regular and appropriate building with one's cognitive faculties, be the mode of representation clear or confused, is quite a different thing from being conscious of this representation with an accompanying sensation of delight. Here the representation is referred wholly to the subject, and what is more to its feeling of life—under the name of the feeling of pleasure or displeasure—and this forms the basis of a quite separate faculty of discriminating and estimating, that contributes nothing to knowledge. All it does is to compare the given representation in the subject with the entire faculty of representations of which the mind is conscious in the feeling of its state. Given representations in a judgement may be empirical, and so aesthetic; but the judgement which is pronounced by their means is logical, provided it refers them to the object. Conversely, be the given representations even rational, but referred in a judgement solely to the subject (to its feeling), they are always to that extent aesthetic.

§2. The delight which determines the judgement of taste is independent of all interest

The delight which we connect with the representation of the real existence of an object is called interest. Such a delight, therefore, always involves a reference to the faculty of desire, either as its determining ground, or else as necessarily implicated with its determining ground. Now, where the question is whether something is beautiful, we do not want to know, whether we, or anyone else, are, or even could be, concerned in the real existence of the thing, but rather what estimate we form of it on mere contemplation (intuition or reflection). If anyone asks me whether I consider that the palace I see before me is beautiful, I may, perhaps, reply that I do not care for things of that sort that are merely made to be gaped at. Or I may reply in the same strain as that Iroquois sachem who said that nothing in Paris pleased him better than the eating-houses. I may even go a step further and inveigh with the vigour of a Rousseau against the vigour of a great against the vanity of the of the people on such superfluous things. Or, in fine, I may quite easily persuade myself that if I found myself on an uninhabited island, without hope of ever again coming among men, and could conjure such a palace into existence by a mere wish, I should still not trouble to do so, so long as I had a hut there that was comfortable enough for me. All this may be admitted and approved; only it is not the point now at issue. All one wants to know is whether the mere representation of the object is to my liking, no matter how indifferent I may be to the real existence of the object of this representation. It is quite plain that in order to say that the object is beautiful, and to show that I have taste, everything turns on the meaning which I can give to this representation, and not on any factor which makes me dependent on the real existence of the object. Everyone must allow that a judgement on the beautiful which is tinged with the slightest interest, is very partial and not a pure judgement of taste. One must not be in the least prepossessed in favour of the real existence of the thing, but must preserve complete indifference in this respect, in order to play the part of judge in matters of taste.

This proposition, which is of the utmost importance, cannot be better explained than by contrasting the pure disinterested delight which appears in the judgement of taste with that allied to an interest—especially if we can also assure ourselves that there are no other kinds of interest beyond those presently to be mentioned.

§3. Delight in the agreeable is coupled with interest

That is agreeable which the senses find pleasing in sensation. This at once affords a convenient opportunity for condemning and directing particular attention to a prevalent confusion of the double meaning of which the word sensation is capable. All delight (as is said or thought) is itself sensation (of a pleasure). Consequently everything that pleases, and for the very reason that it pleases, is agreeable-and according to its different degrees, or its relations to other agreeable sensations, is attractive, charming, delicious, enjoyable, etc. But if this is conceded, then impressions of sense, which determine inclination, or principles of reason, which determine the will, or mere contemplated forms of intuition, which determine judgement, are all on a par in everything relevant to their effect upon the feeling of pleasure, for this would be agreeableness in the sensation of one's state; and since, in the last resort, all the elaborate work of our faculties must issue in and unite in the practical as its goal, we could credit our faculties with no other appreciation of things and the worth of things, than that consisting in the gratification which they promise. How this is attained is in the end immaterial; and, as the choice of the means is here the only thing that can make a difference, men might indeed blame one another for folly or imprudence, but never for baseness or wickedness; for they are all, each according to his own way of looking at things, pursuing one goal, which for each is the gratification in question.

When a modification of the feeling of pleasure or displeasure is termed sensation, this expression is given quite a different meaning to that which it bears when I call the representation of a thing (through sense as a receptivity pertaining to the faculty of knowledge) sensation. For in the latter case the representation is referred to the object, but in the former it is referred solely to the subject and is not available for any cognition, not even for that by which the subject cognizes itself.

Now in the above definition the word sensation is used to denote an objective representation of sense; and, to avoid continually running the risk of misinterpretation, we shall call that which must always remain purely subjective, and is absolutely incapable of forming a representation of an object, by the familiar name of feeling. The green colour of the meadows belongs to objective sensation, as the perception of an object of sense; but its agreeableness to subjective sensation, by which no object is represented; i.e., to feeling, through which the object is regarded as an object of delight (which involves no cognition of the object).

Now, that a judgement on an object by which its agreeableness is affirmed, expresses an interest in it, is evident from the fact that through sensation it provokes a desire for similar objects, consequently the delight presupposes, not the simple judgement about it, but the bearing its real existence has upon my state so far as affected by such an object. Hence we do not merely say of the agreeable that it pleases, but that it gratifies. I do not accord it a simple approval, but inclination is aroused by it, and where agreeableness is of the liveliest type a judgement on the character of the object is so entirely out of place that those who are always intent only on enjoyment (for that is the word used to denote intensity of gratification) would fain dispense with all judgement.

§4. Delight in the good is coupled with interest

That is good which by means of reason commends itself by its mere concept. We call that good for something which only pleases as a means; but that which pleases on its own account we call good in itself. In both cases the concept of an end is implied, and consequently the relation of reason to (at least possible) willing, and thus a delight in the existence of an object or action, i.e., some interest or other.

To deem something good, I must always know what sort of a thing the object is intended to be, i.e., I must have a concept of it. That is not necessary to enable me to see beauty in a thing. Flowers, free patterns, lines aimlessly intertwining-technically termed foliage-have no signification, depend upon no definite concept, and yet please. Delight in the beautiful must depend upon the reflection on an object precursory to some (not definitely determined) concept. It is thus also differentiated from the agreeable, which rests entirely upon sensation.

In many cases, no doubt, the agreeable and the good seem convertible terms. Thus it is commonly said that all (especially lasting) gratification is of itself good; which is almost equivalent to saying that to be permanently agreeable and to be good are identical. But it is readily apparent that this is merely a vicious confusion of words, for the concepts appropriate to these expressions are far from interchangeable. The agreeable, which, as such, represents the object solely in relation to sense, must in the first instance be brought under principles of reason through the concept of an end, to be, as an object of will, called good. But that the reference to delight is wholly different where what gratifies is at the same time called good, is evident from the fact that with the good the question always is whether it is mediately or immediately good, i.e., useful or good in itself; whereas with the agreeable this point can never arise, since the word always means what pleases immediately—and it is just the same with what I call beautiful.

Even in everyday parlance, a distinction is drawn between the agreeable and the good. We do not scruple to say of a dish that stimulates the palate with spices and other condiments that it is agreeable owning all the while that it is not good: because, while it immediately satisfies the senses, it is mediately displeasing, i.e., in the eye of reason that looks ahead to the consequences. Even in our estimate of health, this same distinction may be traced. To all that possess it, it is immediately agreeable-at least negatively, i.e., as remoteness of all bodily pains. But, if we are to say that it is good, we must further apply to reason to direct it to ends, that is, we must regard it as a state that puts us in a congenial mood for all we have to do. Finally, in respect of happiness everyone believes that the greatest aggregate of the pleasures of life, taking duration as well as number into account, merits the name of a true, nay even of the highest, good. But reason sets its face against this too.

Agreeableness is enjoyment. But if this is all that we are bent on, it would be foolish to be scrupulous about the means that procure it for us—whether it be obtained passively by the bounty of nature or actively and by the work of our own hands. But that there is any intrinsic worth in the real existence of a man who merely lives for enjoyment, however busy he may be in this respect, even when in so doing he serves others—all equally with himself intent only on enjoyment—as an excellent means to that one end, and does so, moreover, because through sympathy he shares all their gratifications—this is a view to which reason will never let itself be brought round. Only by what a man does heedless of enjoyment, in complete freedom, and independently of what he can procure passively from the hand of nature, does be give to his existence, as the real existence of a person, an absolute worth. Happiness, with all its plethora of pleasures, is far from being an unconditioned good.

But, despite all this difference between the agreeable and the good, they both agree in being invariably coupled with an interest in their object. This is true, not alone of the agreeable, §3, and of the mediately good, i.e., the useful, which pleases as a means to some pleasure, but also of that which is good absolutely and from every point of view, namely the moral good which carries with it the highest interest. For the good is the object of will, i.e., of a rationally determined faculty of desire). But to will something, and to take a delight in its existence, i.e., to take an interest in it, are identical.

§5. Comparison of the three specifically different kinds of delight

Both the agreeable and the good involve a reference to the faculty of desire, and are thus attended, the former with a delight pathologically conditioned (by stimuli), the latter with a pure practical delight. Such delight is determined not merely by the representation of the object, but also by the represented bond of connection between the subject and the real existence of the object. It is not merely the object, but also its real existence, that pleases. On the other hand, the judgement of taste is simply contemplative, i.e., it is a judgement which is indifferent as to the existence of an object, and only decides how its character stands with the feeling of pleasure and displeasure. But not even is this contemplation itself directed to concepts; for the judgement of taste is not a cognitive judgement (neither a theoretical one nor a practical), and hence, also, is not grounded on concepts, nor yet intentionally directed to them.

The agreeable, the beautiful, and the good thus denote three different relations of representations to the feeling of pleasure and displeasure, as a feeling in respect of which we distinguish different objects or modes of representation. Also, the corresponding expressions which indicate our satisfaction in them are different The agreeable is what GRATIFIES a man; the beautiful what simply PLEASES him; the good what is ESTEEMED (approved), i.e., that on which he sets an objecttive worth. Agreeableness is a significant factor even with irrational animals; beauty has purport and significance only for human beings, i.e., for beings at once animal and rational (but not merely for them as rational—intelligent beings—but only for them as at once animal and rational); whereas the good is good for every rational being in general—a proposition which can only receive its complete justification and explanation in the sequel. Of all these three kinds of delight, that of taste in the beautyful may be said to be the one and only disinterested and free delight; for, with it, no interest, whether of sense or reason, extorts approval. And so we may say that delight, in the three cases mentioned, is related to inclination, to favour, or to respect. For FAVOUR is the only free liking. An object of inclination, and one which a law of reason imposes upon our desire, leaves us no freedom to turn anything into an object of pleasure. All interest presupposes a want, or calls one forth; and, being a ground determining approval, deprives the judgement on the object of its freedom.

So far as the interest of inclination in the case of the agreeable goes, everyone says "Hunger is the best sauce; and people with a healthy appetite relish everything, so long as it is something they can eat." Such delight, consequently, gives no indication of taste having anything to say to the choice. Only when men have got all they want can we tell who among the crowd has taste or not. Similarly there may be correct habits (conduct) without virtue, politeness without good-will, propriety without honour, etc. For where the moral law dictates, there is, objectively, no room left for free choice as to what one has to do; and to show taste in the way one carries out these dictates, or in estimating the way others do so, is a totally different matter from displaying the moral frame of one's mind. For the latter involves a command and produces a need of something, whereas moral taste only plays with the objects of delight without devoting itself sincerely to any. . . .

Definition of the Beautiful derived from the First Moment

Taste is the faculty of estimating an object or a mode of representtation by means of a delight or aversion apart from any interest. The object of such a delight is called beautiful.

SECOND MOMENT. Of the Judgement of Taste: Moment of Quantity

§6. The beautiful is that which, apart from concepts, is represented as the object of a universal delight

This definition of the beautiful is deducible from the foregoing definition of it as an object of delight apart from any interest. For where any one is conscious that his delight in an object is with him independent of interest, it is inevitable that he should look on the object as one containing a ground of delight for all men. For, since the delight is not based on any inclination of the subject (or on any other deliberate interest), but the subject feels himself completely free in respect of the liking which he accords to the object, he can find as reason for his delight no personal conditions to which his own subjective self might alone be party. Hence he must regard it as resting on what he may also presuppose in every other person; and therefore he must believe that he has reason for demanding a similar delight from every one. Accordingly he will speak of the beautiful as if beauty were a quality of the object and the judgement logical (forming a cognition of the object by concepts of it); although it is only aesthetic, and contains merely a reference of the representation of the object to the subject; because it still bears this resemblance to the logical judgement, that it may be presupposed to be valid for all men. But this universality cannot spring from concepts. For from concepts there is no transition to the feeling of pleasure or displeasure (save in the case of pure practical laws, which, however, carry an interest with them; and such an interest does not attach to the pure judgement of taste). The result is that the judgement of taste, with its attendant consciousness of detachment from all interest, must involve a claim to validity for all men, and must do so apart from universality attached to objects, i.e., there must be coupled with it a claim to subjective universality.

§7. Comparison of the beautiful with the agreeable and the good

As regards the agreeable, every one concedes that his judgement, which he bases on a private feeling, and in which he declares that an object pleases him, is restricted merely to himself personally. Thus he does not take it amiss if, when he says that Canary-wine is agreeable, another corrects the expression and reminds him that he ought to say: "It is agreeable to me." This applies not only to the taste of the tongue, the palate, and the throat, but to what may with any one be agreeable to eye or ear. A violet colour is to one soft and lovely: to another dull and faded. One man likes the tone of wind instruments, another prefers that of string instruments. To quarrel over such points with the idea of condemning another's judgement as incorrect when it differs from our own, as if the opposition between the two judgements were logical, would be folly. With the agreeable, therefore, the axiom holds good: Everyone has his own taste (that of sense).

The beautiful stands on quite a different footing. It would, on the contrary, be ridiculous if any one who plumed himself on his taste were to think of justifying himself by saying: "This object (the building we see, the dress that person has on, the concert we hear, the poem submitted to our criticism) is beautiful for me." For if it merely pleases him, be must not call it beautiful. Many things may for him possess charm and agreeableness —no one cares about that; but when he puts a thing on a pedestal and calls it beautiful, he demands the same delight from others. He judges not merely for himself, but for all men, and then speaks of beauty as if it were a property of things. Thus he says the thing is beautiful; and it is not as if he counted on others agreeing in his judgement of liking owing to his having found them in such agreement on a number of occasions, but he demands this agreement of them. He blames them if they judge differently, and denies them taste, which he still requires of them as something they ought to have; and to this extent it is not open to men to say: "Every one has his own taste." This would be equivalent to saying that there is no such thing at all as taste, i.e., no aesthetic judgement capable of making a rightful claim upon the assent of all men.

Yet even in the case of the agreeable, we find that the estimates men form do betray a prevalent agreement among them, which leads to our crediting some with taste and denying it to others, and that, too, not as an organic sense but as a critical faculty in respect of the agreeable generally. So of one who knows how to entertain his guests with pleasures (of enjoyment through all the senses) in such a way that one and all are pleased, we say that he has taste. But the universality here is only understood in a comparative sense; and the rules that apply are, like all empirical rules, general only, not universal, the latter being what the judgement of taste upon the beautiful deals or claims to deal in. It is a judgement in respect of sociability so far as resting on empirical rules. In respect of the good, it is true that judgements also rightly assert a claim to validity for every one; but the good is only represented as an object of universal delight by means of a concept, which is the case neither with the agreeable nor the beautiful.

§8. In a judgement of taste the universality of delight is only represented as subjective

This particular form of the universality of an aesthetic judgement, which is to be met in a judgement of taste, is a significant feature, not for the logician certainly, but for the transcendental philosopher. It calls for no small effort on his part to discover its origin, but in return it brings to light a property of our cognitive faculty which, without this analysis, would have remained unknown.

First, one must get firmly into one's mind that by the judgement of taste (upon the beautiful) the delight in an object is imputed to everyone, yet without being founded on a concept (for then it would be the good), and that this claim to universality is such an essential factor of a judgement by which we describe anything as beautiful, that were it not for its being present to the mind it would never enter into any one's head to use this expression, but everything that pleased without a concept would be ranked as agreeable. For in respect of the agreeable, everyone is allowed to have his own opinion, and no one insists upon others agreeing with his judgement of taste, which is what is invariably done in the judgement of taste about beauty. The first of these I may call the taste of sense, the second, the taste of reflection: the first laying down judgements merely private, the second, on the other hand, judgements ostensibly of general validity (public), but both alike being aesthetic (not practical) judgements about an object merely in respect of the bearings of its representation on the feeling of pleasure or displeasure.

Now it does seem strange that while with the taste of sense it is not alone experience that shows that its judgement (of pleasure or displeasure in something) is not universally valid, but every one willingly refrains from imputing this agreement to others (despite the frequent actual prevalence of a considerable consensus of general opinion even in these judgements), the taste of reflection, which, as experience teaches, has often enough to put up with a rude dismissal of its claims to universal validity of its judgement (upon the beautiful), can (as it actually does) find it possible for all that to formulate judgements capable of demanding this agreement in its universality. Such agreement it does in fact require from every one for each of its judgements of taste the persons who pass these judgements not quarreling over the possibility of such a claim, but only failing in particular cases to come to terms as to the correct application of this faculty.

First of all we have here to note that a universality which does not rest upon concepts of the object (even though these are only empirical) is in no way logical, but aesthetic, i.e., does not involve any objective quantity of the judgement, but only one that is subjective. For this universality I use the expression general validity, which denotes the validity of the reference of a representation, not to the cognitive faculties, but to the feeling of pleasure or displeasure for every subject. (The same expression, however, may also be employed for the logical quantity of the judgement, provided we add objective universal validity, to distinguish it from the merely subjective validity which is always aesthetic.)

Now a judgement that has objective universal validity has always got the subjective also, i.e., if the judgement is valid for everything which is contained under a given concept, it is valid also for all who represent an object by means of this concept. But from a subjective universal validity, i.e., the aesthetic, that does not rest on any concept, no conclusion can be drawn to the logical; because judgements of that kind have no bearing upon the object. But for this very reason the aesthetic universality attributed to a judgement must also be of a special kind, seeing that it does not join the predicate of beauty to the concept of the object taken in its entire logical sphere, and yet does extend this predicate over the whole sphere of judging subjects.

In their logical quantity, all judgements of taste are singular judgements. For, since I must present the object immediately to my feeling of pleasure or displeasure, and that, too, without the aid of concepts, such judgements cannot have the quantity of judgements with objective general validity. Yet by taking the singular representation of the object of the judgement of taste, and by comparison converting it into a concept according to the conditions determining that judgement, we can arrive at a logically universal judgement. For instance, by a judgement of the taste I describe the rose at which I am looking as beautiful. The judgement, on the other hand, resulting from the comparison of a number of singular representations: "Roses in general are beautiful," is no longer pronounced as a purely aesthetic judgement, but as a logical judgement founded on one that is aesthetic. Now the judgement, "The rose is agreeable" (to smell) is also, no doubt, an aesthetic and singular judgement, but then it is not one of taste but of sense. For it has this point of difference from a judgement of taste, that the latter imports an aesthetic quantity of universality, i.e., of validity for everyone which is not to be met with in a judgement upon the agreeable. It is only judgements upon the good which, while also determining the delight in an object, possess logical and not mere aesthetic universality; for it is as involving a cognition of the object that "they are valid of it, and on that account valid for everyone.

In forming an estimate of objects merely from concepts, all representation of beauty goes by the board. There can, therefore, be no rule according to which any one is to be compelled to recognize anything as beautiful. Whether a dress, a house, or a flower is beautiful is a matter upon which one declines to allow one's judgement to be swayed by any reasons or principles. We want to get a look at the object with our own eyes, just as if our delight depended on sensation. And yet, if upon so doing, we call the object beautiful, we believe ourselves to be speaking with a universal voice, and lay claim to the concurrence of everyone, whereas no private sensation would be decisive except for the observer alone and his liking.

Here, now, we may perceive that nothing is postulated in the judgement of taste but such a universal voice in respect of delight that it is not mediated by concepts; consequently, only the possibility of an aesthetic judgement capable of being at the same time deemed valid for everyone. The judgement of taste itself does not postulate the agreement of everyone (for it is only competent for a logically universal judgement to do this, in that it is able to bring forward reasons); it only imputes this agreement to everyone, as an instance of the rule in respect of which it looks for confirmation, not from concepts, but from the concurrence of others. The universal voice is, therefore, only an idea—resting upon grounds the investigation of which is here postponed. It may be a matter of uncertainty whether a person who thinks he is laying down a judgement of taste is, in fact, judging in conformity with that idea; but that this idea is what is contemplated in his judgement, and that, consequently, it is meant to be a judgement of taste, is proclaimed by his use of the expression "beauty." For himself he can be certain on the point from his mere consciousness of the separation of everything belonging to the agreeable and the good from the delight remaining to him; and this is all for which be promises himself the agreement of everyone—a claim which, under these conditions, he would also be warranted in making, were it not that he frequently sinned against them, and thus passed an erroneous judgement of taste.

§9. Investigation of the question of the relative priority in a judgement of taste of the feeling of pleasure and the estimating of the object

The solution of this problem is the key to the Critique of taste, and so is worthy of all attention.

Were the pleasure in a given object to be the antecedent, and were the universal communicability of this pleasure to be all that the judgement of taste is meant to allow to the representation of the object, such a sequence would be self-contradictory. For a pleasure of that kind would be nothing but the feeling of mere agreeableness to the senses, and so, from its very nature, would possess no more than private validity, seeing that it would be immediately dependent on the representation through which the object is given.

Hence it is the universal capacity for being communicated incident to the mental state in the given representation which, as the subjective condition of the judgement of taste, must be, fundamental, with the pleasure in the object as its consequent. Nothing, however, is capable of being universally communicated but cognition and representation so far as appurtenant to cognition. For it is only as thus appurtenant that the representation is objective, and it is this alone that gives it a universal point of reference with which the power of representation of every one is obliged to harmonize. If, then, the determining ground of the judgement as to this universal communicability of the representation is to be merely subjective, that is to say, to be conceived independently of any concept of the object, it can be nothing else than the mental state that presents itself in the mutual relation of the powers of representation so far as they refer a given representation to cognition in general.

The cognitive powers brought into play by this representation are here engaged in a free play, since no definite concept restricts them to a particular rule of cognition. Hence the mental state in this representation must be one of a feeling of the free play of the powers of representation in a given representation for a cognition in general. Now a representation, whereby an object is given, involves, in order that it may become a source of cognition at all, imagination for bringing together the manifold of intuition, and understanding for the unity of the concept uniting the representations. This state of free play of the cognitive faculties attending a representation by which an object is given must admit of universal communication: because cognition, as a definition of the object with which given representations (in any subject whatever) are to accord, is the one and only representation which is valid for everyone.

As the subjective universal communicability of the mode of representation in a judgement of taste is to subsist apart from the presupposition of any definite concept, it can be nothing else than the mental state present in the free play of imagination and understanding (so far as these are in mutual accord, as is requisite for cognition in general); for we are conscious that this subjective relation suitable for a cognition in general must be just as valid for everyone, and consequently as universally communicable, as is any indeterminate cognition, which always rests upon that relation as its subjective condition.

Now this purely subjective (aesthetic) estimating of the object, or of the representation through which it is given, is antecedent to the pleasure in it, and is the basis of this pleasure in the harmony of the cognitive faculties. Again, the above-described universality of the subjecttive conditions of estimating objects forms the sole foundation of this universal subjective validity of the delight which we connect with the representation of the object that we call beautiful.

That an ability to communicate one's mental state, even though it be only in respect of our cognitive faculties, is attended with a pleasure, is a fact which might easily be demonstrated from the natural propensity of mankind to social life, i.e., empirically and psychologically. But what we have here in view calls for something more than this. In a judgement of taste, the pleasure felt by us is exacted from everyone else as necessary, just as if, when we call something beautiful, beauty was to be regarded as a quality of the object forming part of its inherent determination according to concepts; although beauty is for itself, apart from any reference to the feeling of the subject, nothing. But the discussion of this question must be reserved until we have answered the further one of whether, and how, aesthetic judgements are possible a priori.

At present we are exercised with the lesser question of the way in which we become conscious, in a judgement of taste, of a reciprocal subjective common accord of the powers of cognition. Is it aesthetically by sensation and our mere internal sense? Or is it intellectually by consciousness of our intentional activity in bringing these powers into play?

Now if the given representation occasioning the judgement of taste were a concept which united understanding and imagination in the estimate of the object so as to give a cognition of the object, the consciousness of this relation would be intellectual (as in the objective schematism of judgement dealt with in the *Critique of Pure Reason*). But, then, in that case the judgement would not be laid down with respect to pleasure and displeasure, and so would not be a judgement of taste. But, now, the judgement of taste determines the object, independently of concepts, in respect of delight and of the predicate of beauty.

There is, therefore, no other way for the subjective unity of the relation in question to make itself known than by sensation. The quickening of both faculties (imagination and understanding) to an indefinite, but yet, thanks to the given representation, harmonious activity, such as belongs to cognition generally, is the sensation whose universal communicability is postulated by the judgement of taste. An objective relation can, of course, only be thought, yet in so far as, in respect of its conditions, it is subjective, it may be felt in its effect upon the mind, and, in the case of a relation (like that of the powers of representation to a faculty of cognition generally) which does not rest on any concept, no other consciousness of it is possible beyond that through sensation of its effect upon the mind—an effect consisting in the more facile play of both mental powers (imagination and understanding) as quickened by their mutual accord. A representation which is singular and independent of comparison with other representations, and, being such, yet accords with the conditions of the universality that is the general concern of understanding, is one that brings the cognitive faculties into that proportionate accord which we require for all cognition and which we therefore deem valid for everyone who is so constituted as to judge by means of understanding and sense conjointly (i.e., for every man).

Definition of the Beautiful drawn from the Second Moment

The beautiful is that which, apart from a concept, pleases universally.

THIRD MOMENT. Of Judgements of Taste: Moment of the relation of the Ends brought under Review in such Judgements

§10. Finality in general

Let us define the meaning of "an end" in transcendental terms (i.e., without presupposing anything empirical, such as the feeling of pleasure). An end is the object of a concept so far as this concept is regarded as the cause of the object (the real ground of its possibility); and the causality of a concept in respect of its object is finality (*forma finalis*). Where, then, not the cognition of an object merely, but the object itself (its form or real existence) as an effect, is thought to be possible only through a concept of it, there we imagine an end. The representation of the effect is here the determining ground of its cause and takes the lead of it. The consciousness of the causality of a representation in respect of the state of the subject as one tending to preserve a continuance of that state, may here be said to denote in a general way what is called pleasure; whereas displeasure is that representation which contains the ground for converting the state of the representations into their opposite (for hindering or removing them).

The faculty of desire, so far as determinable only through concepts, i.e., so as to act in conformity with the representation of an end, would be the Will. But an object, or state of mind, or even an action may, although its possibility does not necessarily presuppose the representation of an end, be called final simply on account of its possibility being only explicable and intelligible for us by virtue of an assumption on our part of fundamental causality according to ends, i.e., a will that would have so ordained it according to a certain represented rule. Finality, therefore, may exist apart from an end, in so far as we do not locate the causes of this form in a will, but yet are able to render the explanation of its possibility intelligible to ourselves only by deriving it from a will. Now we are not always obliged to look with the eye of reason into what we observe (i.e., to consider it in its possibility). So we may at least observe a finality of form, and trace it in objects—though by reflection only—without resting it on an end (as the material of the *nexus finalis*).

§11. The sole foundation of the judgement of taste is the form of finality of an object (or mode of representing it)

Whenever an end is regarded as a source of delight, it always imports an interest as determining ground of the judgement on the object of pleasure. Hence the judgement of taste cannot rest on any subjective end as its ground. But neither can any representation of an objective end, i.e., of the possibility of the object itself on principles of final connection, determine the judgement of taste, and, consequently, neither can any concept of the good. For the judgement of taste is an aesthetic and not a cognitive judgement, and so does not deal with any concept of the nature or of the internal or external possibility, by this or that cause, of the object, but simply with the relative bearing of the representative powers so far as determined by a representation.

Now this relation, present when an object is characterized as beautiful, is coupled with the feeling of pleasure. This pleasure is by the judgement of taste pronounced valid for every one; hence an agreeableness attending the representation is just as incapable of containing the determining ground of the judgement as the representation of the perfection of the object or the concept of the good. We are thus left with the subjective finality in the representation of an object, exclusive of any end (objective or subjective)—consequently the bare form of finality in the representation whereby an object is given to us, so far as we are conscious of it as that which is alone capable of constituting the delight which, apart from any concept, we estimate as universally communicable, and so of forming the determining ground of the judgement of taste.

§12. The judgement of taste rests upon a priori grounds

To determine a priori the connection of the feeling of pleasure or displeasure as an effect, with some representation or other (sensation or concept) as its cause, is utterly impossible; for that would be a causal relation which (with objects of experience) is always one that can only be cognized a posteriori and with the help of experience. True, in the *Critique of Practical Reason* we did actually derive a priori from universal moral concepts the feeling of respect (as a particular and peculiar modification of this feeling which does not strictly answer either to the pleasure or displeasure which we receive from empirical objects). But there we were further able to cross the border of experience and call in aid a causality resting on a supersensible attribute of the subject, namely that of freedom. But even there it was not this feeling exactly that we deduced from the idea of the moral as cause, but from this was derived simply the determination of the will. But the mental state present in the determination of the will by any means is at once in itself a feeling of pleasure and identical with it, and so does not issue from it as an effect. Such an effect must only be assumed where the concept of the moral as a good precedes the determination of the will by the law; for in that case it would be futile to derive the pleasure combined with the concept from this concept as a mere cognition.

Now the pleasure in aesthetic judgements stands on a similar footing: only that here it is merely contemplative and does not bring about an interest in the object; whereas in the moral judgement it is practical, The consciousness of mere formal finality in the play of the cognitive faculties of the subject attending a representation whereby an object is given, is the pleasure itself, because it involves a determining ground of the subject's activity in respect of the quickening of its cognitive powers, and thus an internal causality (which is final) in respect of cognition generally, but without being limited to a definite cognition, and consequently a mere form of the subjective finality of a representation in an aesthetic judgement. This pleasure is also in no way practical, neither resembling that form the pathological ground of agreeableness nor that from the intellectual ground of the represented good. But still it involves an inherent causality, that, namely, of preserving a continuance of the state of the representation itself and the active engagement of the cognitive powers without ulterior aim. We dwell on the contemplation of the beautiful because this contemplation strengthens and reproduces itself. The case is analogous (but analogous only) to the way we linger on a charm in the representation of an object which keeps arresting the attention, the mind all the while remaining passive.

§13. The pure judgement of taste is independent of charm and emotion

Every interest vitiates the judgement of taste and robs it of its impartiality. This is especially so where, instead of, like the interest of reason, making finality take the lead of the lead of the feeling of pleasure, it grounds it upon this feeling-which is what always happens in aesthetic judgements upon anything so far as it gratifies or pains. Hence judgements so influenced can either lay no claim at all to a universally valid delight, or else must abate their claim in proportion as sensations of the kind in question enter into the determining grounds of taste. Taste that requires an added element of charm and emotion for its delight, not to speak of adopting this as the measure of its approval, has not yet emerged from barbarism.

And yet charms are frequently not alone ranked with beauty (which ought properly to be a question merely of the form) as supplementary to the aesthetic universal delight, but they have been accredited as intrinsic beauties, and consequently the matter of delight passed off for the form. This is a misconception which, like many others that have still an underlying element of truth, may be removed by a careful definition of these concepts.

A judgement of taste which is uninfluenced by charm or emotion (though these may be associated with the delight in the beautiful), and whose determining ground, therefore, is simply finality of form, is a pure judgement of taste.

§14. Exemplification

Aesthetic, just like theoretical (logical) judgements, are divisible into empirical and pure. The first are those by which agreeableness or disagreeableness, the second those by which beauty is predicated of an object or its mode of representation. The former are judgements of sense (material aesthetic judgements), the latter (as formal) alone judgements of taste proper.

A judgement of taste, therefore, is only pure so far as its determining ground is tainted with no merely empirical delight. But such a taint is always present where charm or emotion have a share in the judgement by which something is to be described as beautiful.

Here now there is a recrudescence of a number of specious pleas that go the length of putting forward the case that charm is not merely a necessary ingredient of beauty, but is even of itself sufficient to merit the name of beautiful. A mere colour, such as the green of a plot of grass, or a mere tone (as distinguished from sound or noise), like that of a violin, is described by most people as in itself beautiful, notwithstanding the fact that both seem to depend merely on the matter of the representations in other words, simply on sensation —which only entitles them to be called agreeable. But it will at the same time be observed that sensations of colour as well as of tone are only entitled to be immediately regarded as beautiful where, in either case, they are pure. This is a determination which at once goes to their form, and it is the only one which these representations possess that admits with certainty of being universally communicated. For it is not to be assumed that even the quality of the sensations agrees in all subjects, and we can hardly take it for granted that the agreeableness of a colour, or of the tone of a musical instrument, which we judge to be preferable to that of another, is given a like preference in the estimate of every one.

Assuming vibrations vibration sound, and, what is most important, that the mind not alone perceives by sense their effect in stimulating the organs, but also, by reflection, the regular play of the impressions (and consequently the form in which different representations are united)—which I, still, in no way doubt—then colour and tone would not be mere sensations. They would be nothing short of formal determinations of the unity of a manifold of sensations, and in that case could even be ranked as intrinsic beauties.

But the purity of a simple mode of sensation means that its uniformity is not disturbed or broken by any foreign sensation. It belongs merely to the form; for abstraction may there be made from the quality of the mode of such sensation (what colour or tone, if any, it represents). For this reason, all simple colours are regarded as beautiful so far as pure. Composite colours have not this advantage, because, not being simple, there is no standard for estimating whether they should be called pure or impure.

But as for the beauty ascribed to the object on account of its form, and the supposition that it is capable of being enhanced by charm, this is a common error and one very prejudicial to genuine, uncorrupted, sincere taste. Nevertheless charms may be added to beauty to lend to the mind, beyond a bare delight, an adventitious interest in the representation of the object, and thus to advocate taste and its cultivation. This applies especially where taste is as yet crude and untrained. But they are positively subversive of the judgement of taste, if allowed to obtrude themselves as grounds of estimating beauty. For so far are they from contributing to beauty that it is only where taste is still weak and untrained that, like aliens, they are admitted as a favour, and only on terms that they do not violate that beautiful form.

In painting, sculpture, and in fact in all the formative arts, in architecture and horticulture, so far as fine arts, the design is what is essential. Here it is not what gratifies in sensation but merely what pleases by its form, that is the fundamental prerequisite for taste. The colours which give brilliancy to the sketch are part of the charm. They may no doubt, in their own way, enliven the object for sensation, but make it really worth looking at and beautiful they cannot. Indeed, more often than not the requirements of the beautiful form restrict them to a very narrow compass, and, even where charm is admitted, it is only this form that gives them a place of honour.

All form of objects of sense (both of external and also, mediately, of internal sense) is either figure or play. In the latter case it is either play of figures (in space: mimic and dance), or mere play of sensations (in time). The charm of colours, or of the agreeable tones of instruments, may be added: but the design in the former and the composition in the latter constitute the proper object of the pure judgement of taste. To say that the purity alike of colours and of tones, or their variety and contrast, seem to contribute to beauty, is by no means to imply that, because in themselves agreeable, they therefore yield an addition to the delight in the form and one on a par with it. The real meaning rather is that they make this form more clearly, definitely, and completely intuitable, and besides stimulate the representation by their charm, as they excite and sustain the attention directed to the object itself.

Even what is called ornamentation (*parerga*), i.e., what is only an adjunct and not an intrinsic constituent in the complete representation of the object, in augmenting the delight of taste does so only by means of its form. Thus it is with the frames of pictures or the drapery on statues, or the colonnades of palaces. But if the ornamentation does not itself enter into the composition of the beautiful form—if it is introduced like a gold frame merely to win approval for the picture by means of its charm—it is then called finery and takes away from the genuine beauty.

Emotion—a sensation where an agreeable feeling is produced merely by means of a momentary check followed by a more powerful outpouring of the vital force—is quite foreign to beauty. Sublimity (with which the feeling of emotion is connected) requires, however, a different standard of estimation from that relied upon by taste. A pure judgement of taste has, then, for its determining ground neither charm nor emotion, in a word, no sensation as matter of the aesthetic judgement.

§15. The judgement of taste is entirely independent of the concept of perfection

Objective finality can only be cognized by means of a reference of the manifold to a definite end, and hence only through a concept. This alone makes it clear that the beautiful, which is estimated on the ground of a mere formal finality, i.e., a finality apart from an end, is wholly independent of the representation of the good. For the latter presupposes an objective finality, i.e., the reference of the object to a definite end.

Objective finality is either external, i.e., the utility, or internal, i.e., the perfection, of the object. That the delight in an object on account of which we call it beautiful is incapable of resting on the representation of its utility, is abundantly evident from the two preceding articles; for in that case, it would not be an immediate delight in the object, which latter is the essential condition of the judgement upon beauty. But in an objecttive, internal finality, i.e., perfection, we have what is more akin to the predicate of beauty, and so this has been held even by philosophers of reputation to be convertible with beauty, though subject to the qualification: where it is thought in a confused way. In a critique of taste it is of the utmost importance to decide whether beauty is really reducible to the concept of perfection.

For estimating objective finality we always require the concept of an end, and, where such finality has to be, not an external one (utility), but an internal one, the concept of an internal end containing the ground of the internal possibility of the object. Now an end is in general that, the concept of which may be regarded as the ground of the possibility of the object itself. So in order to represent an objective finality in a thing we must first have a concept of what sort of a thing it is to be. The agreement of the manifold in a thing with this concept (which supplies the rule of its synthesis) is the qualitative perfection of the thing. Quantitative perfection is entirely distinct from this. It consists in the completeness of anything after its kind, and is a mere concept of quantity (of totality). In its case the question of what the thing is to be is regarded as definitely disposed of, and we only ask whether it is possessed of all the requisites that go to make it such. What is formal in the representation of a thing, i.e., the agreement of its manifold with a unity (i.e., irrespective of what it is to be), does not, of itself, afford us any cognition whatsoever of objective finality. For since abstraction is made from this unity as end (what the thing is to be), nothing is left but the subjective finality of the representations in the mind of the subject intuiting.

This gives a certain finality of the representative state of the subject, in which the subject feels itself quite at home in its effort to grasp a given form in the imagination, but no perfection of any object, the latter not being here thought through any concept. For instance, if in a forest I light upon a plot of grass, round which trees stand in a circle, and if I do not then form any representation of an end, as that it is meant to be used, say, for country dances, then not the least hint of a concept of perfection is given by the mere form. To suppose a formal objective finality that is yet devoid of an end, i.e., the mere form of a perfection (apart from any matter or concept of that to which the agreement relates, even though there was the mere general idea of a conformity to law) is a veritable contradiction.

Now the judgement of taste is an aesthetic judgement, one resting on subjective grounds. No concept can be its determining ground, and hence not on of a definite end. Beauty, therefore, as a formal subjective finality, involves no thought whatsoever of a perfection of the object, as a would-be formal finality which yet, for all that, is objective: and the distinction between the concepts of the beautiful and the good, which represents both as differing only in their logical form, the first being merely a confused, the second a clearly defined, concept of perfection, while otherwise alike in content and origin, all goes for nothing: for then there would be no specific difference between them, but the judgement of taste would be just as much a cognitive judgement as one by which something is described as good—just as the man in the street, when be says that deceit is wrong, bases his judgement on confused, but the philosopher on clear grounds, while both appeal in reality to identical principles of reason.

But I have already stated that an aesthetic judgement is quite unique, and affords absolutely no (not even a confused) knowledge of the object. It is only through a logical judgement that we get knowledge. The aesthetic judgement, on the other hand, refers the representation, by which an object is given, solely to the subject, and brings to our notice no quality of the object, but only the final form in the determination of the powers of representation engaged upon it. The judgement is called aesthetic for the very reason that its determining ground cannot be a concept, but is rather the feeling (of the internal sense) of the concert in the play of the mental powers as a thing only capable of being felt.

If, on the other hand, confused concepts, and the objective judgement based on them, are going to be called aesthetic, we shall find ourselves with an understanding judging by sense, or a sense representing its objects by concepts—a mere choice of contradictions. The faculty of concepts, be they confused or be they clear, is understanding; and although understanding has (as in all judgements) its role in the judgement of taste, as an aesthetic judgement, its role there is not that of a faculty for cognizing an object, but of a faculty for determining that judgement and its representation (without a concept) according to its relation to the subject and its internal feeling, and for doing so in so far as that judgement is possible according to a universal rule.

§16. A judgement of taste by which an object is described as beautiful, under the condition of a definite concept, is not pure

There are two kinds of beauty: free beauty (*pulchritudo vaga*), or beauty which is merely dependent (*pulchritudo adhaerens*). The first presupposes no concept of what the object should be; the second does presuppose such a concept and, with it, an answering perfection of the object. Those of the first kind are said to be (self-subsisting) beauties of this thing or that thing; the other kind of beauty, being attached to a concept (conditioned beauty), is ascribed to objects which come under the concept of a particular end.

Flowers are free beauties of nature. Hardly anyone but a botanist knows the true nature of a flower, and even he, while recognizing in the flower the reproductive organ of the plant, pays no attention to this natural end when using his taste to judge of its beauty. Hence no perfection of any kind-no internal finality, as something to which the arrangement of the manifold is related-underlies this judgement. Many birds (the parrot, the humming-bird, the bird of paradise), and a number of crustacea, are self-subsisting beauties which are not appurtenant to any object defined with respect to its end, but please freely and on their own account. So designs a la grecque, foliage for framework or on wall-papers, etc., have no intrinsic meaning; they represent nothing—no object under a definite concept-and are free beauties. We may also rank in the same class what in music are called fantasias (without a theme), and, indeed, all music that is not set to words.

In the estimate of a free beauty (according to mere form) we have the pure judgement of taste. No concept is here presupposed of any end for which the manifold should serve the given object, and which the latter, therefore, should represent—an incumbrance which would only restrict the freedom of the imagination that, as it were, is at play in the contemplation of the outward form.

But the beauty of man (including under this head that of a man, woman, or child), the beauty of a horse, or of a building (such as a church, palace, arsenal, or summer-house), presupposes a concept of the end that defines what the thing has to be, and consequently a concept of its perfection; and is therefore merely attendant beauty. Now, just as it is a clog on the purity of the judgement of taste to have the agreeable (of sensation) joined with beauty to which properly only the form is relevant, so to combine the good with beauty (the good, namely, of the manifold to the thing itself according to its end) mars its purity.

Much might be added to a building that would immediately please the eye, were it not intended for a church. A figure might be beautified with all manner of flourishes and light but regular lines, as is done by the New Zealanders with their tattooing, were we dealing with anything but the figure of a human being. And here is one whose rugged features might be softened and given a more pleasing aspect, only he has got to be a man, or is, perhaps, a warrior that has to have a warlike appearance.

Now the delight in the manifold of a thing, in reference to the internal end that determines its possibility, is a delight based on a concept, whereas delight in the beautiful is such as does not presuppose any concept, but is immediately coupled with the representation through which the object is given (not through which it is thought). If, now, the judgement of taste in respect of the latter delight is made dependent upon the end involved in the former delight as a judgement of reason, and is thus placed under a restriction, then it is no longer a free and pure judgement of taste.

Taste, it is true, stands to gain by this combination of intellectual delight with the aesthetic. For it becomes fixed, and, while not universal, it enables rules to be prescribed for it in respect of certain definite final objects. But these rules are then not rules of taste, but merely rules for establishing a union of taste with reason, i.e., of the beautiful with the good-rules by which the former becomes available as an intentional instrument in respect of the latter, for the purpose of bringing that temper of the mind which is self-sustaining and of subjective universal validity to the support and maintenance of that mode of thought which, while possessing objective universal validity, can only be preserved by a resolute effort. But, strictly speaking, perfection neither gains by beauty, nor beauty by perfection. The truth is rather this, when we compare the representation through which an object is given to us with the object (in respect of what it is meant to be) by means of a concept, we cannot help reviewing it also in respect of the sensation in the subject. Hence there results a gain to the entire faculty of our representative power when harmony prevails between both states of mind.

In respect of an object with a definite internal end, a judgement of taste would only be pure where the person judging either has no concept of this end, or else makes abstraction from it in his judgement. But in cases like this, although such a person should lay down a correct judgement of taste, since he would be estimating the object as a free beauty, he would still be found fault with by another who saw nothing in its beauty but a dependent quality (i.e., who looked to the end of the object) and would be accused by him of false taste, though both would, in their own way, be judging correctly: the one according to what he had present to his senses, the other according to what was present in his thoughts. This distinction enables us to settle many disputes about beauty on the part of critics; for we may show them how one side is dealing with free beauty, and the other with that which is dependent: the former passing a pure judgement of taste, the latter one that is applied intentionally.

Definition of the Beautiful Derived from this Third Moment

Beauty is the form of finality in an object, so far as perceived in it apart from the representation of an end.

FOURTH MOMENT. Of the Judgement of Taste: Moment of the Modality of the Delight in the Object

§18. Nature of the modality in a judgement of taste

I may assert in the case of every representation that the synthesis of a pleasure with the representation (as a cognition) is at least possible. Of what I call agreeable I assert that it actually causes pleasure in me. But what we have in mind in the case of the beautiful is a necessary reference on its part to delight. However, this necessity is of a special kind. It is not a theoretical objective necessity—such as would let us cognize a priori that everyone will feel this delight in the object that is called beautiful by me. Nor yet is it a practical necessity, in which case, thanks to concepts of a pure rational will in which free agents are supplied with a rule, this delight is the necessary consequence of an objective law, and simply means that one ought absolutely (without ulterior object) to act in a certain way. Rather, being such a necessity as is thought in an aesthetic judgement, it can only be termed exemplary. In other words it is a necessity of the assent of all to a judgement regarded as exemplifying a universal rule incapable of formulation. Since an aesthetic judgement is not an objective or cognitive judgement, this necessity is not derivable from definite concepts, and so is not apodeictic. Much less is it inferable from universality of experience (of a thoroughgoing agreement of judgements about the beauty of a certain object). For, apart from the fact that experience would hardly furnish evidences sufficiently numerous for this purpose, empirical judgements do not afford any foundation for a concept of the necessity of these judgements.

§19. The subjective necessity attributed to a judgement of taste is conditioned

The judgement of taste exacts agreement from every one; and a person who describes something as beautiful insists that everyone ought to give the object in question his approval and follow suit in describing it as beautiful. The ought in aesthetic judgements, therefore, despite an accordance with all the requisite data for passing judgement, is still only pronounced conditionally. We are suitors for agreement from everyone else, because we are fortified with a ground common to all. Further, we would be able to count on this agreement, provided we were always assured of the correct subsumption of the case under that ground as the rule of approval.

§20. The condition of the necessity advanced by a judgement of taste is the idea of a common sense

Were judgements of taste (like cognitive judgements) in possession of a definite objective principle, then one who in his judgement followed such a principle would claim unconditioned necessity for it. Again, were they devoid of any principle, as are those of the mere taste of sense, then no thought of any necessity on their part would enter one's head. Therefore they must have a subjective principle, and one which determines what pleases or displeases, by means of feeling only and not through concepts, but yet with universal validity. Such a principle, however, could only be regarded as a common sense. This differs essentially from common understanding, which is also sometimes called common sense (*sensus communis*): for the judgement of the latter is not one by feeling, but always one by concepts, though usually only in the shape of obscurely represented principles.

The judgement of taste, therefore, depends on our presupposing the existence of a common sense. (But this is not to be taken to mean some external sense, but the effect arising from the free play of our powers of cognition.) Only under the presupposition, I repeat, of such a common sense, are we able to lay down a judgement of taste.

§21. Have we reason for presupposing a common sense?

Cognitions and judgements must, together with their attendant conviction, admit of being universally communicated; for otherwise a correspondence with the object would not be due to them. They would be a conglomerate constituting a mere subjective play of the powers of representation, just as scepticism would have it. But if cognitions are to admit of communication, then our mental state, i.e., the way the cognitive powers are attuned for cognition generally, and, in fact, the relative proportion suitable for a representation (by which an object is given to us) from which cognition is to result, must also admit of being universally communicated, as, without this, which is the subjective condition of the act of knowing, knowledge, as an effect, would not arise. And this is always what actually happens where a given object, through the intervention of sense, sets the imagination at work in arranging the manifold, and the imagination, in turn, the understanding in giving to this arrangement the unity of concepts. But this disposition of the cognitive powers has a relative proportion differing with the diversity of the objects that are given.

However, there must be one in which this internal ratio suitable for quickening (one faculty by the other) is best adapted for both mental powers in respect of cognition (of given objects) generally; and this disposition can only be determined through feeling (and not by concepts). Since, now this disposition itself must admit of being universally communicated, and hence also the feeling of it (in the case of a given representation), while again, the universal communicability of a feeling presupposes a common sense: it follows that our assumption of it is well founded. And here, too, we do not have to take our stand on psychological observations, but we assume a common sense as the necessary condition of the universal communicability of our knowledge, which is presupposed in every logic and every principle of knowledge that is not one of scepticism. . . . .

Definition of the Beautiful drawn from the Fourth Moment

The beautiful is that which, apart from a concept, is cognized as object of a necessary delight.

BOOK II. Analytic of the Sublime

§23. Transition from the faculty of estimating the beautiful to that of estimating the sublime

The beautiful and the sublime agree on the point of pleasing on their own account. Further they agree in not presupposing either a judgement of sense or one logically determinant, but one of reflection. Hence it follows that the delight does not depend upon a sensation, as with the agreeable, nor upon a definite concept, as does the delight in the good, although it has, for all that, an indeterminate reference to concepts. Consequently the delight is connected with the mere presentation or faculty of presentation, and is thus taken to express the accord, in a given intuition, of the faculty of presentation, or the imagination, with the faculty of concepts that belongs to understanding or reason, in the sense of the former assisting the latter. Hence both kinds of judgements are singular, and yet such as profess to be universally valid in respect of every subject, despite the fact that their claims are directed merely to the feeling of pleasure and not to any knowledge of the object.

There are, however, also important and striking differences between the two. The beautiful in nature is a question of the form of object, and this consists in limitation, whereas the sublime is to be found in an object even devoid of form, so far as it immediately involves, or else by its presence provokes a representation of limitlessness, yet with a superadded thought of its totality. Accordingly, the beautiful seems to be regarded as a presentation of an indeterminate concept of understanding, the sublime as a presentation of an indeterminate concept of reason. Hence the delight is in the former case coupled with the representation of quality, but in this case with that of quantity. Moreover, the former delight is very different from the latter in kind. For the beautiful is directly attended with a feeling of the furtherance of life, and is thus compatible with charms and a playful imagination. On the other hand, the feeling of the sublime is a pleasure that only arises indirectly, being brought about by the feeling of a momentary check to the vital forces followed at once by a discharge all the more powerful, and so it is an emotion that seems to be no sport, but dead earnest in the affairs of the imagination.

Hence charms are repugnant to it; and, since the mind is not simply attracted by the object, but is also alternately repelled thereby, the delight in the sublime does not so much involve positive pleasure as admiration or respect, i.e., merits the name of a negative pleasure.

But the most important and vital distinction between the sublime and the beautiful is certainly this: that if, as is allowable, we here confine our attention in the first instance to the sublime in objects of nature (that of art being always restricted by the conditions of an agreement with nature), we observe that whereas natural beauty (such as is self-subsisting) conveys a finality in its form making the object appear, as it were, preadapted to our power of judgement, so that it thus forms of itself an object of our delight, that which, without our indulging in any refinements of thought, but, simply in our apprehension of it, excites the feeling of the sublime, may appear, indeed, in point of form to contravene the ends of our power of judgement, to be ill-adapted to our faculty of presentation, and to be, as it were, an outrage on the imagination, and yet it is judged all the more sublime on that account.

From this it may be seen at once that we express ourselves on the whole inaccurately if we term any object of nature sublime, although we may with perfect propriety call many such objects beautiful. For how can that which is apprehended as inherently contra-purposive be noted with an expression of approval? All that we can say is that the object lends itself to the presentation of a sublimity discoverable in the mind.

For the sublime, in the strict sense of the word, cannot be contained in any sensuous form, but rather concerns ideas of reason, which, although no adequate presentation of them is possible, may be excited and called into the mind by that very inadequacy itself which does admit of sensuous presentation. Thus the broad ocean agitated by storms cannot be called sublime. Its aspect is horrible, and one must have stored one's mind in advance with a rich stock of ideas, if such an intuition is to raise it to the pitch of a feeling which is itself sublime—sublime because the mind has been incited to abandon sensibility and employ itself upon ideas involving higher finality.

Self-subsisting natural beauty reveals to us a technic of nature which shows it in the light of a system ordered in accordance with laws the principle of which is not to be found within the range of our entire faculty of understanding. This principle is that of a finality relative to the employment of judgement in respect of phenomena which have thus to be assigned, not merely to nature regarded as aimless mechanism, but also to nature regarded after the analogy of art. Hence it gives a veritable extension, not, of course, to our knowledge of objects of nature, but to our conception of nature itself—nature as mere mechanism being enlarged to the conception of nature as art—an extension inviting profound inquiries as to the possibility of such a form. But in what we are wont to call sublime in nature there is such an absence of anything leading to particular objective principles and corresponding forms of nature that it is rather in its chaos, or in its wildest and most irregular disorder and desolation, provided it gives signs of magnitude and power, that nature chiefly excites the ideas of the sublime.

Hence we see that the concept of the sublime in nature is far less important and rich in consequences than that of its beauty. It gives on the whole no indication of anything final in nature itself, but only in the possible employment of our intuitions of it in inducing a feeling in our own selves of a finality quite independent of nature. For the beautiful in nature we must seek a ground external to ourselves, but for the sublime one merely in ourselves and the attitude of mind that introduces sublimity into the representation of nature. This is a very needful preliminary remark. It entirely separates the ideas of the sublime from that of a finality of nature, and makes the theory of the sublime a mere appendage to the aesthetic estimate of the finality of nature, because it does not give a representation of any particular form in nature, but involves no more than the development of a final employment by the imagination of its own representation.

A. THE MATHEMATICALLY SUBLIME

§25. Definition of the term "sublime"

Sublime is the name given to what is absolutely great. But to be great and to be a magnitude are entirely different concepts (*magnitudo* and *quantitas*). In the same way, to assert without qualification (*simpliciter*) that something is great is quite a different thing from saying that it is absolutely great (absolute, *non-comparative magnum*). The latter is what is beyond all comparison great. What, then, is the meaning of the assertion that anything is great, or small, or of medium size? What is indicated is not a pure concept of understanding, still less an intuition of sense; and just as little is it a concept of reason, for it does not import any principle of cognition. It must, therefore, be a concept of judgement, or have its source in one, and must introduce as basis of the judgement a subjective finality of the representation with reference to the power of judgement. Given a multiplicity of the homogeneous together constituting one thing, and we may at once cognize from the thing itself that it is a magnitude (*quantum*). No comparison with other things is required. But to determine how great it is always requires something else, which itself has magnitude, for its measure. Now, since in the estimate of magnitude we have to take into account not merely the multiplicity (number of units) but also the magnitude of the unit (the measure), and since the magnitude of this unit in turn always requires something else as its measure and as the standard of its comparison, and so on, we see that the computation of the magnitude of phenomena is, in all cases, utterly incapable of affording us any absolute concept of a magnitude, and can, instead, only afford one that is always based on comparison.

If, now, I assert without qualification that anything is great, it would seem that I have nothing in the way of a comparison present to my mind, or at least nothing involving an objective measure, for no attempt is thus made to determine how great the object is. But, despite the standard of comparison being merely subjective, the claim of the judgement is none the less one to universal agreement; the judgements: "that man is beautiful" and "He is tall," do not purport to speak only for the judging subject, but, like theoretical judgements, they demand the assent of everyone.

Now in a judgement that without qualification describes anything as great, it is not merely meant that the object has a magnitude, but greatness is ascribed to it preeminently among many other objects of a like kind, yet without the extent of this preeminence being determined. Hence a standard is certainly laid at the basis of the judgement, which standard is presupposed to be one that can be taken as the same for everyone, but which is available only for an aesthetic estimate of the greatness, and not for one that is logical (mathematically determined), for the standard is a merely subjective one underlying the reflective judgement upon the greatness. Furthermore, this standard may be empirical, as, let us say, the average size of the men known to us, of animals of a certain kind, of trees, of houses, of mountains, and so forth. Or it may be a standard given a priori, which by reason of the imperfecttions of the judging subject is restricted to subjective conditions of presentation *in concreto*; as, in the practical sphere, the greatness of a particular virtue, or of public liberty and justice in a country; or, in the theoretical sphere, the greatness of the accuracy or inaccuracy of an experiment or measurement, etc.

Here, now, it is of note that, although we have no interest whatever in the object, i.e., its real existence may be a matter of no concern to us, still its mere greatness, regarded even as devoid of form, is able to convey a universally communicable delight and so involve the consciousness of a subjective finality in the employment of our cognitive faculties, but not, be it remembered, a delight in the object, for the latter may be formless, but, in contradistinction to what is the case with the beautiful, where the reflective judgement finds itself set to a key that is final in respect of cognition generally, a delight in an extension affecting the imagination itself.

If (subject as above) we say of an object, without qualification, that it is great, this is not a mathematically determinant, but a mere reflective judgement upon its representation, which is subjectively final for a particular employment of our cognitive faculties in the estimation of magnitude, and we then always couple with the representation a kind of respect, just as we do a kind of contempt with what we call absolutely small. Moreover, the estimate of things as great or small extends to everything, even to all their qualities. Thus we call even their beauty great or small. The reason of this is to be found in the fact that we have only got to present a thing in intuition, as the precept of judgement directs (consequently to represent it aesthetically), for it to be in its entirety a phenomenon, and hence a quantum.

If, however, we call anything not alone great, but, without qualification, absolutely, and in every respect (beyond all comparison) great, that is to say, sublime, we soon perceive that for this it is not permissible to seek an appropriate standard outside itself, but merely in itself. It is a greatness comparable to itself alone. Hence it comes that the sublime is not to be looked for in the things of nature, but only in our own ideas. But it must be left to the deduction to show in which of them it resides.

The above definition may also be expressed in this way: that is sublime in comparison with which all else is small. Here we readily see that nothing can be given in nature, no matter how great we may judge it to be, which, regarded in some other relation, may not be degraded to the level of the infinitely little, and nothing so small which in comparison with some still smaller standard may not for our imagination be enlarged to the greatness of a world. Telescopes have put within our reach an abundance of material to go upon in making the first observation, and microscopes the same in making the second. Nothing, therefore, which can be an object of the senses is to be termed sublime when treated on this footing. But precisely because there is a striving in our imagination towards progress ad infinitum, while reason demands absolute totality, as a real idea, that same inability on the part of our faculty for the estimation of the magnitude of things of the world of sense to attain to this idea, is the awakening of a feeling of a supersensible faculty within us; and it is the use to which judgement naturally puts particular objects on behalf of this latter feeling, and not the object of sense, that is absolutely great, and every other contrasted employment small. Consequently it is the disposition of soul evoked by a particular representation engaging the attention of the reflective judgement, and not the object, that is to be called sublime.

The foregoing formulae defining the sublime may, therefore, be supplemented by yet another: The sublime is that, the mere capacity of thinking which evidences a faculty of mind transcending every standard of sense.

B. THE DYNAMICALLY SUBLIME

§28. Nature as Might

Might is a power which is superior to great hindrances. It is termed dominion if it is also superior to the resistance of that which itself possesses might. Nature, considered in an aesthetic judgement as might that has no dominion over us, is dynamically sublime.

If we are to estimate nature as dynamically sublime, it must be represented as a source of fear (though the converse, that every object that is a source of fear, in our aesthetic judgement, sublime, does not hold). For in forming an aesthetic estimate (no concept being present) the superiority to hindrances can only be estimated according to the greatness of the resistance. Now that which we strive to resist is an evil, and, if we do not find our powers commensurate to the task, an object of fear. Hence the aesthetic judgement can only deem nature a might, and so dynamically sublime, in so far as it is looked upon as an object of fear.

But we may look upon an object as fearful, and yet not be afraid of it, if, that is, our estimate takes the form of our simply picturing to ourselves the case of our wishing to offer some resistance to it and recognizing that all such resistance would be quite futile. So the righteous man fears God without being afraid of Him, because he regards the case of his wishing to resist God and His commandments as one which need cause him no anxiety. But in every such case, regarded by him as not intrinsically impossible, he cognizes Him as One to be feared.

One who is in a state of fear can no more play the part of a judge of the sublime of nature than one captivated by inclination and appetite can of the beautiful. He flees from the sight of an object filling him with dread; and it is impossible to take delight in terror that is seriously entertained. Hence the agreeableness arising from the cessation of an uneasiness is a state of joy. But this, depending upon deliverance from a danger, is a rejoicing accompanied with a resolve never again to put oneself in the way of the danger: in fact we do not like bringing back to mind how we felt on that occasion not to speak of going in search of an opportunity for experiencing it again.

Bold, overhanging, and, as it were, threatening rocks, thunderclouds piled up the vault of heaven, borne along with flashes and peals, volcanos in all their violence of destruction, hurricanes leaving desolation in their track, the boundless ocean rising with rebellious force, the high waterfall of some mighty river, and the like, make our power of resistance of trifling moment in comparison with their might. But, provided our own position is secure, their aspect is all the more attractive for its fearfulness; and we readily call these objects sublime, because they raise the forces of the soul above the height of vulgar commonplace, and discover within us a power of resistance of quite another kind, which gives us courage to be able to measure ourselves against the seeming omnipotence of nature.

In the immeasurableness of nature and the incompetence of our faculty for adopting a standard proportionate to the aesthetic estimation of the magnitude of its realm, we found our own limitation. But with this we also found in our rational faculty another non-sensuous standard, one which has that infinity itself under it as a unit, and in comparison with which everything in nature is small, and so found in our minds a preeminence over nature even in it immeasurability. Now in just the same way the irresistibility of the might of nature forces upon us the recognition of our physical helplessness as beings of nature, but at the same time reveals a faculty of estimating ourselves as independent of nature, and discovers a preeminence above nature that is the foundation of a self-preservation of quite another kind from that which may be assailed and brought into danger by external nature.

This saves humanity in our own person from humiliation, even though as mortal men we have to submit to external violence. In this way, external nature is not estimated in our aesthetic judgement as sublime so far as exciting fear, but rather because it challenges our power (one not of nature) to regard as small those things of which we are wont to be solicitous (worldly goods, health, and life), and hence to regard its might (to which in these matters we are no doubt subject) as exercising over us and our personality no such rude dominion that we should bow down before it, once the question becomes one of our highest principles and of our asserting or forsaking them. Therefore nature is here called sublime merely because it raises the imagination to a presentation of those cases in which the mind can make itself sensible of the appropriate sublimity of the sphere of its own being, even above nature.

This estimation of ourselves loses nothing by the fact that we must see ourselves safe in order to feel this soul-stirring delight—a fact from which it might be plausibly argued that, as there is no seriousness in the danger, so there is just as little seriousness in the sublimity of our faculty of soul. For here the delight only concerns the province of our faculty disclosed in such a case, so far as this faculty has its root in our nature; notwithstanding that its development and exercise is left to ourselves and remains an obligation. Here indeed there is truth—no matter how conscious a man, when he stretches his reflection so far abroad, may be of his actual present helplessness.

This principle has, doubtless, the appearance of being too far-fetched and subtle, and so of lying beyond the reach of an aesthetic judgement. But observation of men proves the reverse, and that it may be the foundation of the commonest judgements, although one is not always conscious of its presence. For what is it that, even to the savage, is the object of the greatest admiration? It is a man who is undaunted, who knows no fear, and who, therefore, does not give way to danger, but sets manfully to work with full deliberation. Even where civilization has reached a high pitch, there remains this special reverence for the soldier; only that there is then further required of him that he should also exhibit all the virtues of peace—gentleness, sympathy, and even becoming thought for his own person; and for the reason that in this we recognize that his mind is above the threats of danger.

And so, comparing the statesman and the general, men may argue as they please as to the preeminent respect which is due to either above the other; but the verdict of the aesthetic judgement is for the latter. War itself, provided it is conducted with order and a sacred respect for the rights of civilians, has something sublime about it, and gives nations that carry it on in such a manner a stamp of mind only the more sublime the more numerous the dangers to which they are exposed, and which they are able to meet with fortitude. On the other hand, a prolonged peace favours the predominance of a mere commercial spirit, and with it a debasing self-interest, cowardice, and effeminacy, and tends to degrade the character of the nation.

So far as sublimity is predicated of might, this solution of the concept of it appears at variance with the fact that we are wont to represent God in the tempest, the storm, the earthquake, and the like, as presenting Himself in His wrath, but at the same time also in His sublimity, and yet here it would be alike folly and presumption to imagine a preeminence of our minds over the operations and, as it appears, even over the direction of such might. Here, instead of a feeling of the sublimity of our own nature, submission, prostration, Aristotle's remarks on courage, in the utter helplessness seem more to constitute the attitude of mind befitting the manifestation of such an object, and to be that also more customarily associated with the idea of it on the occasion of a natural phenomenon of this kind. In religion, as a rule, prostration, adoration with bowed head, coupled with contrite, timorous posture and voice, seems to be the only becoming demeanour in presence of the Godhead, and accordingly most nations have assumed and still observe it. Yet this cast of mind is far from being intrinsically and necessarily involved in the idea of the sublimity of a religion and of its object.

The man that is actually in a state of fear, finding in himself good reason to be so, because he is conscious of offending with his evil disposition against a might directed by a will at once irresistible and just, is far from being in the frame of mind for admiring divine greatness, for which a temper of calm reflection and a quite free judgement are required. Only when he becomes conscious of having a disposition that is upright and acceptable to God, do those operations of might serve, to stir within him the idea of the sublimity of this Being, so far as he recognizes the existence in himself of a sublimity of disposition consonant with His will, and is thus raised above the dread of such operations of nature, in which he no longer sees God pouring forth the vials of the wrath. Even humility, taking the form of an uncompromising judgement upon his shortcomings, which, with consciousness of good intentions, might readily be glossed over on the ground of the frailty of human nature, is a sublime temper of the mind voluntarily to undergo the pain of remorse as a means of more and more effectually eradicating its cause. In this way religion is intrinsically distinguished from superstition, which latter rears in the mind, not reverence for the sublime, but dread and apprehension of the all-powerful Being to whose will terror-stricken man sees himself subjected, yet without according Him due honour. From this nothing can arise but grace-begging and vain adulation, instead of a religion consisting in a good life.

Sublimity, therefore, does not reside in any of the things of nature, but only in our own mind, in so far as we may become conscious of our superiority over nature within, and thus also over nature without us (as exerting influence upon us). Everything that provokes this feeling in us, including the might of nature which challenges our strength, is then, though improperly, called sublime, and it is only under presupposition of this idea within us, and in relation to it, that we are capable of attaining to the idea of the sublimity of that Being which inspires deep respect in us, not by the mere display of its might in nature, but more by the faculty which is planted in us of estimating that might without fear, and of regarding our estate as exalted above it. . . .

§43. Art in general

(1) Art is distinguished from nature as making (*facere*) is from acting or operating in general (*agere*), and the product or the result of the former is distinguished from that of the latter as work (*opus*) from operation (*effectus*).

By right it is only production through freedom, i.e., through an act of will that places reason at the basis of its action, that should be termed art. For, although we are pleased to call what bees produce (their regularly constituted cells) a work of art, we only do so on the strength of an analogy with art; that is to say, as soon as we call to mind that no rational deliberation forms the basis of their labour, we say at once that it is a product of their nature (of instinct), and it is only to their Creator that we ascribe it as art.

If, as sometimes happens, in a search through a bog, we light on a piece of hewn wood, we do not say it is a product of nature but of art. Its producing cause had an end in view to which the object owes its form. Apart from such cases, we recognize an art in everything formed in such a way that its actuality must have been preceded by a representation of the thing in its cause (as even in the case of the bees), although the effect could not have been thought by the cause. But where anything is called absolutely a work of art, to distinguish it from a natural product, then some work of man is always understood.

(2) Art, as human skill, is distinguished also from science (as ability from knowledge), as a practical from a theoretical faculty, as technic from theory (as the art of surveying from geometry). For this reason, also, what one can do the' moment one only knows what is to be done, hence without—anything more than sufficient knowledge of the desired result, is not called art. To art that alone belongs which the possession of the most complete knowledge does not involve one's having then and there the skill to do it. Camper, describes very exactly how the best shoe must be made, but he, doubtless, was not able to turn one out himself.

(3) Art is further distinguished from handicraft. The first is called free, the other may be called industrial art. We look on the former as something which could only prove final (be a success) as play, i.e., an occupation which is agreeable on its own account; but on the second as labour, i.e., a business, which on its own account is disagreeable (drudgery), and is only attractive by means of what it results in (e.g., the pay), and which is consequently capable of being a compulsory imposition.

Whether in the list of arts and crafts we are to rank watchmakers as artists, and smiths on the contrary as craftsmen, requires a standpoint different from that here adopted—one, that is to say, taking account of the proposition of the talents which the business undertaken in either case must necessarily involve. Whether, also, among the so-called seven liberal arts some may not have been included which should be reckoned as sciences, and many, too, that resemble handicraft, is a matter I will not discuss here. It is not amiss, however, to remind the reader of this: that in all free arts something of a compulsory character is still required, or, as it is called, a mechanism, without which the soul, which in art must be free, and which alone gives life to the work, would be bodyless and evanescent (e.g., in the poetic art there must be correctness and wealth of language, likewise prosody and metre). For not a few leaders of a newer school believe that the best way to promote a free art is to sweep away all restraint and convert it from labour into mere play.

§44. Fine art

There is no science of the beautiful, but only a critique. Nor, again, is there an elegant (*schone*) science, but only a fine (*schone*) art. For a science of the beautiful would have to determine scientifically, i.e., by means of proofs, whether a thing was to be considered beautiful or not; and the judgement upon beauty, consequently, would, if belonging to science, fail to be a judgement of taste. As for a beautiful science—a science which, as such, is to be beautiful, is a nonentity. For if, treating it as a science, we were to ask for reasons and proofs, we would be put off with elegant phrases (*bons mots*). What has given rise to the current expression elegant sciences is, doubtless, no more than this, that common observation has, quite accurately, noted the fact that for fine art, in the fulness of its perfection, a large store of science is required, as, for example, knowledge of ancient languages, acquaintance with classical authors, history, antiquarian learning, etc. Hence these historical sciences, owing to the fact that they form the necessary preparation and groundwork for fine art, and partly also owing to the fact that they are taken to comprise even the knowledge of the products of fine art (rhetoric and poetry), have by a confusion of words actually got the name of elegant sciences.

Where art, merely seeking to actualize a possible object to the cognition of which it is adequate, does whatever acts are required for that purpose. then it is mechanical. But should the feeling of pleasure be what it has immediately in view, it is then termed aesthetic art. As such it may be either agreeable or fine art. The description "agreeable art" applies where the end of the art is that the pleasure should accompany the representations considered as mere sensations, the description "fine art" where it is to accompany them considered as modes of cognition.

Agreeable arts are those which have mere enjoyment for their object. Such are all the charms that can gratify a dinner party: entertaining narrative, the art of starting the whole table in unrestrained and sprightly conversation, or with jest and laughter inducing a certain air of gaiety. Here, as the saying goes, there may be much loose talk over the glasses, without a person wishing to be brought to book for all he utters, because it is only given out for the entertainment of the moment, and not as a lasting matter to be made the subject of reflection or repetition. (Of the same sort is also the art of arranging the table for enjoyment, or, at large banquets, the music of the orchestra—a quaint idea intended to act on the mind merely as an agreeable noise fostering a genial spirit, which, without any one paying the smallest attention to the composition, promotes the free flow of conversation between guest and guest.) In addition must be included play of every kind which is attended with no further interest than that of making the time pass by unheeded.

Fine art, on the other hand, is a mode of representation which is intrinsically final, and which, although devoid of an end, has the effect of advancing the culture of the mental powers in the interests of social communication.

The universal communicability of a pleasure involves in its very concept that the pleasure is not one of enjoyment arising out of mere sensation, but must be one of reflection. Hence aesthetic art, as art which is beautiful, is one having for its standard the reflective judgement and not organic sensation.

§45. Fine art is an art, so far as it has at the same time the appearance of being nature

A product of fine art must be recognized to be art and not nature. Nevertheless the finality in its form must appear just as free from the constraint of arbitrary rules as if it were a product of mere nature. Upon this feeling of freedom in the play of our cognitive faculties— which play has at the same time to be final rests that pleasure which alone is universally communicable without being based on concepts. Nature proved beautiful when it wore the appearance of art; and art can only be termed beautiful, where we are conscious of its being art, while yet it has the appearance of nature.

For, whether we are dealing with beauty of nature or beauty of art, we may make the universal statement: That is beautiful which pleases in the mere estimate of it (not in sensation or by means of a concept). Now art has always got a definite intention of producing something. Were this "something," however, to be mere sensation (something merely subjective), intended to be accompanied with pleasure, then such product would, in our estimation of it, only please through the agency of the feeling of the senses. On the other hand, were the intention one directed to the production of a definite object, then, supposing this were attained by art, the object would only please by means of a concept. But in both cases the art would please, not in the mere estimate of it, i.e., not as fine art, but rather as mechanical art.

Hence the finality in the product of fine art, intentional though it be, must not have the appearance of being intentional; i.e., fine art must be clothed with the aspect of nature, although we recognize it to be art. But the way in which a product of art seems like nature is by the presence of perfect exactness in the agreement with rules prescribing how alone the product can be what it is intended to be, but with an absence of laboured effect (without academic form betraying itself), i.e., without a trace appearing of the artist having always had the rule present to him and of its having fettered his mental powers.

§46. Fine art is the art of genius

Genius is the talent (natural endowment) which gives the rule to art. Since talent, as an innate productive faculty of the artist, belongs itself to nature, we may put it this way: Genius is the innate mental aptitude (*ingenium*) through which nature gives the rule to art.

Whatever may be the merits of this definition, and whether it is merely arbitrary, or whether it is adequate or not to the concept usually associated with the word genius (a point which the following sections have to clear up), it may still be shown at the outset that, according to this acceptation of the word, fine arts must necessarily be regarded as arts of genius.

For every art presupposes rules which are laid down as the foundation which first enables a product, if it is to be called one of art, to be represented as possible. The concept of fine art, however, does not permit of the judgement upon the beauty of its product being derived from any rule that has a concept for its determining ground, and that depends, consequently, on a concept of the way in which the product is possible. Consequently fine art cannot of its own self excogitate the rule according to which it is to effectuate its product. But since, for all that, a product can never be called art unless there is a preceding rule, it follows that nature in the individual (and by virtue of the harmony of his faculties) must give the rule to art, i.e., fine art is only possible as a product of genius.

From this it may be seen that genius (1) is a talent for producing that for which no definite rule can be given, and not an aptitude in the way of cleverness for what can be learned according to some rule; and that consequently originality must be its primary property. (2) Since there may also be original nonsense, its products must at the same time be models, i.e., be exemplary; and, consequently, though not themselves derived from imitation, they must serve that purpose for others, i.e., as a standard or rule of estimating. (3) It cannot indicate scientifically how it brings about its product, but rather gives the rule as nature. Hence, where an author owes a product to his genius, he does not himself know how the ideas for it have entered into his head, nor has he it in his power to invent the like at pleasure, or methodically, and communicate the same to others in such precepts as would put them in a position to produce similar products. (Hence, presumably, our word *Genie* is derived from genius, as the peculiar guardian and guiding spirit given to a man at his birth, by the inspiration of which those original ideas were obtained.) (4) Nature prescribes the rule through genius not to science but to art, and this also only in so far as it is to be fine art. . . .

§49. Of the faculties of the mind that constitute Genius

We say of certain products of which we expect that they should at least in part appear as beautiful art, they are without *spirit*; although we find nothing to blame in them on the score of taste. A poem may be very neat and elegant, but without spirit. A history may be exact and well arranged, but without spirit. A festal discourse may be solid and at the same time elaborate, but without spirit. Conversation is often not devoid of entertainment, but yet without spirit: even of a woman we say that she is pretty, an agreeable talker, and courteous, but without spirit. What then do we mean by spirit?

Spirit, in an aesthetical sense, is the name given to the animating principle of the mind. But that whereby this principle animates the soul, the material which it applies to that purpose, is that which puts the mental powers purposively into swing, i.e. into such a play as maintains itself and strengthens the mental powers in their exercise.

Now I maintain that this principle is no other than the faculty of presenting aesthetical Ideas. And by an aesthetical Idea I understand that representation of the Imagination which occasions much thought, without, however, any definite thought, i.e. any concept, being capable of being adequate to it; it consequently cannot be completely compassed and made intelligible by language. We easily see that it is the counterpart (pendant) of a rational Idea, which conversely is a concept to which no intuition (or representation of the Imagination) can be adequate.

The Imagination (as a productive faculty of cognition) is very powerful in creating another nature, as it were, out of the material that actual nature gives it. We entertain ourselves with it when experience proves too commonplace, and by it we remould experience, always indeed in accordance with analogical laws, but yet also in accordance with principles which occupy a higher place in Reason (laws too which are just as natural to us as those by which Understanding comprehends empirical nature). Thus we feel our freedom from the law of association (which attaches to the empirical employment of Imagination), so that the material which we borrow from nature in accordance with this law can be worked up into something different which surpasses nature.

Such representations of the Imagination we may call Ideas, partly because they at least strive after something which lies beyond the bounds of experience, and so seek to approximate to a presentation of concepts of Reason (intellectual Ideas), thus giving to the latter the appearance of objective reality, but especially because no concept can be fully adequate to them as internal intuitions. The poet ventures to realise to sense, rational Ideas of invisible beings, the kingdom of the blessed, hell, eternity, creation, etc.; or even if he deals with things of which there are examples in experience—e.g., death, envy and all vices, also love, fame, and the like—he tries, by means of Imagination, which emulate the play of Reason in its quest after a maximum, to go beyond the limits of experience and to present them to Sense with a completeness of which there is no example in nature. It is, properly speaking, in the art of the poet, that the faculty of aesthetical Ideas can manifest itself in its full measure. But this faculty, considered in itself, is properly only a talent (of the Imagination).

If now we place under a concept a representation of the Imagination belonging to its presentation, but which occasions solely by itself more thought than can ever be comprehended in a definite concept, and which therefore enlarges aesthetically the concept itself in an unbounded fashion, the Imagination is here creative, and it brings the faculty of intellectual Ideas (the Reason) into movement; i.e. a movement, occasioned by a representation, towards more thought (though belonging, no doubt, to the concept of the object) than can be grasped in the representation or made clear.

Those forms which do not constitute the presentation of a given concept itself but only, as approximate representations of the Imagination, express the consequences bound up with it and its relationship to other concepts, are called (aesthetical) attributes of an object, whose concept as a rational Idea cannot be adequately presented. Thus Jupiter's eagle with the lightning in its claws is an attribute of the mighty king of heaven, as the peacock is of its magnificent queen. They do not, like logical attributes, represent what lies in our concepts of the sublimity and majesty of creation, but something different, which gives occasion to the Imagination to spread itself over a number of kindred representations, that arouse more thought than can be expressed in a concept determined by words. They furnish an aesthetical Idea, which for that rational Idea takes the place of logical presentation; and thus as their proper office they enliven the mind by opening out to it the prospect into an illimitable field of kindred representations. But beautiful art does this not only in the case of painting or sculpture (in which the term "attribute" is commonly employed): poetry and rhetoric also get the spirit that animates their works simply from the aesthetical attributes of the object, which accompany the logical and stimulate the Imagination, so that it thinks more by their aid, although in an undeveloped way, than could be comprehended in a concept and therefore in a definite form of words. For the sake of brevity I must limit myself to a few examples only....

An intellectual concept may serve conversely as an attribute for a representation of sense and so can quicken this latter by means of the Idea of the supersensible; but only by the aesthetical element, that subjectively attaches to the concept of the latter, being here employed. Thus, for example, a certain poet says, in his description of a beautiful morning:

> The sun arose
> As calm from virtue springs.

The consciousness of virtue, even if one only places oneself in thought in the position of a virtuous man, diffuses in the mind a multitude of sublime and restful feelings and a boundless prospect of a joyful future, to which no expression measured by a definite concept completely attains.

In a word the aesthetical Idea is a representation of the Imagination associated with a given concept, which is bound up with such a multiplicity of partial representations in its free employment, that for it no expression marking a definite concept can be found; and such a representation, therefore, adds to a concept much ineffable thought, the feeling of which quickens the cognitive faculties, and with language, which is the mere letter, binds up spirit also.

The mental powers, therefore, whose union (in a certain relation) constitutes genius are Imagination and Understanding. In the employment of the Imagination for cognition it submits to the constraint of the Understanding and is subject to the limitation of being conformable to the concept of the latter. On the other hand, in an aesthetical point of view it is free to furnish unsought, over and above that agreement with a concept, abundance of undeveloped material for the Understanding; to which the Understanding paid no regard in its concept, but which it applies, though not objectively for cognition, yet subjectively to quicken the cognitive powers and therefore also indirectly to cognitions.

Thus genius properly consists in the happy relation between these faculties, which no science can teach and no industry can learn, by which Ideas are found for a given concept; and on the other hand, we thus find for these Ideas the expression, by means of which the subjective state of mind brought about by them, as an accompaniment of the concept, can be communicated to others. The latter talent is properly speaking what is called spirit; for to express the ineffable element in the state of mind implied by a certain representation and to make it universally communicable —whether the expression be in speech or painting or statuary—this requires a faculty of seizing the quickly passing play of Imagination and of unifying it in a concept (which is even on that account original and discloses a new rule that could not have been inferred from any preceding principles or examples), that can be communicated without any constraint of rules.

If after this analysis we look back to the explanation given above of what is called genius, we find:

First, that it is a talent for Art, not for Science, in which clearly known rules must go beforehand and determine the procedure.

Secondly, as an artistic talent it presupposes a definite concept of the product, as the purpose, and therefore Understanding; but it also presupposes a representation (although an indeterminate one) of the material, i.e., of the intuition, for the presentment of this concept; and, therefore, a relation between the Imagination and the Understanding.

Thirdly, it shows itself not so much in the accomplishment of the proposed purpose in a presentment of a definite concept, as in the enunciation or expression of aesthetical Ideas, which contain abundant material for that very design; and consequently it represents the Imagination as free from all guidance of rules and yet as purposive in reference to the presentment of the given concept.

Finally, in the fourth place, the unsought undesigned subjective purposiveness in the free accordance of the Imagination with the [requirements] of the Understanding presupposes such a proportion and disposition of these faculties as no following of rules, whether of science or of mechanical imitation, can bring about, but which only the nature of the subject can produce.

In accordance with these suppositions genius is the exemplary originality of the natural gifts of a subject in the free employment of his cognitive faculties. In this way the product of a genius (as regards what is to be ascribed to genius and not to possible learning or schooling) is an example, not to be imitated (for then that which in it is genius and constitutes the spirit of the work would be lost), but to be followed, by another genius; whom it awakens to a feeling of his own originality and whom it stirs so to exercise his art in freedom from the constraint of rules, that thereby a new rule is gained for art, and thus his talent shows itself to be exemplary. But because a genius is a favourite of nature and must be regarded by us as a rare phenomenon, his example produces for other good heads a school, i.e. a methodical system of teaching according to rules, so far as these can be derived from the peculiarities of the products of his spirit. For such persons beautiful art is so far imitation, to which nature through the medium of a genius supplied the rule.

But this imitation becomes a mere aping, if the scholar copies everything down to the deformities, which the genius must have let pass only because he could not well remove them without weakening his Idea. This mental characteristic is meritorious only in the case of a genius. A certain audacity in expression—and in general many a departure from common rules—becomes him well, but it is in no way worthy of imitation. It always remains a fault in itself which we must seek to remove, though the genius is as it were privileged to commit it, because the inimitable rush of his spirit would suffer from over-anxious carefulness. Mannerism is another kind of aping, viz. of mere peculiarity (originality) in general; by which a man separates himself as far as possible from imitators, without however possessing the talent to be at the same time exemplary.

There are indeed in general two ways in which such a man may put together his notions of expressing himself; the one is called a manner (*modus aestheticus*), the other a method (*modus logicus*). They differ in this, that the former has no other standard than the feeling of unity in the presentment, but the latter follows definite principles; hence the former alone avails for beautiful art. But an artistic product is said to show mannerism only when the exposition of the artist's Idea is founded on its very singularity, and is not made appropriate to the Idea itself. The ostentatious, contorted, and affected manner, adopted to differentiate oneself from ordinary persons (though devoid of spirit) is like the behaviour of a man of whom we say, that he hears himself talk, or who stands and moves about as if he were on a stage in order to be stared at; this always betrays a bungler. . . .

§59. Beauty as the symbol of morality

Intuitions are always required to verify the reality of our concepts. If the concepts are empirical, the intuitions are called examples: if they are pure concepts of the understanding, the intuitions go by the name of schemata. But to call for a verification of the objective reality of rational concepts, i.e., of ideas, and, what is more, on behalf of the theoretical cognition of such a reality, is to demand an impossibility, because absolutely no intuition adequate to them can be given.

All hypotyposis (presentation) as a rendering in terms of sense, is twofold. Either it is schematic, as where the intuition corresponding to a concept comprehended by the understanding is given a priori, or else it is symbolic, as where the concept is one which only reason can think, and to which no sensible intuition can be adequate. In the latter case the concept is supplied with an intuition such that the procedure of judgement in dealing with it is merely analogous to that which it observes in schematism. In other words, what agrees with the concept is merely the rule of this procedure, and not the intuition itself. Hence the agreement is merely in the form of reflection, and not in the content.

Notwithstanding the adoption of the word symbolic by modern logicians in a sense opposed to an intuitive mode of representation, it is a wrong use of the word and subversive of its true meaning; for the symbolic is only a mode of any intrinsic connection with the intuition of sensetion is, in fact, divisible into the schematic and the symbolic. Both are hypotyposes, i.e., presentations, not mere marks. Marks are merely designations of concepts by the aid of accompanying sensible signs devoid of any intrinsic connection with the intuition of the object. Their sole function is to afford a means of reinvoking the concepts according to the imagination's law of association—a purely subjective role. Such marks are either words or visible (algebraic or even mimetic) signs, simply as expressions for concepts.

All intuitions by which a priori concepts are given a foothold are, therefore, either schemata or symbols. Schemata contain direct, symbols indirect, presentations of the concept. Schemata effect this presentation demonstratively, symbols by the aid of an analogy (for which recourse is had even to empirical intuitions), in which analogy judgement performs a double function: first in applying the concept to the object of a sensible intuition, and then, secondly, in applying the mere rule of its reflection upon that intuition to quite another object, of which the former is but the symbol. In this way, a monarchical state is represented as a living body when it is governed by constitutional laws, but as a mere machine (like a hand-mill) when it is governed by an individual absolute will; but in both cases the representation is merely symbolic. For there is certainly no likeness between a despotic state and a hand-mill, whereas there surely is between the rules of reflection upon both and their causality.

Hitherto this function has been but little analysed, worthy as it is of a deeper study. Still this is not the place to dwell upon it. In language we have many such indirect presentations modeled upon an analogy enabling the expression in question to contain, not the proper schema for the concept, but merely a symbol for reflection. Thus the words ground (support, basis), to depend (to be held up from above), to flow from (instead of to follow), substance (as Locke puts it: the support of accidents), and numberless others, are not schematic, but rather symbolic hypotyposes, and express concepts without employing a direct intuition for the purpose, but only drawing upon an analogy with one, i.e., transferring the reflection upon an object of intuition to quite a new concept, and one with which perhaps no intuition could ever directly correspond.

Supposing the name of knowledge may be given to what only amounts to a mere mode of representation (which is quite permissible where this is not a principle of the theoretical determination of the object in respect of what it is in itself, but of the practical determination of what the idea of it ought to be for us and for its final employment), then all our knowledge of God is merely symbolic; and one who takes it, with the properties of understanding, will, and so forth, which only evidence their objective reality in beings of this world, to be schematic, falls into anthropomorphism, just as, if he abandons every intuitive element, he falls into Deism which furnishes no knowledge whatsoever-not even from a practical point of view.

Now, I say, the beautiful is the symbol of the morally good, and only in this light (a point of view natural to everyone, and one which everyone exacts from others as a duty) does it give us pleasure with an attendant claim to the agreement of everyone else, whereupon the mind becomes conscious of a certain ennoblement and elevation above mere sensibility to pleasure from impressions of sense, and also appraises the worth of others on the score of a like maxim of their judgement. This is that intelligible to which taste, as noticed in the preceding paragraph, extends its view. It is, that is to say, what brings even our higher cognitive faculties into common accord, and is that apart from which sheer contradiction would arise between their nature and the claims put forward by taste.

In this faculty, judgement does not find itself subjected to a heteronomy of laws of experience as it does in the empirical estimate of things-in respect of the objects of such a pure delight it gives the law to itself, just as reason does in respect of the faculty of desire. Here, too, both on account of this inner possibility in the subject, and on account of the external possibility of a nature harmonizing therewith, it finds a reference in itself to something in the subject itself and outside it, and which is not nature, nor yet freedom, but still is connected with the ground of the latter, i.e., the supersensible—a something in which the theoretical faculty gets bound up into unity with the practical in an intimate and obscure manner. We shall bring out a few points of this analogy, while taking care, at the same time, not to let the points of difference escape us.

(1) The beautiful pleases immediately (but only in reflective intuition, not, like morality, in its concept).

(2) It pleases apart from all interest (pleasure in the morally good is no doubt necessarily bound up with an interest, but not with one of the kind that are antecedent to the judgement upon the delight, but with one that judgement itself for the first time calls into existence).

(3) The freedom of the imagination (consequently of our faculty in respect of its sensibility) is, in estimating the beautiful, represented as in accord with the understanding's conformity to law (in moral judgements the freedom of the will is thought as the harmony of the latter with itself according to universal laws of Reason).

(4) The subjective principles of the estimate of the beautiful is represented as universal, i.e., valid for every man, but as incognizable by means of any universal concept (the objective principle of morality is set

forth as also universal, i.e., for all individuals, and, at the same time, for all actions of the same individual, and, besides, as cognizable by means of a universal concept). For this reason the moral judgement not alone admits of definite constitutive principles, but is only possible by adopting these principles and their universality as the ground of its maxims.

Even common understanding is wont to pay regard to this analogy; and we frequently apply to beautiful objects of nature or of art names that seem to rely upon the basis of a moral estimate. We call buildings or trees majestic and stately, or plains laughing and gay; even colours are called innocent, modest, soft, because they excite sensations containing something analogous to the consciousness of the state of mind produced by moral judgements. Taste makes, as it were, the transition from the charm of sense to habitual moral interest possible without too violent a leap, for it represents the imagination, even in its freedom, as amenable to a final determination for understanding, and teaches us to find, even in sensuous objects, a free delight apart from any charm of sense.

GEORG WILHELM FRIEDRICH HEGEL
INTRODUCTION TO THE PHILOSOPHY OF FINE ART

Translated by J. Loewenberg

THE MEANING OF ART

The appropriate expression for our subject is the "Philosophy of Art," or, more precisely, the "Philosophy of Fine Arts." By this expression we wish to exclude the beauty of nature. In common life we are in the habit of speaking of beautiful color, a beautiful sky, a beautiful river, beautiful flowers, beautiful animals, and beautiful human beings. But quite aside from the question, which we wish not to discuss here, how far beauty may be predicated of such objects, or how far natural beauty may be placed side by side with artistic beauty, we must begin by maintaining that artistic beauty is higher than the beauty of nature. For the beauty of art is beauty born—and born again—of the spirit. And as spirit and its products stand higher than nature and its phenomena, by so much the beauty that resides in art is superior to the beauty of nature.

To say that spirit and artistic beauty stand higher than natural beauty, is to say very little, for "higher" is a very indefinite expression, which states the difference between them as quantitative and external. The "higher" quality of spirit and of artistic beauty does not at all stand in a merely relative position to nature. Spirit only is the true essence and content of the world, so that whatever is beautiful is truly beautiful only when it partakes of this higher essence and is produced by it. In this sense natural beauty appears only as a reflection of the beauty that belongs to spirit; it is an imperfect and incomplete expression of the spiritual substance.

Confining ourselves to artistic beauty, we must first consider certain difficulties. The first that suggests itself is the question whether art is at all worthy of a philosophic treatment. To be sure, art and beauty pervade, like a kindly genius, all the affairs of life, and joyously adorn all its inner and outer phases, softening the gravity and the burden of actual existence, furnishing pleasure for idle moments, and, where it can accomplish nothing positive, driving evil away by occupying its place. Yet, although art wins its way everywhere with its pleasing forms, from the crude adornment of the savages to the splendor of the temple with its marvelous wealth of decoration, art itself appears to fall outside the real aims of life. And though the creations of art cannot be said to be directly disadvantageous to the serious purposes of life, nay, on occasion actually further them by holding evil at bay, on the whole, art belongs to the relaxation and leisure of the mind, while the substantial interests of life demand its exertion. At any rate, such a view renders art a superfluity, though the tender and emotional influence which is wrought upon the mind by occupation with art is not thought necessarily detrimental, because effeminate.

There are others, again, who, though acknowledging art to be a luxury, have thought it necessary to defend it by pointing to the practical necessities of the fine arts and to the relation they bear to morality and piety. Very serious aims have been ascribed to art. Art has been recommended as a mediator between reason and sensuousness, between inclination and duty, as the reconcilor of all these elements constantly warring with one another. But it must be said that, by making art serve two masters, it is not rendered thereby more worthy of a philosophic treatment. Instead of being an end in itself, art is degraded into a means of appealing to higher aims, on the one hand, and to frivolity and idleness on the other.

Art considered as means offers another difficulty which springs from its form. Granting that art can be subordinated to serious aims and that the results which it thus produces will be significant, still the means used by art is deception, for beauty is appearance, its form is its life; and one must admit that a true and real purpose should not be achieved through deception. Even if a good end is thus, now and then, attained by art its success is rather limited, and even then deception cannot be recommended as a worthy means; for the means should be adequate to the dignity of the end, and truth can be produced by truth alone and not by deception and semblance.

It may thus appear as if art were not worthy of philosophic consideration because it is supposed to be merely a pleasing pastime; even when it pursues more serious aims it does not correspond with their nature. On the whole, it is conceived to serve both grave and light interests, achieving its results by means of deception and semblance.

As for the worthiness of art to be philosophically considered, it is indeed true that art can be used as a casual amusement, furnishing enjoyment and pleasure, decorating our surroundings, lending grace to the external conditions of life, and giving prominence to other objects through ornamentation. Art thus employed is indeed not an independent or free, but rather a subservient art. That art might serve other purposes and still retain its pleasure-giving function, is a relation which it has in common with thought. For science, too, in the hands of the servile understanding is used for finite ends and accidental means, and is thus not self-sufficient, but is determined by outer objects and circumstances.

On the other hand, science can emancipate itself from such service and can rise in free independence to the pursuit of truth, in which the realization of its own aims is its proper function.

Art is not genuine art until it has thus liberated itself. It fulfils its highest task when it has joined the same sphere with religion and philosophy and has become a certain mode of bringing to consciousness and expression the divine meaning of things, the deepest interests of mankind, and the most universal truths of the spirit. Into works of art the nations have wrought their most profound ideas and aspirations. Fine Art often constitutes the key, and with many nations it is the only key, to an understanding of their wisdom and religion. This character art has in common with religion and philosophy. Art's peculiar feature, however, consists in its ability to represent in sensuous form even the highest ideas, bringing them thus nearer to the character of natural phenomena, to the senses, and to feeling. It is the height of a supra-sensuous world into which thought reaches, but it always appears to immediate consciousness and to present experience as an alien beyond. Through the power of philosophic thinking we are able to soar above what is merely here, above sensuous and finite experience. But spirit can heal the breach between the supra-sensuous and the sensuous brought on by its own advance; it produces out of itself the world of fine art as the first reconciling medium between what is merely external, sensuous, and transient, and the world of pure thought, between nature with its finite reality and the infinite freedom of philosophic reason.

Concerning the unworthiness of art because of its character as appearance and deception, it must be admitted that such criticism would not be without justice, if appearance could be said to be equivalent to falsehood and thus to something that ought not to be. Appearance is essential to reality; truth could not be, did it not shine through appearance. Therefore not appearance in general can be objected to, but merely the particular kind of appearance through which art seeks to portray truth. To charge the appearance in which art chooses to embody its ideas as deception, receives meaning only by comparison with the external world of phenomena and its immediate materiality, as well as with the inner world of sensations and feelings. To these two worlds we are wont, in our empirical work-a-day life, to attribute the value of actuality, reality, and truth, in contrast to art, which is supposed to be lacking such reality and truth. But, in fact, it is just the whole sphere of the empirical inner and outer world that is not the world of true reality; indeed it may be called a mere show and a cruel deception in a far stricter sense than in the case of art.

Only beyond the immediacy of sense and of external objects is genuine reality to be found. Truly real is but the fundamental essence and the underlying substance of nature and of spirit, and the universal element in nature and in spirit is precisely what art accentuates and makes visible. This essence of reality appears also in the common outer and inner world, but it appears in the form of a chaos of contingencies, distorted by the immediateness of sense perception, and by the capriciousness of conditions, events, characters, etc. Art frees the true meaning of appearances from the show and deception of this bad and transient world, and invests it with a higher reality, born of the spirit. Thus, far removed from being mere appearances, the products of art have a higher reality and a more genuine being than the things of ordinary life.

THE CONTENT AND IDEAL OF ART

The content of art is spiritual, and its form is sensuous; both sides art has to reconcile into a united whole. The first requirement is that the content, which art is to represent, must be worthy of artistic representation; otherwise we obtain only a bad unity, since a content not capable of artistic treatment is made to take on an artistic form, and a matter prosaic in itself is forced into a form quite opposed to its inherent nature.

The second requirement demands of the content of art that it shall be no abstraction. By this is not meant that it must be concrete, as the sensuous is alleged to be concrete in contrast to everything spiritual and intellectual. For everything that is genuinely true, in the realm of thought as well as in the domain of nature, is concrete, and has, in spite of universality, nevertheless, a particular and subjective character. By saying, for example, that God is simply One, the Supreme Being as such, we express thereby nothing but a lifeless abstraction of an understanding devoid of reason. Such a God, as indeed he is not conceived in his concrete truth, can furnish no content for art, least of all for plastic art. Thus the Jews and the Turks have not been able to represent their God, who is still more abstract, in the positive manner in which the Christians have represented theirs. For in Christianity God is conceived in his truth, and therefore concrete, as a person, as a subject, and, more precisely still, as Spirit. What he is as spirit appears to the religious consciousness as a Trinity of persons, which at the same time is One. Here the essence of God is the reconciled unity of universality and particularity, such unity alone being concrete. Hence, as a content in order to be true must be concrete in this sense, art demands the same concreteness; because a mere abstract idea, or an abstract universal, cannot manifest itself in a particular and sensuous unified form.

If a true and therefore concrete content is to have its adequate sensuous form and shape, this sensuous form must—this being the third requirement—also be something individual, completely concrete, and one. The nature of concreteness belonging to both the content and the representation of art, is precisely the point in which both can coincide and correspond to each other. The natural shape of the human body, for example, is a sensuous concrete object, which is perfectly adequate to represent the spiritual in its concreteness; the view should therefore be abandoned that an existing object from the external world is accidentally chosen by art to express a spiritual idea.

Art does not seize upon this or that form either because it simply finds it or because it can find no other, but the concrete spiritual content itself carries with it the element of external, real, yes, even sensuous, representation. And this is the reason why a sensuous concrete object, which bears the impress of an essentially spiritual content, addresses itself to the inner eye; the outward shape whereby the content is rendered visible and imaginable aims at an existence only in our heart and mind. For this reason alone are content and artistic shape harmoniously wrought. The mere sensuously concrete external nature as such has not this purpose for its only origin. The gay and variegated plumage of the birds shines unseen, and their song dies away unheard; the torch-thistle which blossoms only for a night withers without having been admired in the wilds of southern forests; and these forests, groves of the most beautiful and luxuriant vegetation, with the most odorous and fragrant perfumes, perish and waste, no more enjoyed. The work of art is not so unconsciously self-immersed, but it is essentially a question, an address to the responsive soul, an appeal to the heart and to the mind.

Although the sensuous form in which art clothes its content is not accidental, yet it is not the highest form whereby the spiritually concrete may be grasped. A higher mode than representation through a sensuous form, is thought. True and rational thinking, though in a relative sense abstract, must not be one-sided, but concrete. How far a definite content can be adequately treated by art and how far it needs, according to its nature, a higher and more spiritual form, is a distinction which we see at once if, for example, the Greek gods are compared with God as conceived in accordance with Christian notions. The Greek god is not abstract but individual, closely related to the natural human form. The Christian God is also a concrete personality, but he is pure spiritually, and can be known only as spirit and in spirit. His sphere of existence is therefore essentially inner knowledge, and not the outer natural shape through which he can be represented but imperfectly and not in the whole depth of his essence.

But the task of art is to represent a spiritual idea to direct contemplation in sensuous form, and not in the form of thought or of pure spirituality. The value and dignity of such representation lies in the correspondence and unity of the two sides, of the spiritual content and its sensuous embodiment, so that the perfection and excellency of art must depend upon the grade of inner harmony and union with which the spiritual idea and the sensuous form interpenetrate.

The requirement of the conformity of spiritual idea and sensuous form might at first be interpreted as meaning that any idea whatever would suffice, so long as the concrete form represented this idea and no other. Such a view, however, would confound the ideal of art with mere correctness, which consists in the expression of any meaning in its appropriate form. The artistic ideal is not to be thus understood. For any content whatever is capable, according to the standard of its own nature, of adequate representation, but yet it does not for that reason lay claim to artistic beauty in the ideal sense. Judged by the standard of ideal beauty, even such correct representation will be defective.

In this connection we may remark that the defects of a work of art are not to be considered simply as always due to the incapacity of the artist; defectiveness of form has also its root in defectiveness of content. Thus, for instance, the Chinese, Indians, Egyptians, in their artistic objects, their representations of the gods, and their idols, adhered to formlessness, or to a vague and inarticulate form, and were not able to arrive at genuine beauty, because their mythological ideas, the content and conception of their works of art, were as yet vague and obscure. The more perfect in form works of art are, the more profound is the inner truth of their content and thought. And it is not merely a question of the greater or lesser skill with which the objects of external nature are studied and copied, for, in certain stages of artistic consciousness and artistic activity, the misrepresentation and distortion of natural objects are not unintentional technical inexpertness and incapacity, but conscious alteration, which depends upon the content that is in consciousness, and is, in fact, demanded by it.

We may thus speak of imperfect art, which, in its own proper sphere, may be quite perfect both technically and in other respects. When compared with the highest idea and ideal of art, it is indeed defective. In the highest art alone are the idea and its representation in perfect congruity, because the sensuous form of the idea is in itself the adequate form, and because the content, which that form embodies, is itself a genuine content.

The higher truth of art consists, then, in the spiritual having attained a sensuous form adequate to its essence. And this also furnishes the principle of division for the philosophy of art. For the Spirit, before it wins the true meaning of its absolute essence, has to develop through a series of stages which constitute its very life. To this universal evolution there corresponds a development of the phases of art, under the form of which the Spirit—as artist— attains to a comprehension of its own meaning.

This evolution within the spirit of art has two sides. The development is, in the first place, a spiritual and universal one, in so far as a gradual series of definite conceptions of the universe—of nature, man, and God—finds artistic representation. In the second place, this universal development of art, embodying itself in sensuous form, determines definite modes of artistic expression and a totality of necessary distinctions within the sphere of art. These constitute the particular arts.

We have now to consider three definite relations of the spiritual idea to its sensuous expression.

SYMBOLIC ART

Art begins when the spiritual idea, being itself still indefinite and obscure and ill-comprehended, is made the content of artistic forms. As indefinite, it does not yet have that individuality which the artistic ideal demands; its abstractness and one-sidedness thus render its shape defective and whimsical. The first form of art is therefore rather a mere search after plasticity than a capacity of true representation. The spiritual idea has not yet found its adequate form, but is still engaged in striving and struggling after it. This form we may, in general, call the symbolic form of art; in such form the abstract idea assumes a shape in natural sensuous matter which is foreign to it; with this foreign matter the artistic creation begins, from which, however, it seems unable to free itself. The objects of external nature are reproduced unchanged, but at the same time the meaning of the spiritual idea is attached to them. They thus receive the vocation of expressing it, and must be interpreted as if the spiritual idea were actually present in them. It is indeed true that natural objects possess an aspect which makes them capable of representing a universal meaning, but in symbolic art a complete correspondence is not yet possible. In it the correspondence is confined to an abstract quality, as when, for example, a lion is meant to stand for strength.

This abstract relation brings also to consciousness the foreignness of the spiritual idea to natural phenomena. And the spiritual idea, having no other reality to express its essence, expatiates in all these natural shapes, seeks itself in their unrest and disproportion, but finds them inadequate to it. It then exaggerates these natural phenomena and shapes them into the huge and the boundless. The spiritual idea revels in them, as it were, seethes and ferments in them, does violence to them, distorts and disfigures them into grotesque shapes, and endeavors by the diversity, hugeness, and splendor of such forms to raise the natural phenomena to the spiritual level. For here it is the spiritual idea which is more or less vague and non-plastic, while the objects of nature have a thoroughly definite form.

The incongruity of the two elements to each other makes the relation of the spiritual idea to objective reality a negative one. The spiritual as a wholly inner element and as the universal substance of all things, is conceived unsatisfied with all externality, and in its sublimity it triumphs over the abundance of unsuitable forms. In this conception of sublimity the natural objects and the human shapes are accepted and left unaltered, but at the same time recognized as inadequate to their own inner meaning; it is this inner meaning which is glorified far and above every worldly content.

These elements constitute, in general, the character of the primitive artistic pantheism of the Orient, which either invests even the lowest objects with absolute significance, or forces all phenomena with violence to assume the expression of its world-view. This art becomes therefore bizarre, grotesque, and without taste, or it represents the infinite substance in its abstract freedom turning away with disdain from the illusory and perishing mass of appearances. Thus the meaning can never be completely molded into the expression, and, notwithstanding all the aspiration and effort, the incongruity between the spiritual idea and the sensuous form remains insuperable. This is, then, the first form of art—symbolic art with its endless quest, its inner struggle, its sphinx-like mystery, and its sublimity.

CLASSICAL ART

In the second form of art, which we wish to designate as the classical, the double defect of symbolic art is removed. The symbolic form is imperfect, because the spiritual meaning which it seeks to convey enters into consciousness in but an abstract and vague manner, and thus the congruity between meaning and form must always remain defective and therefore abstract. This double aspect disappears in the classical type of art; in it we find the free and adequate embodiment of the spiritual idea in the form most suitable to it, and with it meaning and expression are in perfect accord. It is classical art, therefore, which first affords the creation and contemplation of the completed ideal, realizing it as a real fact in the world.

But the congruity of idea and reality in classical art must not be taken in a formal sense of the agreement of a content with its external form; otherwise every photograph of nature, every picture of a countenance, landscape, flower, scene, etc., which constitutes the aim of a representation, would, through the conformity of content and form, be at once classical. The peculiarity of classical art, on the contrary, consists in its content being itself a concrete idea, and, as such, a concrete spiritual idea, for only the spiritual is a truly essential content. For a worthy object of such a content, Nature must be consulted as to whether she contains anything to which a spiritual attribute really belongs.

It must be the World-Spirit itself that invented the proper form for the concrete spiritual ideal—the subjective mind—in this case the spirit of art—has only found it, and given it natural plastic existence in accordance with free individual spirituality. The form in which the idea, as spiritual and individual, clothes itself when revealed as a temporal phenomenon, is the human form. To be sure, personification and anthropomorphism have frequently been decried as a degradation of the spiritual; but art, in so far as its task is to bring before direct contemplation the spiritual in sensuous form, must advance to such anthropomorphism, for only in its body can mind appear in an adequately sensuous fashion. The migration of souls is, in this respect, an abstract notion, and physiology should make it one of its fundamental principles that life has necessarily, in its evolution, to advance to the human shape as the only sensuous phenomenon appropriate to the mind.

The human body as portrayed by classical art is not represented in its mere physical existence, but solely as the natural and sensuous form and garb of mind; it is therefore divested of all the defects that belong to the merely sensuous and of all the finite contingencies that appertain to the phenomenal. But if the form must be thus purified in order to express the appropriate content, and, furthermore, if the conformity of meaning and expression is to be complete, the content which is the spiritual idea must be perfectly capable of being expressed through the bodily form of man, without projecting into another sphere beyond the physical and sensuous representation. The result is that Spirit is characterized as a particular form of mind, namely, as human mind, and not as simply absolute and eternal; but the absolute and eternal Spirit must be able to reveal and express itself in a manner far more spiritual.

This latter point brings to light the defect of classical art, which demands its dissolution and its transition to a third and higher form, to wit, the romantic form of art.

ROMANTIC ART

The romantic form of art destroys the unity of the spiritual idea and its sensuous form, and goes back, though on a higher level, to the difference and opposition of the two, which symbolic art left unreconciled. The classical form of art attained, indeed, the highest degree of perfection which the sensuous process of art was capable of realizing; and, if it shows any defects, the defects are those of art itself, due to the limitation of its sphere. This limitation has its root in the general attempt of art to represent in sensuous concrete form the infinite and universal

Spirit, and in the attempt of the classical type of art to blend so completely spiritual and sensuous existence that the two appear in mutual conformity. But in such a fusion of the spiritual and sensuous aspects Spirit cannot be portrayed according to its true essence, for the true essence of Spirit is its infinite subjectivity; and its absolute internal meaning does not lend itself to a full and free expression in the confinement of the bodily form as its only appropriate existence.

Now, romantic art dissolves the inseparable unity which is the ideal of the classical type, because it has won a content which goes beyond the classical form of art and its mode of expression. This content—if familiar ideas may be recalled—coincides with what Christianity declares to be true of God as Spirit, in distinction to the Greek belief in gods which constitutes the essential and appropriate subject for classical art. The concrete content of Hellenic art implies the unity of the human and divine nature, a unity which, just because it is merely implied and immediate, permits of a representation in an immediately visible and sensuous mold.

The Greek god is the object of naïve contemplation and sensuous imagination; his shape is, therefore, the bodily shape of man; the circle of his power and his essence is individual and confined. To man the Greek god appears as a being and a power with whom he may feel a kinship and unity, but this kinship and unity, are not reflected upon or raised into definite knowledge. The higher stage is the knowledge of this unconscious unity, which underlies the classical form of art and which it has rendered capable of complete plastic embodiment. The elevation of what is unconscious and implied into self-conscious knowledge brings about an enormous difference; it is the infinite difference which, for example, separates man from the animal. Man is an animal, but, even in his animal functions, does not rest satisfied with the potential and the unconscious as the animal does, but becomes conscious of them, reflects upon them, and raises them—as, for instance, the process of digestion—into self-conscious science. And it is thus that man breaks through the boundary of his merely immediate and unconscious existence, so that, just because he knows himself to be animal, he ceases in virtue of such knowledge to be animal, and, through such self-knowledge only, can characterize himself as mind or spirit.

If in the manner just described the unity of the human and divine nature is raised from an immediate to a conscious, unity, the true mold for the reality of this content is no longer the sensuous, immediate existence of the spiritual, the bodily frame of man, but self-consciousness and internal contemplation. For this reason Christianity, in depicting God as Spirit—not as particularized individual mind, but as absolute and universal Spirit—retires from the sensuousness of imagination into the sphere of inner being, and makes this, and not the bodily form, the material and mold of its content; and thus the unity of the human and divine nature is a conscious unity, capable of realization only by spiritual knowledge. The new content, won by this unity, is not dependent upon sensuous representation; it is now exempt from such immediate existence. In this way, however, romantic art becomes art which transcends itself, carrying on this process of self-transcendence within its own artistic sphere and artistic form.

Briefly stated, the essence of romantic art consists in the artistic object being the free, concrete, spiritual idea itself, which is revealed in its spirituality to the inner, and not the outer, eye. In conformity with such a content, art can, in a sense, not work for sensuous perception, but must aim at the inner mood, which completely fuses with its object, at the most subjective inner shrine, at the heart, the feeling, which, as spiritual feeling, longs for freedom within itself and seeks and finds reconciliation only within the inner recesses of the spirit. This inner world is the content of romantic art, and as such an inner life, or as its reflection, it must seek embodiment. The inner life thus triumphs over the outer world—indeed, so triumphs over it that the outer world itself is made to proclaim its victory, through which the sensuous appearance sinks into worthlessness.

On the other hand, the romantic type of art, like every other, needs an external mode of expression. But the spiritual has now retired from the outer mode into itself, and the sensuous externality of form assumes again, as it did in symbolic art, an insignificant and transient character. The subjective, finite mind and will, the peculiarity and caprice of the individual, of character, action, or of incident and plot, assume likewise the character they had in symbolic art. The external side of things is surrendered to accident and committed to the excesses of the imagination, whose caprice now mirrors existence as it is, now chooses to distort the objects of the outer world into a bizarre and grotesque medley, for the external form no longer possesses a meaning and significance, as in classical art, on its own account and for it own sake. Feeling is now everything. It finds its artistic reflection, not in the world of external things and their forms, but in its own expression; and in every incident and accident of life, in every misfortune, grief, and even crime, feeling preserves or regains its healing power of reconciliation.

Hence, the indifference, incongruity, and antagonism of spiritual idea and sensuous form, the characteristics of symbolic art, reappear in the romantic type, but with this essential difference. In the romantic realm, the spiritual idea, to whose defectiveness was due the defective forms of symbolic art, now reveals itself in its perfection within mind and feeling. It is by virtue of the higher perfection of the idea that it shuns any adequate union with an external form, since it can seek and attain its true reality and expression best within itself.

This, in general terms, is the character of the symbolic, classical, and romantic forms of art, which stand for the three relations of the spiritual idea to its expression in the realm of art. They consist in the aspiration after, and the attainment and transcendence of, the ideal as the true idea of beauty.

THE PARTICULAR ARTS

But, now, there inhere in the idea of beauty different modifications which art translates into sensuous forms. And we find a fundamental principle by which the several particular arts may be arranged and defined—that is, the species of art contain in themselves the same essential differences which we have found in the three general types of art. External objectivity, moreover, into which these types are molded by means of a sensuous and particular material, renders them independent and separate means of realizing different artistic functions, as far as each type finds its definite character in some one definite external material whose mode of portrayal determines its adequate realization. Furthermore, the general types of art correspond to the several particular arts, so that they (the particular arts) belong each of them specifically to one of the general types of art. It is these particular arts which give adequate and artistic external being to the general types.

ARCHITECTURE

The first of the particular arts with which, according to their fundamental principle, we have to begin, is architecture. Its task consists in so shaping external inorganic nature that it becomes homogeneous with mind, as an artistic outer world. The material of architecture is matter itself in its immediate externality as a heavy mass subject to mechanical laws, and its forms remain the forms of inorganic nature, but are merely arranged and ordered in accordance with the abstract rules of the understanding, the rules of symmetry. But in such material and in such forms the ideal as concrete spirituality cannot be realized; the reality which is represented in them remains, therefore, alien to the spiritual idea, as something external which it has not penetrated or with which it has but a remote and abstract relation.

Hence the fundamental type of architecture is the symbolical form of art. For it is architecture that paves the way, as it were, for the adequate realization of the God, toiling and wrestling in his service with external nature, and seeking to extricate it from the chaos of finitude and the abortiveness of chance. By this means it levels a space for the God, frames his external surroundings, and builds him his temple as the place for inner contemplation and for reflection upon the eternal objects of the spirit. It raises an enclosure around those gathered together, as a defense against the threatening of the wind, against rain, the thunder-storm, and wild beasts, and reveals the will to gather together, though externally, yet in accordance with the artistic form.

A meaning such as this, the art of architecture is able to mold into its material and its forms with more or less success, according as the determinate nature of the content which it seeks to embody is more significant or more trivial, more concrete or more abstract, more deeply rooted within its inner being or more dim and superficial. Indeed, it may even advance so far as to endeavor to create for such meaning an adequate artistic expression with its material and forms, but in such an attempt it has already overstepped the bounds of its own sphere, and inclines towards sculpture, the higher phase of art. For the limit of architecture lies precisely in this, that it refers to the spiritual as an internal essence in contrast with the external forms of its art, and thus whatever spirit and soul are possessed it must point to as something other than itself.

SCULPTURE

Architecture, however, has purified the inorganic external world, has given it symmetric order, has impressed upon it the seal of mind, and the temple of the God, the house of his community, stands ready. Into this temple now enters the God himself. The lightning-flash of individuality strikes the inert mass, permeates it, and a form no longer merely symmetrical, but infinite and spiritual, concentrates and molds its adequate bodily shape. This is the task of sculpture.

Inasmuch as in it the inner spiritual element, which architecture can no more than hint at, completely abides with the sensuous form and its external matter, and as both sides are so merged into each other that neither predominates, sculpture has the classical form of art as its fundamental type. In fact, the sensuous realm itself can command no expression which could not be that of the spiritual sphere, just as, conversely, no spiritual content can attain perfect plasticity in sculpture which is incapable of being adequately presented to perception in bodily form. It is sculpture which arrests for our vision the spirit in its bodily frame, in immediate unity with it, and in an attitude of peace and repose; and the form in turn is animated by the content of spiritual individuality. Therefore the external sensuous matter is here not wrought, either according to its mechanical quality alone, as heavy mass, nor in forms peculiar to inorganic nature, nor as indifferent to color, etc., but in ideal forms of the human shape, and in the whole of the spatial dimensions.

In this last respect sculpture should be credited with having first revealed the inner and spiritual essence in its eternal repose and essential self-possession. To such repose and unity with itself corresponds only that external element which itself persists in unity and repose. Such an element is the form taken in its abstract spatiality. The spirit which sculpture represents is that which is solid in itself, not variously broken up in the play of contingencies and passions; nor does its external form admit of the portrayal of such a manifold play, but it holds to this one side only, to the abstraction of space in the totality of its dimensions.

THE DEVELOPMENT OF THE ROMANTIC ARTS

After architecture has built the temple and the hand of sculpture has placed inside it the statue of the God, then this sensuously visible God faces in the spacious halls of his house the community. The community is the spiritual, self-reflecting element in this sensuous realm, it is the animating subjectivity and inner life. A new principle of art begins with it. Both the content of art and the medium which embodies it in outward form now demand particularization, individualization, and the subjective mode of expressing these. The solid unity which the God possesses in sculpture breaks up into the plurality of inner individual lives, whose unity is not sensuous, but essentially ideal.

And now God comes to assume the aspect which makes him truly spiritual. As a hither-and-thither, as an alternation between the unity within himself and his realization in subjective knowledge and individual consciousness, as well as in the common and unified life of the many individuals, he is genuinely Spirit—the Spirit in his community. In his community God is released from the abstractness of a mysterious self-identity, as well as from the naïve imprisonment in a bodily shape, in which he is represented by sculpture. Here he is exalted into spirituality, subjectivity, and knowledge. For this reason the higher content of art is now this spirituality in its absolute form. But since what chiefly reveals itself in this stage is not the serene repose of God in himself, but rather his appearance, his being, and his manifestation to others, the objects of artistic representation are now the most varied subjective expressions of life and activity for their own sake, as human passions, deeds, events, and, in general, the wide range of human feeling, will, and resignation.

In accordance with this content, the sensuous element must differentiate and show itself adequate to the expression of subjective feeling. Such different media are furnished by color, by the musical sound, and finally by the sound as the mere indication of inner intuitions and ideas; and thus as different forms of realizing the spiritual content of art by means of these media we obtain painting, music, and poetry. The sensuous media employed in these arts being individualized and in their essence recognized as ideal, they correspond most effectively to the spiritual content of art, and the union between spiritual meaning and sensuous expression develops, therefore, into greater intimacy than was possible in the case of architecture and sculpture. This intimate unity, however, is due wholly to the subjective side.

Leaving, then, the symbolic spirit of architecture and the classical ideal of sculpture behind, these new arts in which form and content are raised to an ideal level borrow their type from the romantic form of art, whose mode of expression they are most eminently fitted to voice. They form, however, a totality of arts, because the romantic type is the most concrete in itself.

PAINTING

The first art in this totality, which is akin to sculpture, is painting. The material which it uses for its content and for the sensuous expression of that content is visibility as such, in so far as it is individualized, viz., specified as color. To be sure, the media employed in architecture and sculpture are also visible and colored, but they are not, as in painting, visibility as such, not the simple light which contrasts itself with darkness and in combination with it becomes color. This visibility as a subjective and ideal attribute, requires neither, like architecture, the abstract mechanical form of mass which we find in heavy matter, nor, like sculpture, the three dimensions of sensuous space, even though in concentrated and organic plasticity, but the visibility which appertains to painting has its differences on a more ideal level, in the particular kinds of color; and thus painting frees art from the sensuous completeness in space peculiar to material things only, by confining itself to a plane surface.

On the other hand, the content also gains in varied particularization. Whatever can find room in the human heart, as emotion, idea, and purpose, whatever it is able to frame into a deed, all this variety of material can constitute the many-colored content of painting. The whole range of particular existence, from the highest aspirations of the mind down to the most isolated objects of nature, can obtain a place in this art. For even finite nature, in its particular scenes and aspects, can here appear, if only some allusion to a spiritual element makes it akin to thought and feeling.

MUSIC

The second art in which the romantic form finds realization, on still a higher level than in painting, is music. Its material, though still sensuous, advances to a deeper subjectivity and greater specification. The idealization of the sensuous, music brings about by negating space. In music the indifferent extension of space whose appearance painting admits and consciously imitates is concentrated and idealized into a single point. But in the form of a motion and tremor of the material body within itself, this single point becomes a concrete and active process within the idealization of matter. Such an incipient ideality of matter which no longer appears under the spatial form, but as temporal ideality, is sound the sensuous acknowledged as ideal, whose abstract visibility is transformed into audibility. Sound, as it were, exempts the ideal from its absorption in matter.

This earliest animation and inspiration of matter furnishes the medium for the inner and intimate life of the spirit, as yet on an indefinite level; it is through the tones of music that the heart pours out its whole scale of feelings and passions. Thus as sculpture constitutes the central point between architecture and the arts of romantic subjectivity, so music forms the centre of the romantic arts, and represents the point of transition between abstract spatial sensuousness, which belongs to painting, and the abstract spirituality of poetry. Within itself music has, like architecture, an abstract quantitative relation, as a contrast to its inward and emotional quality; it also has as its basis a permanent law to which the tones with their combinations and successions must conform.

POETRY

For the third and most spiritual expression of the romantic form of art, we must look to poetry. Its characteristic peculiarity lies in the power with which it subjugates to the mind and to its ideas the sensuous element from which music and painting began to set art free. For sound, the one external medium of which poetry avails itself, is in it no longer a feeling of the tone itself, but is a sign which is, by itself, meaningless. This sign, moreover, is a sign of an idea which has become concrete, and not merely of indefinite feeling and of its nuances and grades. By this means the tone becomes the word, an articulate voice, whose function it is to indicate thoughts and ideas.

The negative point to which music had advanced now reveals itself in poetry as the completely concrete point, as the spirit or the self-consciousness of the individual, which spontaneously unites the infinite space of its ideas with the time-element of sound. But this sensuous element which, in music, was still in immediate union with inner feelings and moods, is, in poetry, divorced from the content of consciousness, for in poetry the mind determines this content on its own account and for the sake of its ideas, and while it employs sound to express them, yet sound itself is reduced to a symbol without value or meaning.

From this point of view sound may just as well be considered a mere letter, for the audible, like the visible, is now relegated to a mere suggestion of mind. Thus the genuine mode of poetic representation is the inner perception and the poetic imagination itself. And since all types of art share in this mode, poetry runs through them all, and develops itself independently in each. Poetry, then, is the universal art of the spirit which has attained inner freedom, and which does not depend for its realization upon external sensuous matter, but expatiates only in the inner space and inner time of the ideas and feelings. But just in this, its highest phase, art oversteps the bounds of its own sphere by abandoning the harmoniously sensuous mode of portraying the spirit and by passing from the poetry of imagination into the prose of thought.

SUMMARY

Such, then, is the organic totality of the several arts the external art of architecture, the objective art of sculpture, and the subjective arts of painting, music, and poetry. The higher principle from which these are derived we have found in the types of art, the symbolic, the classical, and the romantic, which form the universal phases of the idea of beauty itself.

Thus symbolic art finds its most adequate reality and most perfect application in architecture, in which it is self-complete, and is not yet reduced, so to speak, to the inorganic medium for another art. The classical form of art, on the other hand, attains its most complete realization in sculpture, while it accepts architecture only as forming an enclosure round its products and is as yet not capable of developing painting and music as absolute expressions of its meaning. The romantic type of art, finally, seizes upon painting, music, and poetry as its essential and adequate modes of expression. Poetry, however, is in conformity with all types of the beautiful and extends over them all, because its characteristic element is the esthetic imagination, and imagination is necessary for every product of art, to whatever type it may belong.

Thus what the particular arts realize in individual artistic creations are, according to the philosophic conception, simply the universal types of the self-unfolding idea of beauty. Out of the external realization of this idea arises the wide Pantheon of art, whose architect and builder is the self-developing spirit of beauty, for the completion of which, however, the history of the world will require its evolution of countless ages.

ARTHUR SCHOPENHAUER
THE METAPHYSICS OF FINE ART

Translated by T. B. Saunders

The real problem in the philosophy of Art may be very simply stated thus: How is it possible to take pleasure in something that does not come into any relation with the will?

Let me put this more fully. It is commonly felt that pleasure and enjoyment in a thing can arise only when it comes into some relation with our will, or, as we prefer to say, when it serves some end which we have in view. If this were so, it would seem to be a contradiction to talk of pleasure which did not involve bringing the will into play. And yet it is quite obvious that we derive pleasure and enjoyment from the beautiful as such, quite apart from any connection it may have with our personal aims, or, in other words, with our will.

This problem I have solved in the following way: By the beautiful we mean the essential and original forms of animate and inanimate Nature—in Platonic language, the Ideas; and these can be apprehended only by their essential correlate, a knowing subject free from will; in other words, a pure intelligence without purpose or ends in view. Hence in the act of aesthetic perception the will has absolutely no place in consciousness. But it is the will alone which is the fount of all our sorrows and sufferings, and if it thus vanishes from consciousness, the whole possibility of suffering is taken away. This it is that explains the feeling of pleasure which accompanies the perception of the beautiful.

If it should be objected that to take away the possibility of suffering is also to take away the possibility of enjoyment, it should be remembered that, as I have often explained, happiness and satisfaction are negative in their nature; in other words, they are merely freedom from suffering; whilst pain is the positive element of existence. So that, when will vanishes from consciousness, there yet remains over the state of enjoyment; that is to say, the state in which there is a complete absence, not only of pain, but in this case, even of the very possibility of it.

To be freed from oneself is what is meant by becoming a pure intelligence. It consists in forgetfulness of one's own aims and complete absorption in the object of contemplation; so that all we are conscious of is this one object. And since this is a state of mind unattainable by most men, they are, as a rule, unfitted for an objective attitude towards the world; and it is just this that constitutes the artistic faculty. To the will as it exists in the individual is superadded an intellectual faculty, which enables the will to become conscious of itself and of the objects about it.

This intellectual faculty came into being in order to perform the service of the will. Now, let us suppose that the will sets the intellect at liberty for a while and grants it a full release from its service, so that the intellect may for the moment dismiss its concern for the will; in other words, abandon the personal service which forms its only natural task, and, therefore, its regular occupation. If, at the same time that it is thus released, the intellect does not cease to be active and energetic, and use every endeavour to arrive at a clear apprehension of the world, it becomes completely objective; that is to say, it becomes a faithful mirror of the things about it.

It is only in this way, with a pure intelligence as subject, that the object, pure and simple, can come into existence. For this postulated relation between subject and object to arise at all, it is necessary that the intellectual faculty should not only be withdrawn from its original service and be left altogether to itself, but also that, when released, it should nevertheless preserve its whole energy of activity; in spite of the fact that the stimulus of this activity, the impulse of the will, is now absent.

Therein lies the difficulty, and this is just why the condition of mind necessary in artistic creation is so rare; because all our thoughts and endeavors, our powers of sight and hearing, are always naturally exerted, directly or indirectly, in the service of our numerous personal aims, great and small. It is the will that drives the intellect to the fulfilment of its function, and the intellect flags at once if the spur is withdrawn. Rendered active in this way, the intellect is perfectly sufficient for the needs of practical life, nay, even for the kind of knowledge required in professional business. For there the aim is to understand only the relations of things, not the inner reality peculiar to them; and this kind of knowledge proceeds by applying such principles of reasoning as govern the relations in which things may stand to one another. But though in the conception of a work of art the intellect is all in all, in the execution of it, where the aim is to communicate and represent what has been conceived, the will may, nay, must become active again; just because there is an aim to be carried out. Accordingly, in this sphere, the principles of reasoning which govern the relations of things again comes into play. It is in conformity with these principles that the means used by Art are so contrived as to produce artistic effects. Thus we find the painter concerned with the accuracy of his drawing and the manipulation of his colours, and the poet looking first to the arrangement of his subject and then to a right use of expression and the laws of metre.

In the selection of a theme, both poetry and the plastic arts take some one Individual person or thing and endeavour to present it as a separate entity, with all its peculiarities, even down to the minutest, exhibited with the most accurate precision. Science, on the other hand, works by the treatment of abstract ideas, every one of them representing innumerable individuals; and it proceeds to define and mark out the characteristics of these ideas, so as to fix them once for all. A comparison between these two methods might lead one to suppose that art is an insignificant, petty, nay, almost childish pursuit. But the nature of art is such that with it one case holds good for a thousand; for by a careful and detailed preservation of a single individual person or thing, it aims at revealing the idea of the genus to which that person or thing belongs. Thus some one event or scene in the life of a man, described with complete truth— described, that is to say, so as to exhibit precisely all the individuals which go to make it what it is—gives us a clear and profound insight into the idea of humanity itself, as seen from this particular point of view. But, in spite of this difference of method between science and art, there is some similarity in their treatment of single facts. For just as the botanist picks a single flower from the boundless realm of the vegetable world, and then takes it to pieces in order to demonstrate, from the single specimen, the nature of the plant itself; so the poet chooses out of the endless turmoil of human life as it hurries incessantly on its way, some one scene, nay, often only some one mood, some one sensation, so that he may show us from it what is the life and character of man.

And thus it is that the greatest minds, Shakespeare and Goethe, Raphael and Rembrandt, do not think it unworthy of them to bring some quite ordinary person before us—not even one that is anything beyond the common—to delineate him with the greatest accuracy, in the endeavour to show him to us in the most minute particularity. For it is only when they are put before us in this way that we can apprehend individual and particular facts of life; and that is why I have defined poetry as the art of rousing the imagination by means of words.

If the reader wishes for a direct example of the advantage which intuitive knowledge—the primary and fundamental kind—has over abstract thought, as showing that Art reveals to us more than we can gain from all the sciences, let him look at a beautiful human face, full of expressive emotion; and that too whether in nature itself or as presented to us by the mediation of art. How much deeper is the insight gained into the essential character of man, nay, into nature in general, by this sight than by all the words and abstract expressions which may be used to describe it. When a beautiful face beams with laughter, it is as though a fine landscape were suddenly illuminated by a ray of light darting from the clouds.

Let me here state the general reason why the idea, in the Platonic meaning of the word, may be more easily apprehended from a picture than from reality; in other language, why a picture makes a nearer approach to the idea. A work of art is some objective reality as it appears after it has passed through a subject. From this point of view, it may be said to bear the same relation to the mind as animal food, which is vegetable food already assimilated, bears to the body. But there is another and deeper reason for the fact in question. The product of plastic and pictorial art does not present us, as reality does, with something that exists once only and then is gone for ever—the connection, I mean, between this particular matter and this particular form. It is this connection which is the essence of any concrete individuality, in the strict sense of the word. This kind of art shows us the form alone; and this, if it were given in its whole entirety, would be the Idea. The picture, therefore, leads us at once from the individual to the mere form; and this separation of the form from the matter brings the form very much nearer the Idea. Now every artistic representation, whether painting or statue, is just such a separation; and hence this separation, this disjunction of the form from the matter, is part of the character of a work of aesthetic art, because it is just the aim of such art to bring us to the knowledge of the Idea.

It is, therefore, essential to a work of art that it should give the form alone without the matter; and, further, that it should do so without any possibility of mistake on the part of the spectator. This is really the reason why wax figures produce no aesthetic impression, and therefore are not, in the aesthetic sense, works of art at all; although, if they were well made, they produce an illusion a hundred times greater than the best picture or statue could affect; so that if deceptive imitation of reality were the object of art, they would have to take the first place. For a wax figure of a man appears to give not only the mere form but with it the matter as well, so that it produces the illusion that the man himself is standing before you.

The true work of art should lead us from the individual fact, in other words, that which exists once only, and then is gone for ever, to the mere form or the Idea—in other words, that which always exists an infinite number of times in an infinite number of ways. Instead of doing this, the wax figure appears to present us with the individual himself—in other words, with that which exists once only, and then never again; and yet, at the same time, it fails to represent the life which gives such a fleeting existence its value. This is why a wax figure is repulsive; it is stiff and stark, and reminds us of a corpse. It might be thought that it is sculpture alone which gives form without matter; and that painting gives matter as well as form, by making colour serve to imitate matter and its composition. But this objection would imply that form is to be taken in a purely geometrical sense; and that is not what is here meant. Form must be taken in the philosophical sense of the word, as the opposite of matter; and therefore it includes colour, surface, texture; in short, quality, in whatever it may consist. It is quite true that sculpture alone gives form in the purely geometrical sense, exhibiting it on a matter which the eye can see to be foreign to the form, namely, marble; and in this way the form comes to stand by itself so as to strike the eye at once.

But painting does not give matter at all, and it gives only the mere appearance of the form, not in the geometrical, but in the philosophical, sense just described. Painting, I say, does not give even the form itself, but only the mere appearance of it—that is to say, merely its effect on one of our senses, the sense of sight; and that, too, only in so far as a particular act of vision is concerned. This is why a picture in oils does not really produce the illusion that the thing represented is actually before us, both in form and matter. The imitative truth of a picture is always subordinated to certain admitted conditions of this method of representtation. Thus, by the unavoidable suppression of the parallax of our two eyes, a picture always makes things appear in the way in which a one-eyed person would see them. Therefore painting, equally with sculpture, gives the form alone; for it presents nothing but the effect of the form—an effect confined to one of the senses only, namely, that of sight.

In connection with this subject it is to be observed that copper-plates and monochromes answer to a more noble and elevated taste than chromographs and watercolours; while the latter are preferred by persons of little culture. This is obviously due to the fact that pictures in black and white give the form alone, the form, as it were, in the abstract; and the apprehension of this is, as we know, intellectual, in other words, a matter or the intuitive understanding. Colour, on the other hand, is merely an affair of sense, nay more, of a particular arrangement in the organ of sight which depends upon the activity of the retina. In respect of the taste to which they appeal, coloured prints may be likened to rhymed, and copper-plates to blank, verse. The union of beauty and grace in the human form is the clearest manifestation of the will on the topmost stage of its objectivation, and for that very reason the highest achievement of the plastic and pictorial arts.

But still, everything that is natural is beautiful. If there are some animals of which we find a difficulty in believing this to be true, the reason of it is that we are unable to look at them in a purely objective light, so as to apprehend their Idea. We are prevented from doing so by some unavoidable association of thought, chiefly the result of some similarity which forces itself upon our notice; as, for instance, the similarity of the ape with man; so that instead of apprehending the idea of an ape, what we see is the caricature of a man. In the same way a toad appears to produce an effect upon us similar to that of dirt and slime, and yet this is not enough to explain the unbounded aversion, nay, the feeling of dread and horror, which comes over some people at the sight of this animal, as over others when they see a spider. The feeling appears to be deeper than any mere association can explain, and to be traceable to some mysterious fact of a metaphysical nature.

The inorganic world, so far as it does not consist of mere water, produces a very sad, nay, an oppressive effect upon the feelings, whenever it is presented to us quite by itself. Examples of what I mean are afforded by districts which offer to the eye nothing but a mass of bare crags; that long valley of rocks, for instance, without a trace of vegetation, near Toulon, on the way to Marseilles. The same effect is produced on a large scale, and in a much more striking degree, by the African desert. The melancholy impression which this kind of scenery makes is mainly due to the fact that masses of inorganic matter obey one law only, the law of gravity; and consequently everything is disposed in accordance with it.

Contrarily, the sight of vegetation produces a feeling of direct pleasure, and that too in a high degree; and the pleasure is greater in proportion as the vegetation is rich, various, luxuriant, and left to itself. The more immediate reason of this is that, in the case of vegetation, the law of gravity appears to be overcome, as the vegetable world tends to move in a direction the exact contrary of that taken by gravity. This is, indeed, the direct way in which the phenomenon of life announces its presence, as a new and higher order of things. It is an order to which we ourselves belong: it is something akin to us and the element of our being. And so, at the sight of it, our heart is moved. That straight upward direction is the source of our pleasurable feeling. This is why a fine group of trees looks so much better if a few tall, tapering pines shoot out from the middle of it. On the other head, a tree that has been cut down has lost all its effect upon us: and one that grows obliquely has not so much as one that stands straight up. A tree which bends over the earth with its branches obedient to the law of gravity, makes us melancholy; and we call it the weeping willow. Water neutralises in a great measure the oppressive effect of its inorganic composition by its exceeding mobility, which gives it an appearance of life, and also by its constant interplay of light and shade. Besides, water is absolutely indispensable for the existence of life.

But above and beyond this, the pleasurable feeling which the sight of vegetable nature gives us, comes from that look of rest, peace and satisfaction which it wears; whilst the animal world is mostly presented to us in a state of unrest, pain, even of struggle. This explains why it is so easy for the sight of vegetation to put us into a state where we become a pure intelligence, freed from ourselves. It is a very astonishing thing that vegetation, even of the commonest and humblest kind, is no sooner withdrawn from the capricious influence of man than it straightway groups itself picturesquely and strikes the eye as beautiful. This is true of every little spot of earth that has been left wild and uncultivated, even though thistles, thorns and the commonest flowers of the field were all it bore. Where the ground is tilled—in cornfields, for instance, and kitchen-gardens, the aesthetic element in the vegetable world sinks to a minimum.

It has long been observed that everything constructed for the use of man, whether it is a building or only an utensil, must, if it is to be beautiful, preserve a certain similarity with the works of nature. But a mistake has been made in thinking that the similarity must directly strike the eye and have to do with the shape the thing takes; as, for instance, that pillars should represent trees or human limbs; that receptacles should be shaped like mussels or snail-shells, or the calyx of a flower, and that vegetable or animal forms should be met with everywhere in Art. The similarity should be indirect; that is to say, it should lie not in the shape itself, but in its character. One shape may differ from another in actual appearance and yet be the same in character. Accordingly, buildings and utensils should not be imitated from nature, but should be constructed in the spirit of nature. This will show itself in a perfect adaptation of means to ends, so that the thing itself and every part of it may directly proclaim what its purpose is. This will be effected when that purpose is attained in the shortest way and in the simplest manner. It is just this striking conformity to a certain end that stamps the products of nature.

In Nature the will works from within outwards, after completely dominating its material. But in Art it works from without, by a process of intuition; it may be, by setting up the abstract idea of the purpose which the object of art is to serve; it then attains its end and delivers itself of its meaning by impressing it upon some alien material; that is to say, some material originally devoted to another form of will. Yet for all that, the character I have described as belonging to a product of nature may be preserved. This is shown by the ancient style of architecture, where every part or member is precisely suited to the purpose it is immediately meant to serve—a purpose thus naively brought into view, and where there is a total absence of anything that does not serve some purpose. To this is opposed that Gothic style, which owes its mysterious appearance just to the multitude of aimless ornaments and accessories it displays, where we are obliged to ascribe to them some purpose which we cannot discern; and again, that quite degenerate style of architecture which affects originality by playing, in all sorts of unnecessary and round about ways, with the means used for producing artistic effect, dallying capriciously with them, and at the same time misunderstanding their aim.

The same remark holds good of ancient vessels and utensils, the beauty of which is due to the fact that they so naively express their nature, and the purpose they were meant to serve; and so of all other receptacles made by the ancients. You feel in looking at them that if

Nature bad produced vases, amphora, lamps, tables, stools, helmets, shields, armour and so on, they would be made in that style. As regards the birth of a work of art in a man's mind, if he is only in a susceptible mood, almost any object that comes within his range of perception will begin to speak to him, in other words, will generate in him some lively, penetrating, original thought. So it is that a trivial event may become the seed of a great and glorious work. Jacob Bohme is said to have been enlightened upon some deep point of natural science by the sudden sight of a tin can.

In the end it all depends upon the power a man has in himself; and just as no food or medicine will bestow or take the place of vital energy, so no book or study can give a man a mind of his own.

FRIEDRICH NIETZSCHE
THE BIRTH OF TRAGEDY OUT OF THE SPIRIT OF MUSIC

Translated by Ian Johnston

§1

We will have achieved much for scientific study of aesthetics when we come, not merely to a logical understanding, but also to the certain and immediate apprehension of the fact that the further development of art is bound up with the duality of the Apollonian and the Dionysian, just as reproduction similarly depends upon the duality of the sexes, their continuing strife and only periodically occurring reconciliation. We take these names from the Greeks, who gave a clear voice to the profound secret teachings of their contemplative art, not in ideas, but in the powerfully clear forms of their divine world. With those two gods of art, Apollo and Dionysus, we establish our recognition that in the Greek world there exists a huge contrast, in origin and purposes, between the visual arts, the Apollonian, and the non-visual art of music, the Dionysian. These two very different drives go hand in hand, for the most part in open conflict with each other and simultaneously provoking each other all the time to new and more powerful offspring, in order to perpetuate in them the contest of that opposition, which the common word "Art" only seems to bridge, until at last, through a marvellous metaphysical act of the Greek "will," they appear paired up with each other and, as this pair, finally produce Attic tragedy, as much a Dionysian as an Apollonian work of art.

In order to bring those two drives closer to us, let us think of them first as the separate artistic worlds of dream and of intoxication, physiological phenomena between which we can observe an opposition corresponding to the one between the Apollonian and the Dionysian. According to the idea of Lucretius, the marvellous divine shapes first stepped out before the mind of man in a dream. It was in a dream that the great artist saw the delightful anatomy of superhuman existence, and the Greek poet, questioned about the secrets of poetic creativity, would have also recalled his dreams and given an explanation similar to the one Hans Sachs provides in *Die Meistersinger*:

> My friend, that is precisely the poet's work—
> To figure out his dreams, mark them down.
> Believe me, the truest illusion of mankind
> Is revealed to him in dreams:
> All poetic art and poeticizing
> Is nothing but interpreting true dreams.

The beautiful appearance of the world of dreams, in whose creation each man is a complete artist, is the precondition of all plastic art, and also, in fact, as we shall see, an important part of poetry. We enjoy the form with an immediate understanding; every shape speaks to us; nothing is indifferent and unnecessary. For all the most intense life of this dream reality, we nevertheless have the shimmering sense of their illusory quality: That, at least, is my experience. For the frequency, indeed normality, of this response, I could point to many witnesses and the utterances of poets. Even the philosophical man has the presentiment that under this reality in which we live and have our being lies hidden a second, totally different reality and that thus the former is an illusion. And Schopenhauer specifically designates as the trademark of philosophical talent the ability to recognize at certain times that human beings and all things are mere phantoms or dream pictures.

Now, just as the philosopher behaves in relation to the reality of existence, so the artistically excitable man behaves in relation to the reality of dreams: he looks at them precisely and with pleasure, for from these pictures he fashions his interpretation of life; from these events he rehearses his life for himself. This is not merely a case of the agreeable and friendly images which he experiences in himself with a complete understanding; they also include what is serious, cloudy, sad, dark, sudden scruples, teasing accidents, nervous expectations, in short, the entire "divine comedy" of life, including the Inferno—all this moves past him, not just like a shadow play—for he lives and suffers in the midst of these scenes—and yet also not without that fleeting sense of illusion. And perhaps several people remember, like me, amid the dangers and terrors of a dream, successfully cheering themselves up by shouting: "It is a dream! I want to dream it some more!" I have also heard accounts of some people who had the ability to set out the causality of one and the same dream over three or more consecutive nights. These facts are clear evidence showing that our innermost beings, the secret underground in all of us, experiences its dreams with deep enjoyment and a sense of delightful necessity.

In the same manner the Greeks expressed this joyful necessity of the dream experience in their Apollo. Apollo, as the god of all the plastic arts, is at the same time the god of prophecy. In accordance with the root meaning of his association with "brightness," he is the god of light; he also rules over the beautiful appearance of the inner fantasy world. The higher truth, the perfection of this condition in contrast to the sketchy understanding of our daily reality, as well as the deep consciousness of a healing and helping nature in sleep and dreaming, is at the same time the symbolic analogy to the capacity to prophesy the truth, as well as to art in general, through which life is made possible and worth living. But also that delicate line which the dream image may not cross so that it does not work its effect pathologically— otherwise the illusion would deceive us as crude reality—that line must not be absent from the image of Apollo, that boundary of moderation, that freedom from more ecstatic excitement, that fully wise calm of the god of images. His eye must be "sun-like," in keeping with his origin; even when he is angry and gazes with displeasure, the consecration of the beautiful illusion rests on him.

And so concerning Apollo one could endorse, in an eccentric way, what Schopenhauer says of the man trapped in the veil of Maja: "As on the stormy sea which extends without limit on all sides, howling mountainous waves rise up and sink and a sailor sits in a row boat, trusting the weak craft, so, in the midst of a world of torments, the solitary man sits peacefully, supported by and trusting in the *principium individuationis* [principle of individuation]" (*World as Will and Representation*, I.1.3). In fact, we could say of Apollo that the imperturbable trust in that principle and the calm sitting still of the man caught up in it attained its loftiest expression in him, and we may even designate Apollo himself as the marvellous divine image of the *principium individuationis*, from whose gestures and gaze all the joy and wisdom of "illusion," together with its beauty, speak to us.

In the same place Schopenhauer also described for us the tremendous awe which seizes a man when he suddenly doubts his ways of comprehending illusion, when the principle of reason, in any one of its forms, appears to suffer from an exception. If we add to this awe the ecstatic rapture, which rises up out of the same collapse of the *principium individuationis* from the innermost depths of a human being, indeed, from the innermost depths of nature, then we have a glimpse into the essence of the Dionysian, which is presented to us most closely through the analogy to intoxication. Either through the influence of narcotic drink, of which all primitive men and peoples speak in their hymns, or through the powerful coming on of spring, which drives joyfully through all of nature, that Dionysian excitement arises; as it intensifies, the subjective fades into complete forgetfulness of self. Even in the German Middle Ages, under the same power of Dionysus, constantly growing hordes thronged from place to place, singing and dancing; in these St. John's and St. Vitus's dances we recognize the Bacchic chorus of the

Greeks once again, with its precursors in Asia Minor, right back to Babylon and the orgiastic *Sacaea* [riotous Babylonian festival]. There are people who, from a lack of experience or out of apathy, turn mockingly or pityingly away from such phenomena as from a "sickness of the people," with a sense of their own health. These poor people naturally do not have any sense of how deathly and ghost-like this very "health" of theirs sounds, when the glowing life of the Dionysian throng roars past them.

Under the magic of the Dionysian, not only does the bond between man and man lock itself in place once more, but also nature itself, no matter how alienated, hostile, or subjugated, rejoices again in her festival of reconciliation with her prodigal son, man. The earth freely offers up her gifts, and the beasts of prey from the rocks and the desert approach in peace. The wagon of Dionysus is covered with flowers and wreaths; under his yolk stride panthers and tigers. If someone were to transform Beethoven's Ode to Joy into a painting and not restrain his imagination when millions of people sink dramatically into the dust, then we could come close to the Dionysian. Now the slave a free man; now all the stiff, hostile barriers break apart, those things which necessity and arbitrary power or "saucy fashion" have established between men. Now, with the gospel of world harmony, every man feels himself not only united with his neighbour, reconciled and fused together, but also as one with him, as if the veil of Maja had been ripped apart, with only scraps fluttering around in the face of the mysterious primordial unity.

Singing and dancing, man expresses himself as a member of a higher community: he has forgotten how to walk and talk and is on the verge of flying up into the air as he dances. The enchantment speaks out in his gestures. Just as the animals now speak and the earth gives milk and honey, so something supernatural also echoes out of him: he feels himself a god; he himself now moves in as lofty and ecstatic a way as he saw the gods move in his dream. The man is no longer an artist; he has become a work of art: the artistic power of all of nature, to the highest rhapsodic satisfaction of the primordial unity, reveals itself here in the transports of intoxication. The finest clay, the most expensive marble—man—is here worked and hewn, and the cry of the Eleusinian mysteries rings out to the chisel blows of the Dionysian world artist: "Do you fall down, you millions? World, do you have a sense of your creator?"

§2

Up to this point, we have considered the Apollonian and its opposite, the Dionysian, as artistic forces which break forth out of nature itself, without the mediation of the human artist, and in which the human artistic drives are for the time being satisfied directly—on the one hand, as a world of dream images, whose perfection has no connection with an individual's high level of intellect or artistic education, on the other hand, as the intoxicating reality, which once again does not respect the individual, but even seeks to abolish the individual and to redeem him through a mystical feeling of collective unity. In comparison to these unmediated artistic states of nature, every artist is an "imitator," and, in fact, is an artist either of Apollonian dream or Dionysian intoxication or, finally—as in Greek tragedy, for example— simultaneously an artist of intoxication and of dreams. As the last, it is possible for us to imagine how he sinks down in Dionysian drunkenness and mystical obliteration of the self, alone and apart from the rapturous choruses, and how, through the Apollonian effects of dream, his own state now reveals itself to him, that is, his unity with the innermost basis of the world, in a metaphorical dream picture.

Having set out these general assumptions and comparisons, let us now approach the Greeks, in order to recognize to what degree and to what heights those artistic drives of nature were developed in them: in that way we will be in a position to understand more deeply and to assess the relationship of the Greek artist to his primordial images or, to use Aristotle's expression, his "imitation of nature." In spite of all their literature on dreams and numerous dream anecdotes, we can speak of the dreams of the Greeks only hypothetically, although with a fair degree of certainty. Given the incredibly clear and accurate plastic capability of their eyes, along with their intelligent and open love of colour, one cannot go wrong in assuming that, to the shame all those born later, their dreams also had a logical causality of lines and circumferences, colours, and groupings, a sequence of scenes rather like their best bas reliefs, whose perfection would certainly entitle us, if such a comparison were possible, to describe the dreaming Greek man as Homer and Homer as a dreaming Greek man, in a deeper sense than when modern man, with respect to his dreams, has the temerity to compare himself with Shakespeare.

On the other hand, we do not need to speak merely hypothetically when we are to expose the immense gap which separates the Dionysian Greeks from the Dionysian barbarians. In all quarters of the ancient world—setting aside here the newer worlds—from Rome to Babylon, we can confirm the existence of Dionysian celebrations, of a type, at best, related to the Greek type in much the same way as the bearded satyr, whose name and attributes are taken from the goat, is related to Dionysus himself. Almost everywhere, the central point of these celebrations consisted of an exuberant sexual promiscuity, whose waves flooded over all established family practices and its traditional laws. The very wildest bestiality of nature was here unleashed, creating that abominable mixture of lust and cruelty, which has always seemed to me the real "witches' cauldron." From the feverish excitement of those festivals, knowledge of which reached the Greeks from all directions by land and sea, they were, it seems, for a long time completely secure and protected through the figure of Apollo, drawn up here in all his pride.

Apollo could counter by holding up the head of Medusa, for no power was more dangerous than this massive and grotesque Dionysian force. Doric art has immortalized that majestic bearing of Apollo as he stands in opposition. This resistance became more questionable and even impossible as similar impulses finally broke out from the deepest roots of Hellenic culture itself: now the effect of the Delphic god, in a timely final process of reconciliation, limited itself to taking the destructive weapon out of the hand of the powerful opponent. This reconciliation is the most important moment in the history of Greek culture. Wherever we look, the revolutionary effects of this event manifest themselves. It was the reconciliation of two opponents, who from now on observed their differences with a sharp demarcation of the border line to be kept between them and with occasional gifts sent to honour each other, but basically the gap was not bridged over. However, if we see how, under the pressure of that peace agreement, the Dionysian power revealed itself, then we now understand the meaning of the festivals of world redemption and days of transfiguration in the Dionysian orgies of the Greeks, in compareson with that Babylonian Sacaea, which turned human beings back into tigers and apes.

In these Greek festivals, for the first time nature achieves its artistic jubilee. In them, for the first time, the tearing apart of the *principii individuationis* [principle of individuation] becomes an artistic phenomenon. Here that dreadful witches' cauldron of lust and cruelty was without power. The strange mixture and ambiguity in the emotions of the Dionysian celebrant only remind him—as healing potions remind one of deadly poison—of that phenomenon that pain awakens joy, that the jubilation in his chest rips out cries of agony. From the most sublime joy echoes the cry of horror or the longingly plaintive lament over an irreparable loss. In those Greek festivals it was as if a sentimental feature of nature is breaking out, as if nature has to sigh over her dismemberment into separate individuals. The song and the language of gestures of such a doubly defined celebrant was for the Homeric Greek world something new and unheard of, and in it Dionysian music, in particular, awoke fear and terror.

If music was apparently already known as an Apollonian art, this music, strictly speaking, was a rhythmic pattern like the sound of waves, whose artistic power had been developed for presenting Apollonian states. The music of Apollo was Doric architecture expressed in sound, but only in intimate tones characteristic of the cithara. It kept at a careful distance, as something un-Apollonian, the particular element which constitutes the character of Dionysian music and, along with that, of music generally, the emotionally disturbing tonal power, the unified stream of melody, and the totally incomparable world of harmony.

In the Dionysian dithyramb man is aroused to the highest intensity of all his symbolic capabilities; something never felt forces itself into expression, the destruction of the veil of Maja, the sense of oneness as the presiding genius of form, in fact, of nature itself. Now the essence of nature is to express itself symbolically; a new world of symbols is necessary, the entire symbolism of the body, not just the symbolism of the mouth, of the face, and of the words, but the full gestures of the dance, all the limbs moving to the rhythm. And then the other symbolic powers grow, those of the music, in rhythm, dynamics, and harmony—with sudden violence.

To grasp this total unleashing of all symbolic powers, man must already have attained that high level of freedom from the self which desires to express itself symbolically in those forces. Because of this, the dithyrambic servant of Dionysus will be understood only by someone like himself! With what astonishment must the Apollonian Greek have gazed at him! With an amazement which was all the greater as he sensed with horror that all this might not be really so foreign to him, that, in fact, his Apollonian consciousness was, like a veil, merely covering the Dionysian world in front of him.

§3

In order to grasp this point, we must dismantle that artistic structure of Apollonian culture, as it were, stone by stone, until we see the foundations on which it is built. Here we now become aware for the first time of the marvellous Olympian divine forms, which stand on the pediments of this building and whose actions decorate its friezes all around in illuminating bas relief. If Apollo also stands among them as a single god next to others and without any claim to a pre-eminent position, we should not on that account let ourselves be deceived. The same drive which made itself sensuously perceptible in Apollo gave birth to that entire Olympian world in general, and, in this sense, we are entitled to value Apollo as the father of that world. What was the immense need out of which such an illuminating society of Olympian beings arose?

Anyone who steps up to these Olympians with another religion in his heart and now seeks from them ethical loftiness, even sanctity, non-physical spirituality, loving gazes filled with pity, will soon have to turn his back despondently in disappointment with them. Here there is no reminder of asceticism, spirituality, and duty: here speaks to us only a full, indeed a triumphant, existence, in which everything present is worshipped, no matter whether it is good or evil. And thus the onlooker may well stand in real consternation in front of this fantastic excess of life, to ask himself with what magical drink in their bodies these high-spirited men could have enjoyed life, so that wherever they look, Helen laughs back at them, that ideal image of their own existence, "hovering in sweet sensuousness." However, we must call out to this onlooker who has already turned his back: "Don't leave them. First listen to what Greek folk wisdom expresses about this very life which spreads itself out here before you with such inexplicable serenity.

There is an old legend that king Midas for a long time hunted the wise Silenus, the companion of Dionysus, in the forests, without catching him. When Silenus finally fell into the king's hands, the king asked what was the best thing of all for men, the very finest. The daemon remained silent, motionless and inflexible, until, compelled by the king, he finally broke out into shrill laughter and said these words, "Suffering creature, born for a day, child of accident and toil, why are you forcing me to say what would give you the greatest pleasure not to hear? The very best thing for you is totally unreachable: not to have been born, not to exist, to be nothing. The second best thing for you, however, is this—to die soon."

What is the relationship between the Olympian world of the gods and this popular wisdom? It is like the relationship of the entrancing vision of the tortured martyr to his torments.

Now, as it were, the Olympic magic mountain reveals itself and shows us its roots. The Greek knew and felt the terror and horrors of existence: in order to be able to live at all, he must have placed in front of him the gleaming dream birth of the Olympians. That immense distrust of the titanic forces of nature, that Moira [Fate] enthroned mercilessly above everything which could be known, that vulture of the great friend of man, Prometheus, that fatal lot of wise Oedipus, that family curse on the House of Atreus, which compelled Orestes to kill his mother, in short, that entire philosophy of the woodland god, together with its mythical illustrations, from which the melancholy Etruscans died off—that was overcome time after time by the Greeks, or at least hidden and removed from view, through the artistic middle world of the Olympians. In order to be able to live, the Greeks must have created these gods out of the deepest necessity.

We can readily imagine the sequential development of these gods: through that Apollonian drive for beauty there developed, by a slow transition out of the primordial titanic divine order of terror, the Olympian divine order of joy, just as roses break forth out of thorny bushes. How else could a people so emotionally sensitive, so spontaneously desiring, so singularly capable of suffering, have been able to endure their existence, unless the same qualities, with a loftier glory flowing round them, manifested themselves in their gods. The same impulse which summons art into life as the seductive replenishment for further living and the completion of existence also gave rise to the Olympian world, in which the Hellenic "Will" held before itself a transfiguring mirror.

In this way, the gods justify the lives of men, because they themselves live it—that is the only satisfactory theodicy! Existence under the bright sunshine of such gods is experienced as worth striving for in itself, and the essential pain of the Homeric men refers to separation from that sunlight, above all to the fact that such separation is coming soon, so that people could now say of them, with a reversal of the wisdom of Silenus, "The very worst thing for them was to die soon; the second worst was to die at all." When the laments resound now, they tell once more of short-lived Achilles, of the changes in the race of men, transformed like leaves, of the destruction of the heroic age. It is not unworthy of the greatest hero to long to live on, even as a day labourer. Thus, in the Apollonian stage, the "Will" spontaneously demands to keep on living, the Homeric man feels himself so at one with living, that even his lament becomes a song of praise.

Here we must now point out that this harmony, looked on with such longing by more recent men, in fact, that unity of man with nature, for which Schiller coined the artistic slogan "naive," is in no way such a simple, inevitable, and, as it were, unavoidable condition, like a human paradise, which we necessarily run into at the door of every culture: such a belief is possible only in an age which seeks to believe that Rousseau's Emile is also an artist and which imagines it has found in Homer an artist like Emile raised in the bosom of nature. Wherever we encounter the "naive" in art, we have to recognize the highest effect of Apollonian culture, which always first has to overthrow the kingdom of the Titans and to kill monsters and, through powerfully deluding images and joyful illusions, has to emerge victorious over the horrific depth of what we observe in the world and the most sensitive capacity for suffering.

But how seldom does the naive, that sense of being completely swallowed up in the beauty of appearance, succeed! For that reason, how inexpressibly noble is Homer, who, as a single individual, was related to that Apollonian popular culture as the individual dream artist is to the people's capacity to dream and to nature in general. Homeric "naivete" is only to be understood as the complete victory of the Apollonian illusion. It is the sort of illusion which nature uses so frequently in order to attain her objectives. The true goal is concealed by a deluding image: we stretch our hands out toward this image, and nature reaches its goal through our deception.

With the Greeks the "Will" wished to gaze upon itself through the transforming power of genius and the world of art; in order to glorify itself, its creatures had to sense that they themselves were worthy of being glorified; they had to see themselves again in a higher sphere, without this complete world of contemplation affecting them as an imperative or as a reproach. This is the sphere of beauty, in which they saw their mirror images, the Olympians. With this mirror of beauty, the Hellenic "Will" fought against the talent for suffering, which is bound up with artistic talent, and the wisdom of suffering, and, as a memorial of its victory, Homer stands before us, the naive artist.

§4

Using the analogy of a dream, we can learn something about this naive artist. If we recall how the dreamer, in the middle of his illusory dream world, calls out to himself, without destroying that world, "It is a dream. I want to continue dreaming it," and if we can infer from that, on the one hand, that he has a deep inner delight at the contemplation of the dream, and, on the other, that he must have completely forgotten the day and its terrible demands, in order to be capable of dreaming at all with this inner joy at contemplation, then we may interpret all these phenomena, with the guidance of Apollo, the interpreter of dreams, in something like the manner which follows.

To be sure, with respect to both halves of life, the waking and the dreaming parts, the first one strikes us as disproportionately more privileged, more important, more valuable, more worth living, in fact, the only part which is lived; nevertheless, I would like to assert, something of a paradox to all appearances, for the sake of that secret foundation of our essence, whose manifestation we are, precisely the opposite evaluation of dreams. For the more I become aware of those all-powerful natural artistic impulses and the fervent yearning for illusion contained in them, the desire to be redeemed through appearances, the more I feel myself pushed to the metaphysical assumption that the true being and the primordial oneness, ever-suffering and entirely contradictory, constantly uses the delightful vision, the joyful illusion, to redeem itself; we are compelled to experience this illusion, totally caught up in it and constituted by it, as the truly non-existent, that is, as a continuous development in time, space, and causality, in other words, as empirical reality. But if we momentarily look away from our own "reality," if we grasp our empirical existence and the world in general as an idea of the primordial oneness created in every moment, then we must now consider our dream as the illusion of an illusion, as well as an even higher fulfilment of the original hunger for illusion. For this same reason, the innermost core of nature takes that indescribable joy in the naive artist and naive work of art, which is, in the same way, only "an illusion of an illusion."

Raphael, himself one of those immortal "naive" men, has presented in an allegorical painting that reduction of an illusion into an illusion, the fundamental process of the naive artist and Apollonian culture as well. In his Transfiguration the bottom half shows us, with the possessed boy, the despairing porters, the helplessly frightened disciples, the mirror image of the eternal primordial pain, the sole basis of the world. The "illusion" here is the reflection of the eternal contradiction, of the father of things. Now, out of this illusion there rises up, like an ambrosial fragrance, a new world of illusion, like a vision, invisible to those trapped in the first scene—something illuminating and hovering in the purest painless ecstasy, a shining vision to contemplate with eyes wide open. Here we have before our eyes, in the highest symbolism of art, that Apollonian world of beauty and its foundation, the frightening wisdom of Silenus, and we understand, through intuition, their reciprocal necessity.

But Apollo confronts us once again as the divine manifestation of the *principii individuationis*, the only thing through which the eternally attained goal of the primordial oneness, its redemption through illusion, takes place: he shows us, with awe-inspiring gestures, how the entire world of torment is necessary, so that through it the individual is pushed to the creation of the redemptive vision and then, absorbed in contemplation of that vision, sits quietly in his rowboat, tossing around in the middle of the ocean.

This deification of individuation, if it is thought of in general as commanding and proscriptive, understands only one law, the individual, that is, observing the limits of individualization, moderation in the Greek sense. Apollo, as an ethical divinity, demands moderation from his followers and, so that they can observe self-control, a knowledge of the self. And so alongside the aesthetic necessity of beauty run the demands "Know thyself" and "Nothing too much!"; whereas, arrogance and excess are considered the essentially hostile daemons belonging to the non-Apollonian sphere, and therefore characteristics of the pre-Apollonian period, the age of the Titans, and of the world beyond the Apollonian, that is, the barbarian world. Because of his Titanic love for mankind, Prometheus had to be ripped apart by the vulture. For the sake of his excessive wisdom, which solved the riddle of the sphinx, Oedipus had to be overthrown in a bewildering whirlpool of evil. That is how the Delphic god interpreted the Greek past.

To the Apollonian Greek the effect aroused by the Dionysian also seemed "Titanic" and "barbaric." But he could not, with that response, conceal that he himself was, nonetheless, at the same time also internally related to those deposed Titans and heroes. Indeed, he must have felt even more: his entire existence, with all its beauty and moderation, rested on a hidden underground of suffering and knowledge, which was exposed for him again through that very Dionysian. And look! Apollo could not live without Dionysus! The "Titanic" and the "barbaric" were, in the end, every bit as necessary as the Apollonian! And now let us imagine how in this world, constructed on illusion and moderation and restrained by art, the ecstatic sound of the Dionysian celebration rang out all around with a constantly more enticing magic, how in these celebrations the entire excess of nature made itself known in joy, suffering, and knowledge, even in the most piercing scream. Let us imagine what the psalm-chanting Apollonian artist, with his ghostly harp music could have meant in comparison to this daemonic popular singing! The muses of the art of "illusion" withered away in the face of an art which spoke truth in its intoxicated state: the wisdom of Silenus cried out "Woe! Woe!" against the serene Olympians. The individual, with all his limits and moderation, was destroyed in the self-oblivion of the Dionysian condition and forgot the Apollonian principles.

Excess revealed itself as the truth. The contradiction, the ecstasy born from pain, spoke of itself right out of the heart of nature. And so the Apollonian was cancelled and destroyed everywhere the Dionysian penetrated. But it is just as certain that in those places where the first onslaught was halted, the high reputation and the majesty of the Delphic god manifested itself more firmly and threateningly than ever. For I can explain the Doric state and Doric art only as a constant Apollonian war camp: only through an uninterrupted opposition to the Titanic-barbaric essence of the Dionysian could such a defiantly aloof art, protected on all sides with fortifications, such a harsh upbringing as a preparation for war, and such a cruel and ruthless basis for government endure for a long time.

Up to this point I have set out at some length what I observed at the opening of this essay: how the Dionysian and the Apollonian ruled the Hellenic world in a constantly new sequence of births, one after the other, mutually intensifying each other; how, out of the "first" age, with its battles against the Titans and its austere popular philosophy, the Homeric world developed under the rule of the Apollonian drive for beauty; how this "naive" magnificence was swallowed up once more by the breaking out of the Dionysian torrent; and how, in opposition to this new power, the Apollonian erected the rigid majesty of Doric art and the Doric world view. If in this way the earlier history of the Greeks, in the struggle of those two hostile principles, falls into four major artistic periods, we are now impelled to ask more about the final stage of this development and striving, in case we should consider, for example, the last attained period, the one of Doric art, the summit and intention of those artistic impulses. Here, the lofty and highly praised artistic achievement of Attic tragedy and of the dramatic dithyramb presents itself before our eyes, as the common goal of both impulses, whose secret marriage partnership, after a long antecedent struggle, glorified itself with such a child—at once Antigone and Cassandra.

§5

We are now approaching the essential goal of our undertaking, which aims at a knowledge of the Dionysian-Apollonian genius and its work of art, at least at an intuitive understanding of that mysterious unity. Here now, to begin with, we raise the question of where that new seed first manifests itself in the Hellenic world, the seed which later develops into tragedy and the dramatic dithyramb. On this question, classical antiquity itself gives us illustrative evidence when it places Homer and Archilochus next to each other in paintings, cameos, and so on, as the originators and torchbearers of Greek poetry, in full confidence that only these two should be equally considered completely original natures from whom a firestorm flowed out over the entire later world of the Greeks.

Homer, the ancient, self-absorbed dreamer, the archetype of the naive Apollonian artist, now stares astonished at the passionate head of wild Archilochus, the fighting servant of the Muses, battered by existence. In its interpretative efforts, our more recent aesthetics has known only how to indicate that here the first "subjective" artist stands in contrast to the "objective" artist. This interpretation is of little use to us, since we recognize the subjective artist only as a bad artist and demand in every style of art and every high artistic achievement, first and foremost, a victory over the subjective, redemption from the "I," and the silence of every individual will and desire; indeed, we are incapable of believing the slightest artistic creation true, unless it has objectivity and a purely disinterested contemplation.

Hence, our aesthetic must first solve that problem of how it is possible for the "lyric poet" to be an artist. . . . We can, on the basis of the aesthetic metaphysics we established earlier, now account for the lyric poet in the following manner.

He has, first of all, as a Dionysian artist, become entirely unified with the primordial oneness, with its pain and contradiction, and produces the reflection of this primordial oneness as music, if music can with justice be called a re-working of the world and its second casting. But now this music becomes perceptible to him once again, as in a metaphorical dream image, under the influence of Apollonian dreaming. That reflection, which lacks imagery and ideas, of the original pain in the music, together with its redemption in illusion, gives rise now to a second reflection as a particular metaphor or illustration. The artist has already surrendered his subjectivity in the Dionysian process; the image which now reveals to him his unity with the heart of the world is a dream scene, which symbolizes that original contradiction and pain, together with the primordial joy in illusion.

The "I" of the lyric poet thus echoes out of the abyss of being. . . . The Dionysian musical enchantment of the sleeper now, as it were, flashes around him fiery images, lyrical poems, which are called, in their highest form, tragedies and dramatic dithyrambs. The plastic artist, as well as his relation, the epic poet, is absorbed in the pure contemplation of images. The Dionysian musician totally lacks every image and is in himself only and entirely the original pain and original reverberation of that image. The lyrical genius feels a world of images and metaphors grow up out of the mysterious state of unity and of renunciation of the self. These have a colour, causality, and speed entirely different from that world of the plastic artist and of the writer of epic. While the epic poet lives in these pictures and only in them with joyful contentment and does not get tired of contemplating them with love, right down to the smallest details, and while even the image of the angry Achilles is for him only a picture whose expression of anger he enjoys with that dream joy in illusions—so that he, by this mirror of appearances, is protected against the development of that sense of unity and of being fused together with the forms he has created—the images of the lyric poet are, by contrast nothing but he himself and, as it were, only different objectifications of himself. He can say "I" because he is the moving central point of that world; only this "I" is not the same as the "I" of the awake, empirically real man, but the single "I" of true and eternal being in general, the "I" resting on the foundation of things, through the portrayal of which the lyrical genius looks right into that very basis of things.

Now, let's imagine next how he also looks upon himself among these likenesses, as a non-genius, that is, as his own "Subject," the entire unruly crowd of subjective passions and striving of his will aiming at something particular, which seems real to him. If it now appears as if the lyrical genius and the non-genius bound up with him were one and the same and as if the first of these spoke that little word "I" about himself, then this illusion could now no longer deceive us, not at least in the way it deceived those who have defined the lyricist as a subjective poet. . . .

Schopenhauer, who did not hide from the difficulty which the lyric poet creates for the philosophical observation of art, believed that he had discovered a solution, something which I cannot go along with, when in his profound metaphysics of music he alone found a way of setting that difficulty decisively to one side, as I believe I have done here, in his spirit and with due honour to him. For the sake of comparison, here is how he describes the essential nature of song:

> The consciousness of the singer is filled with the subject of willing, that is, his own willing, often as an unleashed satisfied willing (joy), but also, and more often, as a restricted willing (sorrow), always as emotion, passion, a turbulent state of feeling. However, alongside this condition and simultaneous with it, the singer, through a glimpse at the surrounding nature, becomes aware of himself as a subject of pure, will-less knowledge, whose imperturbable, blessed tranquilly now enters in contrast to the pressure of his always hindered, always still limited willing: the sensation of this contrast, this game back and forth, is basically what expresses itself in the totality of the song and what, in general, creates the lyrical state. In this condition, pure understanding, as it were, comes to us, to save us from willing and the pressure of willing; we follow along, but only moment by moment: the will, the memory of our personal goals, constantly removes this calm contemplation from us, but over and over again the next beautiful setting, in which pure will-less knowledge presents itself to us once again, entices us away from willing. Hence, in the song and the lyrical mood, willing (the personal interest in purposes) and pure contemplation of the setting which reveals itself are miraculously mixed up together: we seek and imagine relationships between them both; the subjective mood, the emotional state of the will, communicates with the surroundings we contemplate, and the latter, in turn, give their colour to our mood, in a reflex action. The true song is the expression of this entire emotional condition, mixed and divided in this way. (*World as Will and Presentation*, I.3.51)

Who can fail to recognize in this description that here the lyric has been characterized as an incompletely realized art, a leap, as it were, which seldom attains its goal, indeed, as a semi-art, whose essence is to consist of the fact that the will and pure contemplation, that is, the unaesthetic and the aesthetic conditions, must be miraculously mixed up together? In contrast to this, we maintain that the entire opposition of the subjective and the objective, which even Schopenhauer still uses as a measurement of value to classify art, has generally no place in aesthetics, since the subject, the willing individual demanding his own egotistical purposes, can only be thought of as an enemy of art, not as its origin.

But insofar as the subject is an artist, he is already released from his individual willing and has become, so to speak, a medium, through which a subject of true being celebrates its redemption in illusion. For we need to be clear on this point, above everything else, to our humiliation and ennoblement: the entire comedy of art does not present itself for us in order to make us, for example, better or to educate us, even less because we are the actual creators of that art world. We are, however, entitled to assume this about ourselves: for the true creator of that world we are already pictures and artistic projections and in the meaning of works of art we have our highest dignity —for only as an aesthetic phenomena are existence and the world eternally justified—while, of course, our consciousness of this significance of ours is scarcely any different from the consciousness which soldiers painted on canvas have of the battle portrayed there.

Hence our entire knowledge of art is basically completely illusory, because, as knowing people, we are not one with and identical to that being who, as the single creator and spectator of that comedy of art, prepares for itself an eternal enjoyment. Only to the extent that the genius in the act of artistic creation is fused with that primordial artist of the world does he know anything about the eternal nature of art, for in that state he is, in a miraculous way, like the weird picture of fairy tales, which can turn its eyes and contemplate itself. Now he is simultaneously subject and object, simultaneously poet, actor, and spectator.

§6

. . . We are thus entitled to consider the lyrical poem as the mimetic efflorescence of music in pictures and ideas, then we can now ask the following question: "What does music look like in the mirror of imagery and ideas?" It appears as the will, taking that word in Schopenhauer's sense, that is, as the opposite to the aesthetic, purely contemplative, will-less state. Here we must now differentiate as sharply as possible the idea of being from the idea of appearance: it is impossible for music, given its nature, to be the will, because if that were the case we would have to ban music entirely from the realm of art—for the will consists of what is inherently unaesthetic—but music appears as the will. For in order to express that appearance in images, the lyric poet needs all the excitements of passion, from the whispers of affection right up to the ravings of lunacy.

Under the impulse to speak of music in Apollonian metaphors, he understands all nature and himself in nature only as eternal willing, desiring, yearning. However, insofar as he interprets music in images, he himself is resting in the still tranquility of the sea of Apollonian observation, no matter how much everything which he contemplates through that medium of music is moving around him, pushing and driving. Indeed, if he looks at himself through that same medium, his own image reveals itself to him in a state of emotional dissatisfaction: his own willing, yearning, groaning, cheering are for him a metaphor with which he interprets the music for himself. This is the phenomenon of the lyric poet: as an Apollonian genius, he interprets the music through the image of the will, while he himself, fully released from the greed of the will, is a pure, untroubled eye of the sun.

This entire discussion firmly maintains that the lyric is just as dependent on the spirit of music as is music itself. In its fully absolute power, music does not need image and idea, but only tolerates them as something additional to itself. The poetry of the lyricist can express nothing which was not already latent in the most immense universality and validity of the music, which forces him to speak in images. The world symbolism of music for this very reason cannot in any way be exhausted by or reduced to language, because music addresses itself symbolically to the primordial contradiction and pain in the heart of the original oneness, and thus presents in symbolic form a sphere which is above all appearances and prior to them. In comparison with music, each appearance is far more a mere metaphor: hence, language, as voice and symbol of appearances, can never ever convert the deepest core of music to something external, but always remains, as long as it involves itself with the imitation of music, only in superficial contact with the music. The full eloquence of lyric poetry cannot bring us one step closer to the deepest meaning of music.

§7

We must now seek assistance from all the artistic principles laid out above, in order to find our way correctly through the labyrinth, a descriptive term we have to use to designate the origin of Greek tragedy. I do not think I am saying anything illogical when I claim that the problem of this origin still has not once been seriously formulated up to now, let alone solved, no matter how frequently the scattered scraps of ancient tradition have already been combined with one another and then torn apart once more. This tradition tells us very emphatically that tragedy developed out of the tragic chorus and originally consisted only of a chorus and nothing else.

. . . The Greek satyr chorus, the chorus of the primitive tragedy, customarily strolled, a stage lifted high over the real strolling stage of mortal men. For this chorus the Greeks constructed a suspended scaffolding of an imaginary state of nature and on it placed imaginary natural beings. Tragedy grew up out of this foundation and, for that very reason, has, from its inception, been spared the embarrassing business of counterfeiting reality. That is not to say, however, that it is a world arbitrarily fantasized somewhere between heaven and earth. It is much rather a world possessing the same reality and credibility as the world of Olympus, together with its inhabitants, had for the devout Greek.

The satyr, as the Dionysian chorus member, lives in a reality granted by religion and sanctioned by myth and ritual. The fact that tragedy begins with him, that out of him the Dionysian wisdom of tragedy speaks, is a phenomenon as foreign to us here as the development of tragedy out of the chorus generally. Perhaps we can reach a starting point for this discussion when I offer the claim that the satyr himself, the imaginary natural being, is related to the cultural person in the same way that Dionysian music is related to civilization. On this last point Richard Wagner states that civilization is neutralized by music in the same way light from a lamp is neutralized by daylight. In just such a manner, I believe, the cultured Greek felt himself neutralized by the sight of the chorus of satyrs, and the next effect of Dionysian tragedy is that the state and society, in general the gap between man and man, give way to an invincible feeling of unity, which leads back to the heart of nature. The metaphysical consolation with which, as I am immediately indicating here, every true tragedy leaves us, that, in spite of all the transformations in phenomena, at the bottom of everything life is indestructibly powerful and delightful, this consolation appears in lively clarity as the chorus of satyrs, as the chorus of natural beings, who live, so to speak, indestructibly behind all civilization, and who, in spite of all the changes in generations and a people's history, always remain the same.

With this chorus, the profound Greek, uniquely capable of the most delicate and the most severe suffering, consoled himself, the man who looked around with a daring gaze in the middle of the terrifying destructive instincts of so-called world history and equally into the cruelty of nature and who is in danger of longing for a Buddhist denial of the will. Art saves him, and through art life saves him.

The ecstasy of the Dionysian state, with its obliteration of the customary manacles and boundaries of existence, contains, of course, for as long as it lasts a lethargic element, in which everything personally experienced in the past is immersed. Because of this gulf of oblivion, the world of everyday reality and the world of Dionysian reality separate from each other. But as soon as that daily reality comes back again into consciousness, one feels it as something disgusting. The fruit of that state is an ascetic condition, in which one denies the power of the will.

In this sense the Dionysian man has similarities to Hamlet: both have had a real glimpse into the essence of things. They have understood, and it disgusts them to act, for their action can change nothing in the eternal nature of things. They perceive as ridiculous or humiliating the fact that they are expected to set right again a world which is out of joint. The knowledge kills action, for action requires a state of being in which we are covered with the veil of illusion—that is what Hamlet has to teach us, not that really venal wisdom about John-a-Dreams, who cannot move himself to act because of too much reflection, because of an excess of possibilities, so to speak. It's not a case of reflection. No!—the true knowledge, the glimpse into the cruel truth overcomes every driving motive to act, both in Hamlet as well as in the Dionysian man. Now no consolation has any effect any more. His longing goes out over a world, even beyond the gods themselves, toward death. Existence is denied, together with its blazing reflection in the gods or in an immortal afterlife. In the consciousness of once having glimpsed the truth, the man now sees everywhere only the horror or absurdity of being; now he understands the symbolism in the fate of Ophelia; now he recognizes the wisdom of the forest god Silenus. It disgusts him.

Here, at a point when the will is in the highest danger, art approaches, as a saving, healing magician. Art alone can turn those thoughts of disgust at the horror or absurdity of existence into imaginary constructs which permit living to continue. These constructs are the Sublime as the artistic mastering of the horrible and the Comic as the artistic release from disgust at the absurd. The chorus of satyrs of the dithyramb is the saving fact of Greek art. Those emotional moods I have just described play themselves out in the middle world of these Dionysian attendants.

§8

The satyr as well as the idyllic shepherd of our more recent times are both the epitomes of a longing directed toward the primordial and natural, but with what a firm, fearless grip the Greek held onto his man from the woods, and how timidly and weakly modern man toys with the flattering image of a delicate and gentle flute-playing shepherd! Nature on which no knowledge had yet worked, in which the walls of culture had still not been thrown up— that's what the Greek saw in his satyr, and so he did not yet mistake him for an ape. Quite the contrary: the satyr was the primordial image of man, the expression of his highest and strongest emotions, as an inspired reveller, enraptured by the approach of the god, as a sympathetic companion, in whom the suffering of the god was repeated, as a messenger bringing wisdom from the deepest heart of nature, as a perceptible image of the sexual omnipotence of nature, which the Greek was accustomed to observing with reverent astonishment.

The satyr was something sublime and divine: that's how he must have seemed, especially to the painfully broken gaze of the Dionysian man, who would have been insulted by our well-groomed fictitious shepherd. His eye lingered with sublime satisfaction on the exposed, vigorous, and magnificent script of nature; here the illusion of culture was wiped away by the primordial image of man; here the real man revealed himself, the bearded satyr, who cried out with joy to his god. In comparison with him, the man of culture was reduced to a misleading caricature.

. . . The chorus is a living wall against the pounding reality, because it—the satyr chorus—presents existence more genuinely, more truly, and more completely than does the civilized person, who generally considers himself the only reality. The sphere of poetry does not lie beyond this world as a fantastic impossibility of a poet's brain; it wants to be exactly the opposite, the unadorned expression of the truth, and it must therefore simply cast off the false costume of that alleged truth of the man of culture. The contrast between this real truth of nature and the cultural lie which behaves as if it is the only reality is similar to the contrast between the eternal core of things, the thing-in-itself, and the total world of appearances.

And just as tragedy, with its metaphysical consolation, draws attention to the eternal life of that existential core in the continuing destruction of appearances, so the symbolism of the satyr chorus already expresses metaphorically that primordial relationship between the thing-in-itself and appearance. That idyllic shepherd of modern man is only a counterfeit, the totality of cultural illusions which he counts as nature. The Dionysian Greek wants truth and nature in their highest power—he sees himself magically changed into the satyr.

The enraptured horde of those who served Dionysus rejoiced under such moods and insights, whose power transformed them even before their very eyes, so that they imagined they saw themselves as restored natural geniuses, as satyrs. The later constitution of the tragic chorus is the artistic imitation of that natural phenomenon, in which now a division was surely necessary between the Dionysian spectators and those under the Dionysian enchantment. But we must always remind ourselves that the public for Attic tragedy rediscovered itself in the chorus of the orchestra, that basically there was no opposition between the public and the chorus: for everything is only a huge sublime chorus of dancing and singing satyrs or of those people who permit themselves to be represented by these satyrs.

. . . A public of spectators, as we are familiar with it, was unknown to the Greeks. In their theatre, given the way the spectators' space was built up in terraces of concentric rings, it was possible for everyone quite literally to look out over the collective cultural world around him and in that complete perspective to imagine himself a member of the chorus. Given this insight, we can call the chorus, in its primitive stages of the prototypical tragedy, the self-reflection of the Dionysian man, a phenomenon which we can make out most clearly in the experience of the actor, who, if he is really gifted, sees perceptibly in front of him the image of the role he has to play, hovering before his eyes, there for him to grasp. The satyr chorus is, first and foremost, a vision of the Dionysian mass, just as, in turn, the world of the stage area is a vision of this satyr chorus: the power of this vision is strong enough to dull and desensitize the impression of "reality," the sight of the cultured people ranged in their rows of seats all around. The form of the Greek theatre is a reminder of a solitary mountain valley: the architecture of the scene appears as an illuminated picture of a cloud, which the Bacchae swarming around in the mountains gaze upon from on high, as the majestic setting in the middle of which the image of Dionysus is revealed to them.

This primitive artistic illusion, which we are putting into words here to explain the tragic chorus, is, from the perspective of our scholarly views about the basic artistic process, almost offensive, although nothing can be more obvious than that the poet is only a poet because of the fact that he sees himself surrounded by shapes which live and act in front of him and into whose innermost being he gazes. Through some peculiar weakness in our modern talent, we are inclined to imagine primitive aesthetic phenomena in too complicated and abstract a manner. For the true poet, metaphor is not a rhetorical trope, but a representative image which really hovers in front of him in the place of an idea. For him the character is not some totality put together from individual traits collected bit by bit, but a living person, insistently there before his eyes, which differs from the similar vision of the painter only through its continued further living and acting.

Why does Homer give us descriptions so much more vivid than all the poets? Because he sees so much more around him. We speak about poetry so abstractly because we all tend to be poor poets. The aesthetic phenomenon is fundamentally simple: if someone simply possesses the capacity to see a living game going on continually and to live all the time surrounded by hordes of ghosts, then the man is a poet; if someone simply feels the urge to change himself and to speak out from other bodies and souls, then that person is a dramatist.

Dionysian excitement is capable of communicating this artistic talent to an entire multitude, so that they see themselves surrounded by such a horde of ghosts with which they know they are inwardly one. This dynamic of the tragic chorus is the original dramatic phenomenon: to see oneself transformed before one's eyes and now to act as if one really had entered another body, another character. This process stands at the beginning of the development of drama. Here is something different from the rhapsodist, who does not fuse with his images, but, like the painter, sees them with an observing eye outside himself; in the dramatic process there is already a surrender of individuality by the entry into a strange nature.

And, in fact, this phenomenon breaks out like an epidemic; an entire horde feels itself enchanted in this way. For this reason the dithyramb is essentially different from every other choral song. The virgins who move solemnly to Apollo's temple with laurel branches in their hands, singing a processional song as they go, remain who they are and retain their names as citizens. The dithyrambic chorus is a chorus of transformed people, for whom their civic past, their social position, is completely forgotten. They have become their god's timeless servants, living beyond all regions of society. Every other choral lyric of the Greeks is only an immense intensification of the Apollonian solo singer; whereas, in the dithyramb a congregation of unconscious actors stands before us, who look upon each other as transformed.

Enchantment is the precondition for all dramatic art. In this enchantment the Dionysian reveler sees himself as a satyr, and then, in turn, as a satyr he looks at his god; that is, in his transformed state he sees a new vision outside himself as an Apollonian fulfilment of his condition. With this new vision drama is complete.

Keeping this knowledge in mind, we must understand Greek tragedy as the Dionysian chorus which over and over again discharges itself in an Apollonian world of images. Those choral passages interspersed through tragedy are thus, as it were, the maternal womb of the entire dialogue so-called, that is, of the totality of the stage word, the actual drama. This primordial basis of tragedy radiates that vision of drama out in several discharges following one after the other, a vision which is entirely a dream image and, in this respect, epic in nature, but, on the other hand, as an objectification of a Dionysian state, it presents not the Apollonian consolation in illusion, but, by contrast, the smashing of individuality and becoming one with primordial being. Thus, drama is the Apollonian embodiment of Dionysian knowledge and effects, and, hence, is separated as if by an immense gulf from epic.

This conception of ours provides a full explanation for the chorus of Greek tragedy, the symbol for the collectively aroused Dionysian multitude. While we, given what we are used to with the role of the chorus on the modern stage, especially the chorus in opera, have been totally unable to grasp how that tragic chorus of the Greeks could be older, more original, in fact, more important than the actual "action"—as tradition tells us so clearly—while we, in turn, could not figure out why, given that traditionally high importance and original pre-eminence, the chorus would nonetheless be put together only out of lowly serving creatures, in fact, at first only out of goat-like satyrs, and while for us the orchestra in front of the acting area remained a constant enigma, now we have come to the insight that the acting area, together with the action, was basically and originally thought of only as a vision, that the single "reality" is simply the chorus, which creates the vision out of itself and speaks of that with the entire symbolism of dance, tone, and word.

This chorus in its vision gazes at its lord and master Dionysus and is thus always the chorus of servants; the chorus sees how Dionysus, the god, suffers and glorifies himself, and thus it does not itself act. But in this role, as complete servants in relation to the god, the chorus is nevertheless the highest, that is, the Dionysian expression of nature and, like nature, in its frenzy speaks the language of oracular wisdom. As the sympathetic as well as wise person, it announces the truth out of the heart of the world. So arises that fantastic and apparently so offensive figure of the wise and frenzied satyr, who is, at the same time, "the simple man" in contrast to the god: an image of nature and its strongest drives, indeed, a symbol of that and at the same time the announcer of its wisdom and art: musician, poet, dancer, visionary in a single person.

According to this insight and to the tradition, Dionysus, the actual stage hero and central point of the vision, was at first, in the very oldest periods of tragedy, not really present but was only imagined as present. That is, originally tragedy is only "chorus" and not "drama." Later the attempt was made to show the god as real and then to present in a way visible to every eye the form of the vision together with the transfiguring setting. At that point "drama" in the strict sense begins. Now the dithyrambic chorus takes on the task of stimulating the mood of the listeners right up to the Dionysian level, so that when the tragic hero appears on the stage, they do not see something like an awkward masked person but a visionary shape born, as it were, out of their own enchantment. . . .

Spontaneously he transferred the whole picture of the god, magically trembling in front of his soul, onto that masked form and dissolved the reality of that figure, so to speak, in a ghostly unreality. This is the Apollonian dream state, in which the world of day veils itself and a new world, clearer, more comprehensible, more moving than the first, and yet more shadow-like, generates itself anew in a continuing series of changes before our eyes. With this in mind, we can recognize in tragedy a drastic contrast of styles: speech, colour, movement, dynamics of speech appear in the Dionysian lyric of the chorus and, on the other hand, in the Apollonian dream world of the scene as expressive spheres completely separate from each other. The Apollonian illusions, in which Dionysus objectifies himself, are no longer "an eternal sea, a changing weaving motion, a glowing life," as is the case with the music of the chorus, no longer those powers which are only felt and cannot be turned into poetic images, moments when the frenzied servant of Dionysus feels the approach of the god. Now, from the acting area the clarity and solemnity of the epic form speak to him; now Dionysus no longer speaks through forces but as an epic hero, almost with the language of Homer.

§9

. . . Anyone who understands that innermost core of the Prometheus saga, namely, the imperative requirement that the individual striving like a Titan has to fall into crime, must also sense at the same time the un-Apollonian quality of this pessimistic idea, for Apollo wants to make individual beings tranquil precisely because he establishes border lines between them and, with his demands for self-knowledge and moderation, always reminds them once again of the most sacred laws of the world. However, to prevent this Apollonian tendency from freezing form into Egyptian stiffness and frigidity and to make sure the movement of the entire lake does not die away through the attempt of the Apollonian to prescribe to the individual waves their path and their extent, from time to time the high flood of the Dionysian once again destroys all those small circles in which the one-sided Apollonian "will" seeks to confine the Greek spirit.

Now that suddenly rising flood of the Dionysian takes the single small wave crest of the individual on its back, just as the brother of Prometheus, the Titan Atlas, shouldered the Earth. This Titanic impulse to become, as it were, the Atlas of all individuals and to bear them on one's wide back, higher and higher, further and further, is the common link between the Promethean and the Dionysian. In this view, the Aeschylean Prometheus is a Dionysian mask, while, in that previously mentioned deep desire for justice Aeschylus betrays, to the one who understands, his paternal descent from Apollo, the god of individuation and just boundaries. And so the double nature of the Aeschylean Prometheus, his simultaneously Dionysian and Apollonian nature, can be expressed in an understandable formula with the following words: "Everything present is just and unjust and equally justified in both."

That is your world! That's what one calls a world!

§10

It is an incontestable tradition that Greek tragedy in its oldest form had as its subject only the suffering of Dionysus and that for a long time later the individually present stage heroes were simply Dionysus. But with the same certainty we can assert that right up to the time of Euripides Dionysus never ceased being the tragic hero, that all the famous figures of the Greek theatre, like Prometheus, Oedipus, and so on, are only masks of that primordial hero, Dionysus. The fact that behind all these masks stands a divinity, that is the single fundamental reason for the frequently admired characteristic "ideality" of those well-known figures. Someone, I don't know who, made the claim that all individuals, as individuals, are comic and thus untragic, and from that we might gather that the Greeks in general could not tolerate individuals on the tragic stage. In fact, they seem to have felt this way: that Platonic distinction between and evaluation of the "idea" in contrast to the "idol," to copies, in general lies deeply grounded in the nature of the Greeks.

But for us to make use of Plato's terminology, we would have to talk of the tragic figures of the Greek stage in something like the following terms: the one truly real Dionysus appears in a multiplicity of shapes, in the mask of a struggling hero and, as it were, bound up in the net of the individual will. So now the god made manifest talks and acts in such a way that he looks like an erring, striving, suffering individual: the fact that he generally appears with this epic definition and clarity is the effect of Apollo, the interpreter of dreams, who indicates to the chorus its Dionysian state by that metaphorical appearance. In reality, however, that hero is the suffering Dionysus of the mysteries, that god who experiences the suffering of the individual in himself, the god about whom the amazing myths tell how he, as a child, was dismembered by the Titans and now in this condition is venerated as Zagreus. Through this is revealed the idea that this dismemberment, the essentially Dionysian suffering, is like a transformation into air, water, earth, and fire, that we also have to look upon the condition of individuation as the source and basis for all suffering, as something in itself reprehensible.

From the smile of this Dionysus arose the Olympian gods, from his tears arose mankind. In that existence as dismembered god Dionysus has the dual nature of a cruelly savage daemon and a lenient, gentle master. The initiates in the Eleusinian mysteries hoped for a rebirth of Dionysus, which we now can understand as a premonition of the end of individuation: the initiates' thundering song of jubilation cried out to this approaching third Dionysus. And only with this hope was there a ray of joy on the face of the fragmented world, torn apart into individuals, as myth reveals in the picture of Demeter sunk in eternal sorrow, who rejoices again for the first time when someone says to her that she might be able once again to give birth to Dionysus. In these established views we already have assembled all the components of a profound and pessimistic world view, together with the mysterious doctrine of tragedy: the basic acknowledgement of the unity of all existing things, the observation that individuation is the ultimate foundation of all evil, art the joyful hope, that the spell of individuation is there for us to break, as a premonition of a re-established unity.—

It has been pointed out earlier that the Homeric epic is the poetry of Olympian culture, with which it sang its own song of victory over the terrors of the fight against the Titans. Now, under the overwhelming influence of tragic poetry, the Homeric myths were newly reborn and show in this metamorphosis that since then the Olympian culture has also been overcome by an even deeper world view. The defiant Titan Prometheus reported to his Olympian torturer that for the first time his rule was threatened by the highest danger, unless he quickly joined forces with him. In Aeschylus we acknowledge the union of the frightened Zeus, worried about his end, with the Titan. Thus the earlier age of the Titans is belatedly brought back from Tartarus into the light once more.

The philosophy of wild and naked nature looks with the open countenance of truth at the myths of the Homeric world dancing past it: before the flashing eyes of this goddess, those myths grow pale and tremble—until the mighty fist of the Dionysian artist forces them into the service of the new divinity. The Dionysian truth takes over the entire realm of myth as the symbol of its knowledge and speaks of this knowledge, partly in the public culture of tragedy and partly in the secret celebrations of dramatic mystery ceremonies, but always in the disguise of the old myths.

What power was it which liberated Prometheus from his vultures and transformed the myth into a vehicle of Dionysian wisdom? It was the Herculean power of music, which attained its highest manifestation in tragedy and knew how to interpret myth with a new significance in the most profound manner, something we have already described before as the most powerful capacity of music. For it is the lot of every myth gradually to creep into the crevice of an assumed historical reality and to become analyzed as a unique fact in answer to the historical demands of some later time or other. The Greek were already fully on their way to re-labeling cleverly and arbitrarily the completely mythical dreams of their youth as a historical, pragmatic, and youthful history. For this is the way religions tend to die out, namely, when the mythical pre-conditions of a religion, under the strict, rational eyes of an orthodox dogmatism, become systematized as a closed totality of historical events and people begin anxiously defending the credibility of their myths but resisting every naturally continuing life and further growth of those same myths and when the feeling for the myth dies out and in its place the claim to put religion on a historical footing steps forward.

The newly born genius of Dionysian music now seized these dying myths, and in its hands myth blossomed again, with colours which it had never shown before, with a scent which stirred up a longing premonition of a metaphysical world. After this last flourishing, myth collapsed.... Through tragedy myth attains its most profound content, its most expressive form. It lifts itself up again, like a wounded hero, and all the remaining strength and wise tranquilly of a dying man burn in its eyes with its final powerful light. . . .

§11

Greek tragedy died in a manner different from all its ancient sister artistic styles: it died by suicide, as a result of an insoluble, hence tragic, conflict; whereas, all those others passed away in advanced old age with the most beautiful and most tranquil deaths. For if it is an appropriately happy natural condition to depart from life with beautiful descendants and without any painful strain, then the end of those older artistic genres manifests such a fortunate natural state of things. They disappeared slowly, and their more beautiful offspring were already standing there before their dying gazes, impatiently craning their heads with courageous gestures. By contrast, with the death of Greek tragedy there was created an immense emptiness, profoundly felt everywhere. Just as the Greek sailors at the time of Tiberius once heard from some isolated island the shattering cry "Great Pan is dead," so now, like a painful lament, rang throughout the Greek world, "Tragedy is dead! Poetry itself is lost with it! Away, away with you, you stunted, emaciated epigones! Off with you to Hades, so that there you can for once eat your fill of the crumbs from your former masters!"

If now a new form of art still blossomed which paid tribute to tragedy as its predecessor and mistress, it was looked upon with fright, because while it certainly carried the characteristics of its mother, they were the ones she had shown in her long death struggle. This death struggle of tragedy was fought by Euripides. . . .

In Euripides the spectator is brought up onto the stage. Anyone who has recognized the material out of which the Promethean tragedians before Euripides created their heroes and how remote from them lay any intention of bringing the true mask of reality onto the stage will also see clearly the totally deviant tendencies of Euripides. As a result of Euripides, the man of ordinary life pushed his way out of the spectators' space and up onto the acting area. The mirror in which earlier only the great and bold features had been shown now displayed that awkward fidelity which also conscientiously reflected the unsuccessful features of nature. . . .

From that time on there was nothing mysterious any more about how ordinary life could appear on stage and what stock phrases it would use. Middle-class mediocrity, on which Euripides built all his political hopes, now had its say.

§12

... Near the end of his life, Euripides himself proposed as emphatically as possible for his contemporaries the question about the value and meaning of this tendency in a myth. Should the Dionysian exist at all? Should we not eradicate it forcefully from Greek soil? Of course we should, the poet says to us, if only it were possible, but the god Dionysus is too powerful. The most sensible opponent—like Pentheus in the *Bacchae*—is unexpectedly charmed by Dionysus and later runs in this enchanted state to his own destruction. The judgment of the two old men, Cadmus and Tiresias, seems also to be the judgment of the aged poet: the thinking of the cleverest individual does not throw away that old folk tradition, that eternally propagating reverence for Dionysus; indeed, where such amazing powers are concerned, it is appropriate at least to demonstrate a diplomatically prudent show of joining in. But even with that, it is still possible that the god might take offence at such lukewarm participation and in the end transform the diplomat into a dragon—as happens here with Cadmus.

The poet tells us this, a poet who fought throughout his long life against Dionysus with heroic force —only to conclude his life with a glorification of his opponent and a suicide, like a man suffering from vertigo who, in order to escape the dreadful dizziness, which he can no longer endure, throws himself off a tower. That tragedy [Euripides' *Bacchae*] is a protest against the practicality of his artistic program alas, and it had already succeeded! A miracle had taken place: just when the poet recanted, his program had already triumphed. Dionysus had already been chased off the tragic stage, and by a daemonic power speaking out from Euripides. But Euripides was, in a certain sense, only a mask: the divinity which spoke out of him was not Dionysus, and not Apollo, but an entirely new-born daemon called Socrates.

This is the new opposition: the Dionysian and the Socratic. And from this contrast, Greek tragedy perished as a work of art. No matter how much Euripides might now seek to console us with his retraction, he was unsuccessful: the most magnificent temple lay in ruins. What use to us are the laments of the destroyer and his awareness that it had been the most beautiful of all temples?

... The essential quality of Socratic aesthetics, [its] most important law, runs something like this: "Everything must be understandable in order to be beautiful," a corollary to the Socratic saying, "Only the knowledgeable person is virtuous." With this canon in hand, Euripides assessed all the individual features [of drama] and justified them according to this principle: the language, the characters, the dramatic construction, the choral music. ... Euripides undertook the task, as Plato did, too, of showing the world the opposite of the "irrational" poet. His basic aesthetic principle, "Everything must be conscious in order to be beautiful," is, as I have mentioned, the corollary of the Socratic saying, "Everything must be conscious in order to be good."

With this in mind, we are entitled to assess Euripides as the poet of aesthetic Socratism. Socrates . . . did not understand the older tragedy and therefore did not value it. With Socrates as his ally, Euripides dared to be the herald of a new artistic creativity. If the older tragedy perished from this development, then aesthetic Socratism is the murdering principle. But insofar as the fight was directed against the Dionysian of the older art, we recognize in Socrates the enemy of Dionysus, the new Orpheus, who roused himself against Dionysus, and who, although destined to be torn apart by the maenads of the Athenian Court of Justice, nevertheless compelled the overpowering god himself to run away. Dionysus, as before, when he fled from Lycurgus, king of the Edoni, saved himself in the depths of the sea, that is, in the mysterious floods of a secret cult which would gradually overrun the entire world.

§13

. . . I will proceed to demonstrate the close interrelationship between Socrates and Euripides as the ancients saw it. It's important to remember, in this connection, that Socrates, as an opponent of tragic art, did not attended the performances of tragedy and only joined the spectators when a new piece by Euripides was being produced. The best known link, however, is the close juxtaposition of both names in the pronouncements of the Delphic Oracle, which indicated that Socrates was the wisest of men and at the same time delivered the judgment that Euripides captured second prize in the contest for wisdom. . . .

The most pointed statement about that new and unheard of high opinion of knowledge and understanding was uttered by Socrates, when he claimed that he was the only person to assert that he knew nothing; whereas, in his critical wandering about in Athens conversing with the greatest statesmen, orators, poets, and artists, everywhere he ran into people who imagined they knew things. Astonished, he recognized that all these famous people themselves had no correct and clear insight into their careers and carried out their work only instinctually. "Only from instinct"—with this expression we touch upon the heart and centre of the Socratic attitude. Given this, Socratism condemns prevailing art as well as prevailing ethics. Wherever he directs his searching gaze, he sees a lack of insight and the power of delusion, and from this lack he infers the inner falsity and worthlessness of present conditions. On the basis of this one point, Socrates believed he had to correct existence. He, a solitary individual, stepped forward with an expression of contempt and superiority, as the pioneer of an entirely different style of culture, art, and morality, into a world, a scrap of which we would count an honour and the greatest good fortune to catch.

That is the immensely disturbing thing which always grips us about Socrates and which over and over again stimulates us to find out the meaning and intention of this man, the most problematic figure of ancient times. Who is the man who can dare, as an individual, to deny the essence of Greece, which as Homer, Pindar, and Aeschylus, as Phidias, as Pericles, as Pythia, and Dionysus, as the most profound abyss and loftiest height, can count on our astonished veneration? What daemonic force is it that could dare to sprinkle this magic drink in the dust? What demi-god is it to whom the ghostly chorus of the noblest specimens of humanity had to cry out: "Alas, alas! You have destroyed the beautiful world with your mighty fist. It is collapsing, falling to pieces!"

A key to the essence of Socrates is offered to us by that amazing phenomenon indicated by the term "Socrates' daimonon." Under special circumstances, in which his immense reasoning power was gripped by doubt, he got a firm clue from a divine voice which expressed itself at such times. When this voice came, it always sounded a cautionary note. In this totally anomalous character, instinctive wisdom reveals itself only in order to stand up now and then against conscious knowledge as a hindrance. Whereas in all productive men instinct is the truly creative and affirming power, and consciousness acts as a critical and cautioning reaction, in Socrates instinct becomes the critic, consciousness becomes the creator—truly a monstrosity *per defectum* [from some defect]! Indeed, we do perceive here a grotesque *defectus* [defect] of every mystical talent, so that Socrates can be considered a specific case of the non-mystical man, in whom the logical character has become simply too massive through excessive use, just like instinctive wisdom in the mystic.

On the other hand, however, it was utterly impossible for that logical drive, as it appeared in Socrates, to turn against itself. In its unfettered outpouring it demonstrates a natural force of the sort we meet, to our shuddering surprise, only in the very greatest of all instinctive powers. Anyone who has sensed in the Platonic texts the merest scent of that god-like naiveté and confidence in the direction of Socrates' life has also felt how that immense drive wheel of logical Socratism is in motion, as it were, behind Socrates and how we are compelled to see this through Socrates, as if we were looking through a shadow. That he himself had a premonition of this relationship comes out in the dignified seriousness with which he assessed his divine calling everywhere, even before his judges. To censure him for this was basically as impossible as to approve of his influence on the dissolution of instinct.

When Socrates was hauled before the assembly of the Greek state, there was only one single form of sentence for this irreconcilable conflict, namely, banishment: people should have expelled him beyond the borders as something completely enigmatic, unclassifiable, inexplicable, so that some posterity could not justly indict the Athenians for acting shamefully. But the fact that death and not mere exile was pronounced over him Socrates himself appears to have brought about, fully clear about what he was doing and without the natural horror of death: he went to his death with that tranquility Plato describes him showing as he leaves the Symposium, the last drinker in the early light of dawn, to start a new day, while behind him, on the benches and on the ground, his sleeping dinner companions remain, to dream of Socrates, the truly erotic man. The dying Socrates became the new ideal of the noble Greek youth, one never seen before. Above all, the typical Greek youth, Plato, prostrated himself before Socrates' image with all the fervent adoration of his passionately enthusiastic soul.

§14

Let's now imagine that one great Cyclops eye of Socrates focussed on tragedy, that eye in which the beautiful madness of artistic enthuseasm never glowed—let's imagine how it was impossible for that eye to peer into the Dionysian abyss with a feeling of pleasure. What must that eye have actually seen in the "lofty and highly praised" tragic art, as Plato calls it? Something really unreasonable—causes without effects and effects which seemed to have no causes, and the whole so confused and with so many different elements that any reasonable disposition had to reject it, but dangerous tinder for sensitive and susceptible souls. We know which single form of poetry Socrates understood: Aesop's Fables, and he certainly did so with that smiling complacency with which the noble and good Gellert in his fable of the bee and the hen sings the praises of poetry:

> You see in me the use of poetry—
> To tell the man without much sense
> A picture image of the truth of things.

But for Socrates tragic art did not seem "to speak the truth" at all, quite apart from the fact that it addressed itself to the man who "does not possess much sense," and thus not to philosophers, a double excuse to keep one's distance from it. Like Plato, he assigned it to the arts of cosmetics, which present only what is pleasant, not what is useful, and he therefore made the demand that his disciples abstain and strictly stay away from such unphilosophical temptations, with so much success that the youthful poet of tragedy, Plato, immediately burned his poetical writing, so that he could become Socrates' student. But where invincible talents fought against the Socratic instructions, his power, together with the force of that immense personality, was still great enough to force poetry itself into new attitudes, unknown up until then.

An example of this is Plato himself. To be sure, in his condemnation of tragedy and art in general he did not remain back behind the naive cynicism of his master. But completely from artistic necessity he had to create an art form inwardly related to the existing art forms which he had rejected. The major criticism which Plato had made about the older art—that it was the imitation of an illusion and thus belonged to an even lower level than the empirical world—must above all not be directed against the new work of art. And so we see Plato exerting himself to go beyond reality and to present the Idea which forms the basis of that pseudo-reality. With that, however, Plato the thinker reached by a detour the very place where, as a poet, he had always been at home and from where Sophocles and all the older art was solemnly protesting against Plato's criticism.

If tragedy had assimilated into itself all earlier forms of art, so the same again holds true, in an odd way, for the Platonic dialogue, which was created from a mixture of all available styles and forms and hovers between explanation, lyric, drama, between prose and poetry, right in the middle, and in so doing broke through the strict old law about the unity of stylistic form. The Cynic writers went even further along the same path. In the excessive garishness of their style, in their weaving back and forth between prose and metrical forms, they produced the literary image of "raving Socrates," which they were in the habit of depicting in their own lives.

The Platonic dialogue was, so to speak, the boat on which the shipwreck of the older poetry, along with all its children, was saved. Pushed together into a single narrow space and with Socrates at the helm they anxiously and humbly set off now into a new world, which never could get its fill of looking at fantastic images of this procession. Plato truly gave all future generations the image of a new form of art, the image of the novel, which can be characterized as an infinitely intensified Aesopian fable, in which poetry lived on with a relative priority to dialectical philosophy similar to the relative priority of that very philosophy to theology for many centuries, that is, as *ancilla* [subservient maid]. This was poetry's new position, the place into which Plato forced it under the pressure of the daemonic Socrates.

Now philosophical ideas grew up around art and forced it to cling closely to the trunk of dialectic. The Apollonian attitude metamorphosed into logical systematizing, just as we noticed something similar with

Euripides and, in addition, the Dionysian was transformed into naturalistic emotions. Socrates, the dialectical hero in Platonic drama, reminds us of the changed nature of the Euripidean hero, who has to defend his actions with reasons and counter-reasons and thus often runs the risk of losing our tragic sympathy.

For who can fail to recognize the optimistic element in the heart of dialectic, which celebrates a jubilee with every conclusion and can breathe only in cool brightness and consciousness, that optimistic element which, once it has penetrated tragedy, must gradually overrun its Dionysian regions and necessarily drive them to self-destruction—right to their death leap into middle-class drama. Let people merely recall the consequences of the Socratic sayings "Virtue is knowledge; sin arises only from ignorance; the virtuous person is the happy person": in these three basic forms of optimism lies the death of tragedy. For now the virtuous hero must be a dialectician; now there must be a necessarily perceptible link between virtue and knowledge, belief and morality; now the transcendental resolution of justice in Aeschylus is lowered to the flat and impertinent principle of "poetic justice" with its customary *deus ex machina*.

What does this new Socratic optimistic stage world think about the chorus and the whole musical-Dionysian foundation for tragedy in general? As something accidental, as a reminder of the origin of tragedy, which we can well do without. We, by contrast, have come to realize that the chorus can only be understood as the cause of tragedy and of the tragic in general. Already with Sophocles the issue of the chorus reveals something of an embarrassment—an important indication that even with him the Dionysian stage of tragedy is beginning to fall apart. He no longer dares to trust the chorus to carry the major share of the action, but limits its role to such an extent that it now appears almost coordinated with the actors, just as if it had been lifted up out of the orchestra into the scene.

This feature naturally destroys its nature completely, no matter how much Aristotle may have approved of this particular arrangement of the chorus. That displacement of the chorus, which Sophocles certainly recommended through his dramatic practice and, according to tradition, even in a written text, is the first step toward the destruction of the chorus, whose phases in Euripides, Agathon, and the New Comedy followed one after the other with breakneck speed. Optimistic dialectic, with its syllogistic whip, drove music out of tragedy; that is, it destroyed the essence of tragedy, which can be interpreted only as a manifestation and representation of Dionysian states, as a perceptible symbolizing of music, as the dream world of a Dionysian intoxication.

If we have thus noticed an anti-Dionysian tendency already effective even before Socrates, which only in him achieves incredible, brilliant expression, then we must not shrink from the question of where such a phenomenon as Socrates points to. For we are not in a position, given the Platonic dialogues, to see that phenomenon merely as a negative force of dissolution. And so, while it's true that the most immediate effect of the Socratic drive was to bring about the subversion of Dionysian tragedy, a profound living experience of Socrates himself forces us to the question whether there must necessarily be only an antithetical relationship between Socratism and art and whether the birth of an "artistic Socrates" is in general an inherent contradiction.

For where art is concerned, that despotic logician now and then had the feeling of a gap, of an emptiness, of a partial reproach, of a duty he had perhaps neglected. As he explains to his friends in prison, one and the same dream apparition often came to him, always with the same words, "Socrates, practise music!" He calmed himself, right up to his last days, with the interpretation that his practice of philosophy was the highest musical art and believed that it was incorrect that a divinity would remind him of "common, popular music." Finally in prison, in order to relieve his conscience completely, he agreed to practice that music, something he had considered insignificant. And in this mood, he composed a poem to Apollo and rendered a few of Aesop's fables in verse.

What drove him to this practice was something like the voice of his warning daemon: it was his Apollonian insight that, like a barbarian king, he did not understand a noble divine image and was in danger of sinning against a divinity—through his failure to understand. That statement of Socrates's dream vision is the single indication of his thinking about something perhaps beyond the borders of his logical nature. So he had to ask himself: Is something which I do not understand not also something incomprehensible? Perhaps there is a kingdom of wisdom which is forbidden to the logician? Perhaps art is even a necessary correlative and supplement to scientific understanding?

§15

In the sense of this last mysterious question we must now state how the influence of Socrates has spread out over later worlds, right up to this moment and, indeed, into all future ages, like a shadow in the evening sun constantly growing larger, how that influence always makes necessary the re-creation of art—I mean art in its most profound and widest metaphysical sense—and through its own immortality guarantees the immortality of art.

Before we could recognize this fact, before we convincingly established the innermost dependence of every art on the Greeks, from Homer right up to Socrates, we had to treat these Greeks as the Athenians treated Socrates. Almost every era and cultural stage has at some point sought in an profoundly ill-tempered frame of mind to free itself of the Greeks, because in comparison with the Greeks, all their own achievements, apparently fully original and admired in all sincerity, suddenly appeared to lose their colour and life and shrivelled to unsuccessful copies, in fact, to caricatures. And so a heartfelt inner anger always keeps breaking out again against that arrogant little nation which dared to designate for all time everything that was not produced in its own country as "barbaric."

Who were those Greeks, people asked themselves, who, although they had achieved only an ephemeral historical glitter, only ridiculously restricted institutions, only an ambiguous competence in morality, who could even be identified with hateful vices, yet who had nevertheless laid a claim to a dignity and a preeminent place among peoples, appropriate to a genius among the masses? Unfortunately people were not lucky enough to find the cup of hemlock which could easily do away with such a being, for all the poisons which envy, slander, and inner rage created were insufficient to destroy that self-satisfied magnificence. Hence, confronted by the Greeks, people have been ashamed and afraid, unless an individual values the truth above everything else and dares to propose this truth: the notion that the Greeks, as the charioteers of our culture and every other one, hold the reins, but that almost always the wagon and horses are inferior material and do not match the glory of their drivers, who then consider it amusing to whip such a team into the abyss, over which they themselves jump with the leap of Achilles.

To demonstrate that Socrates also merits a place among the drivers of the chariot, it is sufficient to recognize him as typifying a form of existence inconceivable before him, the type known as The Theoretical Man. Our next task is to reach some insight about the meaning and purpose of such a man. The theoretical man, like the artist, also takes an infinite satisfaction in the present and is, like the artist, protected by that satisfaction from the practical ethic of pessimism and from its lynx eyes which glow only in the darkness. For while the artist, with each revelation of the truth, always keeps his enchanted gaze hanging on what still remains hidden after his revelation, theoretical man enjoys and remains satisfied with the covers which have been cast aside and takes as the greatest object of delight the process of continually happy unveiling which his own power has brought about.

There would be no science if it concerned itself only with that one naked goddess and with nothing else. For then its disciples would have to feel like people who wanted to dig a hole straight through the earth, and each of them sees that, even with the greatest lifelong effort, he is in a position to dig through only a really small piece of the immense depths, and that piece will be covered over in front of his eyes by the work of the person who comes after him, so that a third person would apparently do well to select on his own initiative a new place for his tunnelling efforts. Well, if someone now convincingly demonstrates that it is impossible to reach the antipodes by this direct route, who will still want to continue working on in the old depths, unless in the meantime he lets himself be satisfied with the possibility of finding some valuable rock or discovering some natural law?

For that reason, Lessing, the most honest theoretical man, ventured to state that for him the search for the truth counted for more than truth itself. With that statement the fundamental secret of science is unmasked, to the astonishment, indeed, the anger, of scientists. Now, of course, alongside occasional recognitions like Lessing's, prompted by excessive honesty if not high spirits, stands a profound delusion, which first came into the world in the person of Socrates, the unshakeable faith that thinking, guided by the main idea of causality, might reach into the deepest abyss of being and that thinking is capable, not just of understanding being, but even of correcting it. This sublime metaphysical delusion is instinctually part of science and leads it over and over again to its limits, at which point it must turn into art, something which is really predictable with this mechanical process.

With the torch of this idea, let's now look at Socrates: to us he appears as the first person who was capable not only of living by that instinct for science, but also—something much more—of dying by it, and thus the picture of the dying Socrates as a man raised above fear of death by knowledge and reason is the shield hanging over the entranceway to science, reminding every individual of his purpose, namely, to make existence intelligible and thus apparently justified. Of course, when reasoning cannot succeed in this endeavour, myth must also finally serve, something which I have just noted as the necessary consequence, indeed, even the purpose, of science.

Once anyone clearly sees how, after Socrates, that mystagogue of science, one philosophical school succeeds another in sequence, like wave after wave, how a never-imagined universal greed for knowledge throughout the widest extent of the educated world steered science around on the high seas as the essential task for every person of greater capabilities, a greed which it has been impossible since then completely to expel from science, how through this universality a common net of thinking was cast over the entire earth for the first time, with prospects, in fact, of the rule-bound workings of an entire solar system—whoever reminds himself of all this, together with that astonishingly high pyramid of contemporary knowledge, cannot deny the fact that in Socrates we see a turning point and vortex of so-called world history.

Then imagine for a moment if the entire incalculable sum of the energy which has been used in pursuit of that world project were spent, not in the service of knowledge, but on the practical, that is, the egotistical, aims of individuals and peoples, then in all probability the instinctive delight in living would be so weakened by universal wars of destruction and continuing migrations of people that, with suicide being a common occurrence, perhaps the individual would have had to feel the final remnant of a sense of duty, when he, like the inhabitants of the Fiji Islands, as a son would strangle his parents, and as a friend would strangle his friend—a practical pessimism, which could even give rise to a dreadful ethic of mass murder out of sympathy —an ethic which, by the way, is present and has been present all over the world, wherever art has not appeared in some form or other, especially in religion and science, as a remedy and a defence against that miasma.

With respect to this practical pessimism, Socrates is the original picture of the theoretical optimist, who, as I have described, in the belief that we could come to understand the nature of things, thinks that the power of a universal medicine is contained in knowledge and discovery and that evil inherently consists of error. To push forward with that reasoning and to separate true knowledge from appearance and from error seemed to the Socratic man the noblest, even the single truly human, vocation, and so from Socrates on, that mechanism of ideas, judgments, and conclusions has been valued as the highest activity and the most admirable gift of nature, above all other capabilities.

Even the noblest moral deeds, the emotions of pity, of self-sacrifice, of heroism and that calmness in the soul, so difficult to attain, which the Apollonian Greeks called *sophrosyne* —all these were derived by Socrates and his like-minded descendants right up to the present time from the dialectic of knowledge and therefore described as teachable. Whoever has experienced for himself the delight of a Socratic discovery and feels how this, in ever-widening circles, seeks to enclose the entire world of phenomena, will from then on find no spur capable of pushing him into existence more intense than the desire to complete that conquest and to weave a solid impenetrable net. To a man so minded, the Platonic Socrates then appears as the teacher of an entirely new form of "Greek serenity" and of a blissful existence, which seeks to discharge itself in actions and which will find this discharge, for the most part, in those influences which come from acting as a midwife to and educating noble disciples, in order finally to produce a genius.

But now science, incited by its powerful delusion, speeds on inexorably right to its limits, at which point the optimism hidden in the essence of logic breaks down. For the circumference of the circle of science has an infinity of points, and while it is still impossible to see how that circumference could ever be completely measured, nevertheless the noble, talented man, before the middle of his life, inevitably comes up against such a border point on that circumference, where he stares out into something which cannot be illuminated. When, at this point, he sees to his horror how at these limits logic turns around on itself and finally bites its own tail—then a new form of knowledge breaks through, tragic insight, which, in order merely to be endured, requires art as a protector and healer.

If we look at the loftiest realms of that world streaming around us, our eyes strengthened and refreshed by the Greeks, we become aware of that greed of insatiably optimistic knowledge, exemplary in Socrates, turning into tragic resignation and a need for art, even if it's true that this same greed, at its lower levels, must express itself as hostile to art and must inwardly loathe Dionysian tragic art in particular, as I have already explained in the example of the conflict between Aeschylean tragedy and Socratism.

Here we are now knocking, with turbulent feelings, on the doors of the present and future: Will that "turning around" lead to continuously new configurations of genius and straight to the music-playing Socrates? Will that net of art spread out over existence, whether in the name of religion or of science, be woven always more tightly and delicately, or is it determined that it will be ripped to shreds by the restless barbaric impulses and hurly-burly which we now call "the present"?—We are standing here on the sidelines for a little while as lookers on, worried but not without hope, for we are being permitted to witness that immense struggle and transition. Alas! The magic of these battles is that whoever looks at them must also fight them!

§16

. . . What aesthetic effect arises when those inherently separate powers of art, the Apollonian and the Dionysian, come to operate alongside each other? Or, put more briefly, what is the relationship of music to images and ideas? Schopenhauer, whom Richard Wagner applauded on this very point for the unsurpassable clarity and perceptiveness of his explanation, spoke his views on this matter in the greatest detail in the following place, which I will quote again here in full, from *World as Will and Presentation*, I, p. 309:

> We can look upon the world of appearance, or nature, and music as two different expressions of the same thing, which itself is thus

the only mediating factor in the analogy between the two of them; thus, an insight into this mediating factor is required in order to understand that analogy. According to this, music, when considered as an expression of the world, is to the highest degree a universal language, something which even has a relationship with the universality of ideas, rather like the way these are related to particular things. Its universality, however, is in no way that empty universality of abstractions, but something of an entirely different kind, bound up with a thoroughly clear certainty. In this, music is like geometric figures and numbers, which are the universal forms of all possible objects of experience and applicable to them all a priori, not, however, in an abstract manner but vividly and thoroughly fixed. All possible efforts, excitements, and manifestations of the will, all those processes inside human beings, which reason subsumes under the broad negative concept of feelings, can be expressed through the infinite number of possible melodies, but always in the universality of mere form, without matter, always only according to the thing-in-itself, not according to its appearance; they are, so to speak, its innermost soul, without the body. From this intimate relationship which music has with the true essence of all things, we can also account for the fact that when an appropriate music is heard in any scene, business, action, or environment, this music appears to open up to us the most secret sense of these things and comes forward as the most correct and clearest commentary on them, in the same way that for the man who surrenders himself entirely to the experience of a symphony it is as if he saw all possible events of life and of the world drawn over into himself, and yet he cannot, if he thinks about it, perceive any similarity between that play of sounds and the things which are in his mind. For music is, as mentioned, different from all other arts in this sense: it is not a portrayal of appearances, or more correctly, the adequate objectification of the will, but the immediate portrayal of the will itself, as well as the metaphysical complement of all physical things in the world and the thing-in-itself of all appearances. We could, therefore, call the world the embodiment of music just as much as the embodiment of the will. And that is why it is understandable that music is capable of bringing out every painting, indeed, every scene of real life and the world with an immediate and higher significance and, of course, to do that all the more, the closer the analogy of its melody is to the inner spirit of the given phenomenon. On this point we base the fact that we can set a poem to music as a song, or a vivid presentation as a pantomime, or both as an opera. Such individual pictures of human life, given a foundation in the universal language of music, are never bound to music and do not correspond with music by some constant necessity, but stand in relation to music as a random example to a universal idea. They present in the clarity of the real the very thing which music expresses in the universality of mere form. For melodies are, to a certain extent, like general ideas, an *abstractum* [abstraction] from the reality. For reality, that is, the world of individual things, supplies clear phenomena, remarkable and individual things, the single case, to both the universality of ideas and to the universality of melodies. Both of these universals, however, are, from a certain point of view, contrary to each other, since ideas consist only of forms abstracted first of all from perception, the stripped-away outer skin of things, so to speak, and are thus really and entirely *abstractta* [abstractions]; music, by contrast, gives the heart of the thing, the innermost core, which comes before all particular forms. This relationship can be really well expressed in the language of the scholastics, when we say: ideas are the *universalia post rem* [universals after the fact]; music, however, gives the *universalia ante rem* [universals before the fact], and reality the *universalia in re* [universals in the fact]. That in general there can be a connection between a musical composition and a perceptible presentation, however, rests on the point that, as stated, both are only very different expressions of same inner essence of the world. Now, when in a particular case such a connection is truly present, that is, the composer has known how to express in the universal language of music the dynamic of the will, which constitutes the core of an event, then the melody of the song, the music of the opera, is full of expression. But the analogy discovered by the composer between those two must issue from his immediate insight into the world's essence, unknown to his reason, and must not be an imitation, conveyed in ideas with conscious intentionality. Otherwise the music does not express the inner essence, the will itself, but only gives an inadequate imitation of its appearance, the way all essentially imitative music does.

Following what Schopenhauer has taught, we also understand music as the language of the unmediated will and feel our imaginations stirred to shape that spirit world which speaks to us invisibly and nonetheless with such vital movement and to embody it for ourselves in an analogous illustration.

By contrast, image and idea, under the influence of a truly appropriate music, reach an elevated significance. Thus, Dionysian art customarily works in two ways on Apollonian artistic potential: music stimulates us to the metaphorical viewing of the Dionysian universality, and music then permits that metaphorical image to come forward with the highest significance. From this inherently intelligible observation and without any deeper considerations of unapproachable things, I conclude that music is capable of generating myth, that is, the most meaningful example, and of giving birth in particular to the tragic myth, the myth which speaks in metaphors of the Dionysian insight. I have explained in the phenomenon of the lyric poet, how the music in the lyric poet strives to make its essence known through him in Apollonian pictures. If we now imagine that music at its highest intensity must also seek to reach its highest representation, then we must consider it possible that music also knows how to find the symbolic expression for its essentially Dionysian wisdom. And where else will we have to look for this expression, if not in tragedy and in the idea of the tragic generally?

From the essence of art as it is commonly understood according to the single categories of illusion and beauty, it is genuinely impossible to derive the tragic. Only with reference to the spirit of music do we understand a joy in the destruction of the individual. For in particular examples of such a destruction is made clear to us the eternal phenomenon of Dionysian art, which brings into expression the will in its omnipotence out from behind, so to speak, the *principio individuationis*, the eternal life beyond all appearances and in spite of all destruction. The metaphysical joy in the tragic is a translation of the instinctive unconscious Dionysian wisdom into the language of the image: the hero, the highest manifestation of the will, is destroyed, and we are happy at that, because, after all, he is only an illusion, and the eternal life of the will is not disturbed by his destruction.

"We believe in eternal life," so tragedy calls out, while the music is the direct idea of this life. The work of the plastic artist has an entirely different purpose: here Apollo overcomes the suffering of the individual through the bright exaltation in the eternity of the illusion. Here beauty is victorious over the suffering inherent in life. The pain is, in a certain sense, brushed away from the face of nature. In Dionysian art and in its tragic symbolism this same nature speaks to us with its true, undisguised voice: "Be as I am! Under the incessant changes in phenomena, the eternally creative primordial mother, eternally forcing things into existence, eternally satisfied with the changing nature of appearances!"

§17

Dionysian art thus wishes to convince us of the eternal delight in existence: only we are to seek this delight, not in appearances, but behind them; we are to recognize how everything which comes into being must be ready for painful destruction; we are forced to gaze directly into the terror of individual existence—and nonetheless are not to become paralyzed: a metaphysical consolation tears us momentarily out of the hustle and bustle of changing forms. For a short time we really are the primordial essence itself and feel its unbridled lust for and joy in existence; the struggle, the torment, the destruction of appearances now seem to us necessary, on account of the excess of innumerable forms of existence pressing and punching themselves into life and of the exuberant fecundity of the world will. We are transfixed by the raging barbs of this torment in the very moment when we become, as it were, one with the immeasurable primordial delight in existence and when, in Dionysian rapture, we sense the indestructible and eternal nature of this joy. In spite of fear and pity, we are fortunate vital beings, not as individuals, but as the one living being, with whose procreative joy we have been fused.

The story of how Greek tragedy arose tells us now with clear certainty how the Greeks' tragic work of art really was born out of the spirit of music. With this idea we think we have, for the first time, done justice to the original and astonishing meaning of the chorus. At the same time, however, we must concede that the significance of the tragic myth established previously was never conceptually and transparently clear to the Greek poets, to say nothing of the Greek philosophers. Their heroes speak to a certain extent more superficially than they act; the myth really does not find its adequate objectification in the spoken word. The structure of the scenes and the vivid images reveal a deeper wisdom than the poet himself can grasp in words and ideas.

We can make the same observation about Shakespeare, whose Hamlet, for example, in a similar sense speaks more superficially than he acts, so that we derive the doctrine of Hamlet we discussed earlier, not from the words, but from the deeper view and review of the totality of the work. With respect to Greek tragedy, which, of course, comes to us only as a drama of words, I have even suggested that the incongruity between myth and word can easily seduce us into considering it shallower and more empty of meaning than it is and thus also into assuming a more superficial effect than it must have had according to the testimony of the ancients, for we easily forget that what the poet as a wordsmith could not achieve, the attainment of the highest intellectualization and idealization of myth, he could have achieved successfully at any moment as a creative musician!

Admittedly we are almost forced to recreate through scholarship the extraordinary power of the musical effects in order to experience something of that incomparable consolation necessarily characteristic of true tragedy. But we would experience this superior musical power for what it is only if we ourselves were Greeks; whereas, considering the entire development of Greek music in comparison to the music we know and are familiar with—so infinitely richer by comparison—we believe that we are hearing youthful songs of musical genius, sung with only a timid sense of their power. The Greeks are, as the Egyptian priests say, eternal children and, even in tragic art, only children who do not know what a sublime toy has arisen under their hands, something which—will be destroyed.

That struggle of the spirit of music for pictorial and mythic revelation, which becomes increasingly intense from the beginning of the lyric right up to Attic tragedy, suddenly breaks apart, right after it first attained full luxuriant bloom and, so to speak, disappears from the surface of Hellenic art, although the Dionysian world view born out of this struggle lives on in the mysteries and, in the most amazing transformations and degenerations, never stops attracting more serious natures to it. Is it not possible that one day it will rise from its mystic depths as art once more?

At this point we are concerned with the question whether the power whose opposition broke tragedy has sufficient force for all time to hinder the artistic reawakening of tragedy and the tragic world view. If the old tragedy was derailed by the dialectical drive for knowledge and for the optimism of science, we might have to infer from this fact an eternal struggle between the theoretical and the tragic world view, and only after the spirit of science is taken right to its limits and its claim to universal validity destroyed by the proof of those limits would it be possible to hope for a rebirth of tragedy. For a symbol of such a cultural form, we would have to set up Socrates the player of music, in the sense talked about earlier. By this confrontation I understand with respect to the spirit of science that belief, which first came to light in the person of Socrates, that nature can be rationally understood and that knowledge has a universal healing power.

Anyone who remembers the most immediate consequences of this restless, forward-driving spirit of science will immediately recall how it destroyed myth and how, through this destruction, poetry was driven out of its naturally ideal soil as something which from now on was without a home. If we have correctly ascribed to music the power to be able to bring about out of itself a rebirth of myth, then we will also have to seek out the spirit of science on the path where it has its hostile encounter with the myth-creating power of music. This occurred in the development of the new Attic dithyramb, whose music no longer expressed the inner essence, the will itself, but only gave back an inadequate appearance in an imitation delivered through ideas. From such inwardly degenerate music those with a true musical nature turned away with the same aversion which they had shown when confronted by the art-killing attitude of Socrates.

The instinct of Aristophanes, which had such a sure grasp, was certainly right when he linked together Socrates himself, the tragedies of Euripides, and the music of the new writers of dithyrambs, hating each of them equally and smelling in all three phenomena the characteristics of a degenerate culture. Through that newer dithyramb, music was, in an outrageous manner, turned into a mimetic demonstration of appearances, for example, a battle, a storm at sea, and in the process was certainly robbed of all its power to create myths. For when music seeks to arouse our indulgence only by compelling us to look for external analogies between an event in life and nature and certain rhythmic figures and characteristic musical sounds, when our understanding is supposed to be satisfied with the recognition of these analogies, then we are dragged down into a mood in which a conception of the mythic is impossible, for myth desires to be vividly felt as a single instance of universality and truth staring into the infinite. . . .

§18

It is an eternal phenomenon: the voracious will always finds a way to keep its creatures alive and to force them on to further living by an illusion spread over things. One man is fascinated by the Socratic desire for knowledge and the delusion that with it he will be able to heal the eternal wound of existence. Another is caught up by the seductive veil of artistic beauty fluttering before his eyes, still another by the metaphysical consolation that underneath the hurly-burly of appearances eternal life flows on indestructibly, to say nothing of the more common and almost even more powerful illusions which the will holds ready at all times. In general, these three stages of illusion are only for nobly endowed natures, those who especially feel with a more profound reluctance the weight and difficulty of existence and who have to be deceived out of this reluctance by these exquisite stimulants. Everything we call culture consists of these stimulants: depending on the proportions of the mixture we have a predominantly Socratic or artistic or tragic culture—or if you'll permit historical examples— there is either an Alexandrian or a Hellenic or a Buddhist culture.

Our entire modern world is trapped in the net of Alexandrian culture and recognizes as its ideal the theoretical man, equipped with the highest intellectual powers and working in the service of science, a man for whom Socrates is the prototype and progenitor. All our methods of education originally have this ideal in view; every other existence has struggled on with difficulty alongside this ideal as a way of life we permit, not as one we desire. For a long time now, in an almost frightening sense, an educated person here has been found only in the form of the scholar. Even our poetic arts have had to develop out of scholarly imitations, and in the important effect of rhyme we recognize still the development of our poetical form out of artificial experiments with what is essentially a really scholarly language, not one native to us.

To a true Greek how incomprehensible Faust would have to have appeared, the man of modern culture, inherently intelligible to us, who storms dissatisfied through all faculties, that Faust whose drive for knowledge makes him devoted to magic and the devil. We have only to stand him beside Socrates for comparison in order to recognize that modern man is beginning to have a premonition of the limits of that Socratic desire for knowledge and is yearning for a coastline in the wide, desolate sea of knowledge. When Goethe once remarked to Eckermann, with reference to Napoleon, "Yes, my good man, there is also a productivity in actions," in a delightfully naive way he was reminding us that the non-theoretical man is something implausible and astonishing to modern human beings, so that, once again, it required the wisdom of a Goethe to find out that such a strange form of existence is comprehensible, indeed, forgivable.

And now we should not conceal from ourselves what lies hidden in the womb of this Socratic culture! An optimism that thinks itself all-powerful! Well, people should not be surprised when the fruits of this optimism ripen, when a society that has been thoroughly leavened with this kind of culture, right down to the lowest levels, gradually trembles with an extravagant turmoil of desires, when the belief in earthly happiness for everyone, when faith in the possibility of such a universal knowledge culture gradually changes into the threatening demand for such an Alexandrian earthly happiness, into the plea for a Euripidean *deus ex machina*!

People should take note: Alexandrian culture requires a slave class in order to be able to exist over time, but with its optimistic view of existence, it denies the necessity for such a class and thus, when the effect of its beautiful words of seduction and reassurance about the "dignity of human beings" and the "dignity of work" has worn off, it gradually moves towards a horrific destruction. There is nothing more frightening than a barbarian slave class which has learned to think of its existence as an injustice and is preparing to take revenge, not only for itself, but for all generations. In the face of such threatening storms, who dares appeal with sure confidence to our pale and exhausted religions, which themselves in their foundations have degenerated into scholarly religions, so that myth, the essential pre-condition for every religion, is already paralyzed everywhere, and even in this area that optimistic spirit which we have just described as the germ of destruction of our society has gained control.

While the disaster slumbering in the bosom of theoretical culture gradually begins to worry modern man, while he, in his uneasiness, reaches into the treasure of his experience for ways to avert the danger, without himself having any real faith in these means, and while he also begins to have a premonition of the particular consequences for him, some great wide-ranging natures have, with an incredible circumspecttion, known how to use the equipment of science itself to set out the boundaries and restricted nature of knowledge generally and, in the process, decisively to deny the claim of science to universal validity and universal goals. Given proofs like this, the delusion which claims that with the help of causality it can fathom the innermost essence of things has for the first time become recognized for what it is.

The immense courage and wisdom of Kant and Schopenhauer achieved the most difficult victory, the victory over the optimism lying concealed in the essential nature of logic, which is, in turn, the foundation of our culture. While this logic, based on *aeternae veritates* [eternal truths] which it did not consider open to objection, believed that all the riddles of the world could be recognized and resolved and had treated space, time, and causality as totally unconditional laws with the most universal validity, Kant showed how these really served only to raise mere appearance, the work of Maja, to the single, highest reality and to set it in place of the innermost and true essence of things and thus to make true knowledge of this essence impossible, that is, in the words of Schopenhauer, to get the dreamer to sleep even more soundly (*World as Will and Presentation*, I, 498).

With this recognition there is introduced a culture which I venture to describe as a tragic culture. Its most important distinguishing feature is that wisdom replaces science as the highest goal, a wisdom which, undeceived by the seductive diversions of science, turns its unswerving gaze onto the all-encompassing picture of the world and, with a sympathetic feeling of love, seeks in that world to grasp eternal suffering as its own suffering. Let us picture for ourselves a generation growing up with this fearlessness in its gaze, with this heroic push into what is tremendous; let us picture for ourselves the bold stride of these dragon slayers, the proud audacity with which they turn their backs on all the doctrines of weakness associated with that optimism, in order "to live with resolution," fully and completely. Would it not be necessary that the tragic man of this culture, having trained himself for what is serious and frightening, desire a new art, the art of metaphysical consolation, the tragedy, as his own personal Helen of Troy, and to have to cry out with Faust:

> With my desire's power, should I not call
> Into this life the fairest form of all?

However, now that Socratic culture has been shaken on two sides and can hang onto the sceptre of its infallibility only with trembling hands, first of all by the fear of its own consequences, which it is definitely beginning to sense and, in addition, because it is itself no longer convinced with that earlier naive trust of the eternal validity of its foundations, it's a sorry spectacle how the dance of its thinking constantly dashes longingly after new forms in order to embrace them and then how, like Mephistopheles with the seductive Lamias, it suddenly, with a shudder, lets them go again. That is, in fact, the characteristic mark of that "fracture" which everyone is in the habit of talking about as the root malady of modern culture, that theoretical man is afraid of his own consequences and, in his dissatisfaction, no longer dares to commit himself to the fearful ice currents of existence. He runs anxiously up and down along the shore. He no longer wants to have anything completely, any totality with all the natural cruelty of things.

That's how much the optimistic way of seeing things has mollycoddled him. At the same time he feels how a culture which has been built on the principle of science must collapse when it begins to become illogical, that is, when it begins to run back once it is faced with its own consequences. Our art reveals this general distress: in vain people use imitation to lean on all the great productive periods and natures; in vain they gather all "world literature" around modern man to bring him consolation and place him in the middle of artistic styles and artists of all ages, so that he may, like Adam with the animals, give them a name. But he remains an eternally hungry man, the "critic" without joy and power, the Alexandrian man, who is basically a librarian and copy editor and goes miserably blind from the dust of books and printing errors. . . .

§24

Among the characteristic artistic effects of musical tragedy we had to stress an Apollonian illusion through which we are to be rescued from immediate unity of being with the Dionysian music, while our musical excitement can discharge itself in an Apollonian sphere and in a visible middle world which interposed itself. By doing this we thought we had noticed how, simply through this discharge, that middle world of the scenic action, the drama in general, to a certain degree became visible and comprehensible from within, in a way which is unattainable in all other Apollonian art, so that here, where the Apollonian is energized and raised aloft, as it were, through the spirit of the music, we had to acknowledge the highest intensification of its power and, therefore, in that fraternal bond of Apollo and Dionysus the peak of both the Apollonian and the Dionysian artistic aims.

Of course, the projected Apollonian image with this particular inner illumination through the music does not achieve the effect characteristic of the weaker degrees of Apollonian art, what epic or animated stone is capable of, compelling the contemplating eye to that calm delight in the world of the individual—in spite of a higher animation and clarity, that effect will not permit itself to be attained here. We looked at drama and with a penetrating gaze forced our way into the inner moving world of its motives—and nonetheless for us it was as if only an allegorical picture passed before us, whose most profound meaning we thought we could almost guess and which we wanted to pull aside, like a curtain, in order to look at the primordial image behind it. The brightest clarity of the image did not satisfy us, for this seemed to hide just as much as it revealed. And while, with its allegorical-like revelation, it seemed to promise to rip aside the veil, to disclose the mysterious background, once again it was precisely that penetrating light illuminating everything which held the eye in its spell and prevented it from probing more deeply.

Anyone who has not had this experience of having to watch and, at the same time, of yearning to go above and beyond watching will have difficulty imagining how definitely and clearly these two processes exist together and are felt alongside each other, as one observes the tragic myth. However, the truly aesthetic spectators will confirm for me that among the peculiar effects of tragedy that co-existence may be the most remarkable. If we now translate this phenomenon taking place in the aesthetic spectator into an analogous process in the tragic artist, we will have understood the genesis of the tragic myth. He shares with the Apollonian sphere of art the full joy in appearances and in watching—at the same time he denies this joy and has an even higher satisfaction in the destruction of the visible world of appearances.

The content of the tragic myth is at first an epic event with the glorification of the struggling hero. But what is the origin of that inherently mysterious feature, the fact that the suffering in the fate of the hero, the most painful victories, the most agonizing opposition of motives, in short, the exemplification of that wisdom of Silenus, or, expressing it aesthetically, of the ugly and the dissonant, in so many countless forms, is presented with such fondness, always renewed, and precisely in the richest and most youthful age of a people, unless we recognize in all this a higher pleasure?

For the fact that in life things are really so tragic would not in the least account for the development of an art form, if art is not only an imitation of natural reality but a metaphysical supplement to that reality, set beside it in order to overcome it. The tragic myth, insofar as it belongs to art at all, also participates fully in this general purpose of art to provide metaphysical transfiguration. But what does it transfigure, when it leads out the world of appearance in the image of the suffering hero? Least of all the "Reality" of this world of appearances, for it says directly to us: "Look here! Look right here! This is your life! This is the hour hand on the clock of your existence!"

And did the myth show us this life in order to transfigure it in front of us? If not, in what does the aesthetic joy consist with which we allow those images to pass in front of us? I ask about aesthetic delight and know full well that many of these images can in addition now and then still produce a moral pleasure, for example, in the form of pity or a moral triumph. But whoever wants to derive the effect of the tragic merely from these moral origins, as, of course, has been customary in aesthetics for far too long, should not think that, in so doing, he has then done anything for art, which above all must demand purity in its realm.

For an explanation of the tragic myth the very first demand is that he seek that joy characteristic of it in the purely aesthetic sphere, without reaching over into the territory of pity, fear, and the morally sublime. How can the ugly and dissonant, the content of the tragic myth, excite an aesthetic delight?

Here it is necessary for us to vault with a bold leap into a metaphysics of art, when I repeat an earlier sentence—that existence and the world appear justified only as an aesthetic phenomenon. It is in this sense that the tragic myth has to convince us that even the ugly and dissonant are an artistic game, which the will, in the eternal abundance of its joy, plays with itself.

But there is a direct way to make this primordial phenomenon of Dionysian art, which is so difficult to comprehend, completely understandable and to enable one to grasp it immediately, through the miraculous meaning of musical dissonance, the way the music in general, set next to the world, is the only thing that can give an idea of what it means to understand a justification of the world as an aesthetic phenomenon.

The joy which the tragic myth produces has the same homeland as the delightful sensation of dissonance in music. The Dionysian, together with its primordial joy felt even in pain, is the common birth womb of music and the tragic myth. . . .

HENRI BERGSON
LAUGHTER:
AN ESSAY ON THE MEANING OF THE COMIC

Translation by
Cloudesley Brereton and Fred Rothwell

Chapter One
The Comic in General. The Comic Element in Forms and Movements.
Expansive Force of the Comic

What does laughter mean? What is the basal element in the laughable? What common ground can we find between the grimace of a merry-andrew, a play upon words, an equivocal situation in a burlesque and a scene of high comedy? What method of distillation will yield us invariably the same essence from which so many different products borrow either their obtrusive odour or their delicate perfume? The greatest of thinkers, from Aristotle downwards, have tackled this little problem, which has a knack of baffling every effort, of slipping away and escaping only to bob up again, a pert challenge flung at philosophic speculation. Our excuse for attacking the problem in our turn must lie in the fact that we shall not aim at imprisoning the comic spirit within a definition. We regard it, above all, as a living thing.

However trivial it may be, we shall treat it with the respect due to life. We shall confine ourselves to watching it grow and expand. Passing by imperceptible gradations from one form to another, it will be seen to achieve the strangest metamorphoses. We shall disdain nothing we have seen. Maybe we may gain from this prolonged contact, for the matter of that, something more flexible than an abstract definition —a practical, intimate acquaintance, such as springs from a long companionship. And maybe we may also find that, unintentionally, we have made an acquaintance that is useful. For the comic spirit has a logic of its own, even in its wildest eccentricities. It has a method in its madness. It dreams, I admit, but it conjures up, in its dreams, visions that are at once accepted and understood by the whole of a social group. Can it then fail to throw light for us on the way that human imagination works, and more particularly social, collective, and popular imagination? Begotten of real life and akin to art, should it not also have something of its own to tell us about art and life?

At the outset we shall put forward three observations which we look upon as fundamental. They have less bearing on the actually comic than on the field within which it must be sought.

I

The first point to which attention should be called is that the comic does not exist outside the pale of what is strictly *human*. A landscape may be beautiful, charming and sublime, or insignificant and ugly; it will never be laughable. You may laugh at an animal, but only because you have detected in it some human attitude or expression. You may laugh at a hat, but what you are making fun of, in this case, is not the piece of felt or straw, but the shape that men have given it—the human caprice whose mould it has assumed. It is strange that so important a fact, and such a simple one too, has not attracted to a greater degree the attention of philosophers. Several have defined man as "an animal which laughs." They might equally well have defined him as an animal which is laughed at; for if any other animal, or some lifeless object, produces the same effect, it is always because of some resemblance to man, of the stamp he gives it or the use he puts it to.

Here I would point out, as a symptom equally worthy of notice, the *absence of feeling* which usually accompanies laughter. It seems as though the comic could not produce its disturbing effect unless it fell, so to say, on the surface of a soul that is thoroughly calm and unruffled. Indifference is its natural environment, for laughter has no greater foe than emotion. I do not mean that we could not laugh at a person who inspires us with pity, for instance, or even with affection, but in such a case we must, for the moment, put our affection out of court and impose silence upon our pity. In a society composed of pure intelligences there would probably be no more tears, though perhaps there would still be laughter; whereas highly emotional souls, in tune and unison with life, in whom every event would be sentimentally prolonged and re-echoed, would neither know nor understand laughter.

Try, for a moment, to become interested in everything that is being said and done; act, in imagination, with those who act, and feel with those who feel; in a word, give your sympathy its widest expansion: as though at the touch of a fairy wand you will see the flimsiest of objects assume importance, and a gloomy hue spread over everything. Now step aside, look upon life as a disinterested spectator: many a drama will turn into a comedy. It is enough for us to stop our ears to the sound of music, in a room where dancing is going on, for the dancers at once to appear ridiculous. How many human actions would stand a similar test? Should we not see many of them suddenly pass from grave to gay, on isolating them from the accompanying music of sentiment? To produce the whole of its effect, then, the comic demands something like a momentary anesthesia of the heart. Its appeal is to intelligence, pure and simple.

This intelligence, however, must always remain in touch with other intelligences. And here is the third fact to which attention should be drawn. You would hardly appreciate the comic if you felt yourself isolated from others. Laughter appears to stand in need of an echo, Listen to it carefully: it is not an articulate, clear, well-defined sound; it is something which would fain be prolonged by reverberating from one to another, something beginning with a crash, to continue in successive rumblings, like thunder in a mountain. Still, this reverberation cannot go on for ever. It can travel within as wide a circle as you please: the circle remains, none the less, a closed one.

Our laughter is always the laughter of a group. It may, perchance, have happened to you, when seated in a railway carriage or at table d'hote, to hear travellers relating to one another stories which must have been comic to them, for they laughed heartily. Had you been one of their company, you would have laughed like them; but, as you were not, you had no desire whatever to do so. A man who was once asked why he did not weep at a sermon, when everybody else was shedding tears, replied: "I don't belong to the parish!" What that man thought of tears would be still more true of laughter.

However spontaneous it seems, laughter always implies a kind of secret freemasonry, or even complicity, with other laughers, real or imaginary. How often has it been said that the fuller the theatre, the more uncontrolled the laughter of the audience! On the other hand, how often has the remark been made that many comic effects are incapable of translation from one language to another, because they refer to the customs and ideas of a particular social group! It is through not understanding the importance of this double fact that the comic has been looked upon as a mere curiosity in which the mind finds amusement, and laughter itself as a strange, isolated phenomenon, without any bearing on the rest of human activity.

Hence those definitions which tend to make the comic into an abstract relation between ideas: "an intellectual contrast," "a palpable absurdity," etc.—definitions which, even were they really suitable to every form of the comic, would not in the least explain why the comic makes us laugh. How, indeed, should it come about that this particular logical relation, as soon as it is perceived, contracts, expands and shakes our limbs, whilst all other relations leave the body unaffected? It is not from this point of view that we shall approach the problem. To understand laughter, we must put it back into its natural environment, which is society, and above all must we determine the utility of its function, which is a social one. Such, let us say at once, will be the leading idea of all our investigations. Laughter must answer to certain requirements of life in common. It must have a *social* signification.

Let us clearly mark the point towards which our three preliminary observations are converging. The comic will come into being, it appears, whenever a group of men concentrate their attention on one of their number, imposing silence on their emotions and calling into play nothing but their intelligence. What, now, is the particular point on which their attention will have to be concentrated, and what will here be the function of intelligence? To reply to these questions will be at once to come to closer grips with the problem. But here a few examples have become indispensable.

II

A man, running along the street, stumbles and falls; the passers-by burst out laughing. They would not laugh at him, I imagine, could they suppose that the whim had suddenly seized him to sit down on the ground. They laugh because his sitting down is involuntary. Consequently, it is not his sudden change of attitude that raises a laugh, but rather the involuntary element in this change—his clumsiness, in fact. Perhaps there was a stone on the road. He should have altered his pace or avoided the obstacle. Instead of that, through lack of elasticity, through absentmindedness and a kind of physical obstinacy, *as a result, in fact, of rigidity or of momentum*, the muscles continued to perform the same movement when the circumstances of the case called for something else. That is the reason of the man's fall, and also of the people's laughter. Now, take the case of a person who attends to the petty occupations of his everyday life with mathematical precision. The objects around him, however, have all been tampered with by a mischievous wag, the result being that when he dips his pen into the inkstand he draws it out all covered with mud, when he fancies he is sitting down on a solid chair he finds himself sprawling on the floor, in a word his actions are all topsy-turvy or mere beating the air, while in every case the effect is invariably one of momentum.

Habit has given the impulse: what was wanted was to check the movement or deflect it. He did nothing of the sort, but continued like a machine in the same straight line. The victim, then, of a practical joke is in a position similar to that of a runner who falls—he is comic for the same reason. The laughable element in both cases consists of a certain *mechanical inelasticity*, just where one would expect to find the wide-awake adaptability and the living pliableness of a human being. The only difference in the two cases is that the former happened of itself, whilst the latter was obtained artificially. In the first instance, the passer-by does nothing but look on, but in the second the mischievous wag intervenes.

All the same, in both cases the result has been brought about by an external circumstance. The comic is therefore accidental: it remains, so to speak, in superficial contact with the person. How is it to penetrate within? The necessary conditions will be fulfilled when mechanical rigidity no longer requires for its manifestation a stumbling-block which either the hazard of circumstance or human knavery has set in its way, but extracts by natural processes, from its own store, an inexhaustible series of opportunities for externally revealing its presence. Suppose, then, we imagine a mind always thinking of what it has just done and never of what it is doing, like a song which lags behind its accompaniment.

Let us try to picture to ourselves a certain inborn lack of elasticity of both senses and intelligence, which brings it to pass that we continue to see what is no longer visible, to hear what is no longer audible, to say what is no longer to the point: in short, to adapt ourselves to a past and therefore imaginary situation, when we ought to be shaping our conduct in accordance with the reality which is present. This time the comic will take up its abode in the person himself; it is the person who will supply it with everything—matter and form, cause and opportunity.

Is it then surprising that the absent-minded individual—for this is the character we have just been describing—has usually fired the imagination of comic authors? When La Bruyere came across this particular type, he realised, on analysing it, that he had got hold of a recipe for the wholesale manufacture of comic effects. As a matter of fact he overdid it, and gave us far too lengthy and detailed a descripttion of Menalque, coming back to his subject, dwelling and expatiating on it beyond all bounds. The very facility of the subject fascinated him. Absentmindedness, indeed, is not perhaps the actual fountain-head of the comic, but surely it is contiguous to a certain stream of facts and fancies which flows straight from the fountain-head. It is situated, so to say, on one of the great natural watersheds of laughter.

Now, the effect of absentmindedness may gather strength in its turn. There is a general law, the first example of which we have just encountered, and which we will formulate in the following terms: when a certain comic effect has its origin in a certain cause, the more natural we regard the cause to be, the more comic shall we find the effect. Even now we laugh at absentmindedness when presented to us as a simple fact. Still more laughable will be the absentmindedness we have seen springing up and growing before our very eyes, with whose origin we are acquainted and whose life-history we can reconstruct. To choose a definite example: suppose a man has taken to reading nothing but romances of love and chivalry. Attracted and fascinated by his heroes, his thoughts and intentions gradually turn more and more towards them, till one fine day we find him walking among us like a somnambulist. His actions are distractions. But then his distractions can be traced back to a definite, positive cause. They are no longer cases of *absence* of mind, pure and simple; they find their explanation in the *presence* of the individual in quite definite, though imaginary, surroundings.

Doubtless a fall is always a fall, but it is one thing to tumble into a well because you were looking anywhere but in front of you, it is quite another thing to fall into it because you were intent upon a star. It was certainly a star at which Don Quixote was gazing. How profound is the comic element in the over-romantic, Utopian bent of mind! And yet, if you reintroduce the idea of absentmindedness, which acts as a go-between, you will see this profound comic element uniting with the most superficial type. Yes, indeed, these whimsical wild enthusiasts, these madmen who are yet so strangely reasonable, excite us to laughter by playing on the same chords within ourselves, by setting in motion the same inner mechanism, as does the victim of a practical joke or the passer-by who slips down in the street.

They, too, are runners who fall and simple souls who are being hoaxed—runners after the ideal who stumble over realities, child-like dreamers for whom life delights to lie in wait. But, above all, they are past-masters in absentmindedness, with this superiority over their fellows that their absentmindedness is systematic and organised around one central idea, and that their mishaps are also quite coherent, thanks to the inexorable logic which reality applies to the correction of dreams, so that they kindle in those around them, by a series of cumulative effects, a hilarity capable of unlimited expansion.

Now, let us go a little further. Might not certain vices have the same relation to character that the rigidity of a fixed idea has to intellect? Whether as a moral kink or a crooked twist given to the will, vice has often the appearance of a curvature of the soul. Doubtless there are vices into which the soul plunges deeply with all its pregnant potency, which it rejuvenates and drags along with it into a moving circle of reincarnations. Those are tragic vices. But the vice capable of making us comic is, on the contrary, that which is brought from without, like a ready-made frame into which we are to step. It lends us its own rigidity instead of borrowing from us our flexibility. We do not render it more complicated; on the contrary, it simplifies us.

Here, as we shall see later on in the concluding section of this study, lies the essential difference between comedy and drama. A drama, even when portraying passions or vices that bear a name, so completely incorporates them in the person that their names are forgotten, their general characteristics effaced, and we no longer think of them at all, but rather of the person in whom they are assimilated; hence, the title of a drama can seldom be anything else than a proper noun.

On the other hand, many comedies have a common noun as their title: *L'Avare*, *Le Joueur*, etc. Were you asked to think of a play capable of being called le Jaloux, for instance, you would find that *Sganarelle* or *George Dandin* would occur to your mind, but not *Othello*: *Le Jaloux* could only be the title of a comedy. The reason is that, however intimately vice, when comic, is associated with persons, it none the less retains its simple, independent existence, it remains the central character, present though invisible, to which the characters in flesh and blood on the stage are attached. At times it delights in dragging them down with its own weight and making them share in its tumbles. More frequently, however, it plays on them as on an instrument or pulls the strings as though they were puppets.

Look closely: you will find that the art of the comic poet consists in making us so well acquainted with the particular vice, in introducing us, the spectators, to such a degree of intimacy with it, that in the end we get hold of some of the strings of the marionette with which he is playing, and actually work them ourselves; this it is that explains part of the pleasure we feel. Here, too, it is really a kind of automatism that makes us laugh—an automatism, as we have already remarked, closely akin to mere absentmindedness. To realise this more fully, it need only be noted that a comic character is generally comic in proportion to his ignorance of himself. The comic person is unconscious. As though wearing the ring of Gyges¹ with reverse effect, he becomes invisible to himself while remaining visible to all the world.

A character in a tragedy will make no change in his conduct because he will know how it is judged by us; he may continue therein, even though fully conscious of what he is and feeling keenly the horror he inspires in us. But a defect that is ridiculous, as soon as it feels itself to be so, endeavours to modify itself, or at least to appear as though it did. Were Harpagon to see us laugh at his miserliness, I do not say that he would get rid of it, but he would either show it less or show it differently. Indeed, it is in this sense only that laughter "corrects men's manners." It makes us at once endeavour to appear what we ought to be, what some day we shall perhaps end in being.

It is unnecessary to carry this analysis any further. From the runner who falls to the simpleton who is hoaxed, from a state of being hoaxed to one of absentmindedness, from absentmindedness to wild enthuseasm, from wild enthusiasm to various distortions of character and will, we have followed the line of progress along which the comic becomes more and more deeply imbedded in the person, yet without ceasing, in its subtler manifestations, to recall to us some trace of what we noticed in its grosser forms, an effect of automatism and of inelasticity. Now we can obtain a first glimpse—a distant one, it is true, and still hazy and confused—of the laughable side of human nature and of the ordinary function of laughter.

What life and society require of each of us is a constantly alert attention that discerns the outlines of the present situation, together with a certain elasticity of mind and body to enable us to adapt ourselves in consequence. *Tension* and *elasticity* are two forces, mutually complementary, which life brings into play. If these two forces are lacking in the body to any considerable extent, we have sickness and infirmity and accidents of every kind. If they are lacking in the mind, we find every degree of mental deficiency, every variety of insanity. Finally, if they are lacking in the character, we have cases of the gravest inadaptability to social life, which are the sources of misery and at times the causes of crime.

---

¹A ring that made the wearer invisible.

Once these elements of inferiority that affect the serious side of existence are removed—and they tend to eliminate themselves in what has been called the struggle for life—the person can live, and that in common with other persons. But society asks for something more; it is not satisfied with simply living, it insists on living well. What it now has to dread is that each one of us, content with paying attention to what affects the essentials of life, will, so far as the rest is concerned, give way to the easy automatism of acquired habits.

Another thing it must fear is that the members of whom it is made up, instead of aiming after an increasingly delicate adjustment of wills which will fit more and more perfectly into one another, will confine themselves to respecting simply the fundamental conditions of this adjustment: a cut-and-dried agreement among the persons will not satisfy it, it insists on a constant striving after reciprocal adaptation. Society will therefore be suspicious of all *inelasticity* of character, of mind and even of body, because it is the possible sign of a slumbering activity as well as of an activity with separatist tendencies, that inclines to swerve from the common centre round which society gravitates: in short, because it is the sign of an eccentricity. And yet, society cannot intervene at this stage by material repression, since it is not affected in a material fashion.

It is confronted with something that makes it uneasy, but only as a symptom—scarcely a threat, at the very most a gesture. A gesture, therefore, will be its reply. Laughter must be something of this kind, a sort of *social gesture*. By the fear which it inspires, it restrains eccentricity, keeps constantly awake and in mutual contact certain activities of a secondary order which might retire into their shell and go to sleep, and, in short, softens down whatever the surface of the social body may retain of mechanical inelasticity. Laughter, then, does not belong to the province of esthetics alone, since unconsciously (and even immorally in many particular instances) it pursues a utilitarian aim of general improvement.

And yet there is something esthetic about it, since the comic comes into being just when society and the individual, freed from the worry of self-preservation, begin to regard themselves as works of art. In a word, if a circle be drawn round those actions and dispositions—implied in individual or social life—to which their natural consequences bring their own penalties, there remains outside this sphere of emotion and struggle—and within a neutral zone in which man simply exposes himself to man's curiosity—a certain rigidity of body, mind and character, that society would still like to get rid of in order to obtain from its members the greatest possible degree of elasticity and sociability. This rigidity is the comic, and laughter is its corrective.

Still, we must not accept this formula as a definition of the comic. It is suitable only for cases that are elementary, theoretical and perfect, in which the comic is free from all adulteration. Nor do we offer it, either, as an explanation. We prefer to make it, if you will, the leitmotiv which is to accompany all our explanations. We must ever keep it in mind, though without dwelling on it too much, somewhat as a skillful fencer must think of the discontinuous movements of the lesson whilst his body is given up to the continuity of the fencing-match. We will now endeavour to reconstruct the sequence of comic forms, taking up again the thread that leads from the horseplay of a clown up to the most refined effects of comedy, following this thread in its often unforeseen windings, halting at intervals to look around, and finally getting back, if possible, to the point at which the thread is dangling and where we shall perhaps find—since the comic oscillates between life and art—the general relation that art bears to life.

III

Let us begin at the simplest point. What is a comic physiognomy? Where does a ridiculous expression of the face come from? And what is, in this case, the distinction between the comic and the ugly? Thus stated, the question could scarcely be answered in any other than an arbitrary fashion. Simple though it may appear, it is, even now, too subtle to allow of a direct attack. We should have to begin with a definition of ugliness, and then discover what addition the comic makes to it; now, ugliness is not much easier to analyse than is beauty. However, we will employ an artifice which will often stand us in good stead. We will exaggerate the problem, so to speak, by magnifying the effect to the point of making the cause visible. Suppose, then, we intensify ugliness to the point of deformity, and study the transition from the deformed to the ridiculous.

Now, certain deformities undoubtedly possess over others the sorry privilege of causing some persons to laugh; some hunchbacks, for instance, will excite laughter. Without at this point entering into useless details, we will simply ask the reader to think of a number of deformities, and then to divide them into two groups: on the one hand, those which nature has directed towards the ridiculous; and on the other, those which absolutely diverge from it. No doubt he will hit upon the following law: A deformity that may become comic is a deformity that a normally built person, could successfully imitate.

Is it not, then, the case that the hunchback suggests the appearance of a person who holds himself badly? His back seems to have contracted an ugly stoop. By a kind of physical obstinacy, by rigidity, in a word, it persists in the habit it has contracted. Try to see with your eyes alone. Avoid reflection, and above all, do not reason. Abandon all your prepossessions; seek to recapture a fresh, direct and primitive impression. The vision you will reacquire will be one of this kind. You will have before you a man bent on cultivating a certain rigid attitude—whose body, if one may use the expression, is one vast grin.

Now, let us go back to the point we wished to clear up. By toning down a deformity that is laughable, we ought to obtain an ugliness that is comic. A laughable expression of the face, then, is one that will make us think of something rigid and, so to speak, coagulated, in the wonted mobility of the face. What we shall see will be an ingrained twitching or a fixed grimace. It may be objected that every habitual expression of the face, even when graceful and beautiful, gives us this same impression of something stereotyped? Here an important distinction must be drawn. When we speak of expressive beauty or even expressive ugliness, when we say that a face possesses expression, we mean expression that may be stable, but which we conjecture to be mobile. It maintains, in the midst of its fixity, a certain indecision in which are obscurely portrayed all possible shades of the state of mind it expresses, just as the sunny promise of a warm day manifests itself in the haze of a spring morning.

But a comic expression of the face is one that promises nothing more than it gives. It is a unique and permanent grimace. One would say that the person's whole moral life has crystallised into this particular cast of features. This is the reason why a face is all the more comic, the more nearly it suggests to us the idea of some simple mechanical action in which its personality would forever be absorbed. Some faces seem to be always engaged in weeping, others in laughing or whistling, others, again, in eternally blowing an imaginary trumpet, and these are the most comic faces of all. Here again is exemplified the law according to which the more natural the explanation of the cause, the more comic is the effect. Automatism, inelasticity, habit that has been contracted and maintained, are clearly the causes why a face makes us laugh. But this effect gains in intensity when we are able to connect these characteristics with some deep-seated cause, a certain fundamental absentmindedness, as though the soul had allowed itself to be fascinated and hypnotised by the materiality of a simple action.

We shall now understand the comic element in caricature. However regular we may imagine a face to be, however harmonious its lines and supple its movements, their adjustment is never altogether perfect: there will always be discoverable the signs of some impending bias, the vague suggestion of a possible grimace, in short some favourite distortion towards which nature seems to be particularly inclined. The art of the caricaturist consists in detecting this, at times, imperceptible tendency, and in rendering it visible to all eyes by magnifying it. He makes his models grimace, as they would do themselves if they went to the end of their tether. Beneath the skin-deep harmony of form, he divines the deep-seated recalcitrance of matter. He realises disproportions and deformations which must have existed in nature as mere inclinations, but which have not succeeded in coming to a head, being held in check by a higher force. His art, which has a touch of the diabolical, raises up the demon who had been overthrown by the angel.

Certainly, it is an art that exaggerates, and yet the definition would be very far from complete were exaggeration alone alleged to be its aim and object, for there exist caricatures that are more lifelike than portraits, caricatures in which the exaggeration is scarcely noticeable, whilst, inversely, it is quite possible to exaggerate to excess without obtaining a real caricature. For exaggeration to be comic, it must not appear as an aim, but rather as a means that the artist is using in order to make manifest to our eyes the distortions which he sees in embryo. It is this process of distortion that is of moment and interest. And that is precisely why we shall look for it even in those elements of the face that are incapable of movement, in the curve of a nose or the shape of an ear. For, in our eyes, form is always the outline of a movement. The caricaturist who alters the size of a nose, but respects its ground plan, lengthening it, for instance, in the very direction in which it was being lengthened by nature, is really making the nose indulge in a grin.

Henceforth we shall always look upon the original as having determined to lengthen itself and start grinning. In this sense, one might say that Nature herself often meets with the successes of a caricaturist. In the movement through which she has slit that mouth, curtailed that chin and bulged out that cheek, she would appear to have succeeded in completing the intended grimace, thus outwitting the restraining supervision of a more reasonable force. In that case, the face we laugh at is, so to speak, its own caricature.

To sum up, whatever be the doctrine to which our reason assents, our imagination has a very clear-cut philosophy of its own: in every human form it sees the effort of a soul which is shaping matter, a soul which is infinitely supple and perpetually in motion, subject to no law of gravitation, for it is not the earth that attracts it. This soul imparts a portion of its winged lightness to the body it animates: the immateriality which thus passes into matter is what is called gracefulness.

Matter, however, is obstinate and resists. It draws to itself the ever-alert activity of this higher principle, would fain convert it to its own inertia and cause it to revert to mere automatism. It would fain immobilise the intelligently varied movements of the body in stupidly contracted grooves, stereotype in permanent grimaces the fleeting expressions of the face, in short imprint on the whole person such an attitude as to make it appear immersed and absorbed in the materiality of some mechanical occupation instead of ceaselessly renewing its vitality by keeping in touch with a living ideal. Where matter thus succeeds in dulling the outward life of the soul, in petrifying its movements and thwarting its gracefulness, it achieves, at the expense of the body, an effect that is comic.

If, then, at this point we wished to define the comic by comparing it with its contrary, we should have to contrast it with gracefulness even more than with beauty. It partakes rather of the unsprightly than of the unsightly, of *rigidness* rather than of *ugliness*.

IV

We will now pass from the comic element in *forms* to that in *gestures* and *movements*. Let us at once state the law which seems to govern all the phenomena of this kind. It may indeed be deduced without any difficulty from the considerations stated above. *The attitudes, gestures and movements of the human body are laughable in exact proportion as that body reminds us of a mere machine.*

There is no need to follow this law through the details of its immediate applications, which are innumerable. To verify it directly, it would be sufficient to study closely the work of comic artists, eliminating entirely the element of caricature, and omitting that portion of the comic which is not inherent in the drawing itself. For, obviously, the comic element in a drawing is often a borrowed one, for which the text supplies all the stock-in-trade. I mean that the artist may be his own understudy in the shape of a satirist, or even a playwright, and that then we laugh far less at the drawings themselves than at the satire or comic incident they represent. But if we devote our whole attention to the drawing with the firm resolve to think of nothing else, we shall probably find that it is generally comic in proportion to the clearness, as well as the subtleness, with which it enables us to see a man as a jointed puppet.

The suggestion must be a clear one, for inside the person we must distinctly perceive, as though through a glass, a set-up mechanism. But the suggestion must also be a subtle one, for the general appearance of the person, whose every limb has been made rigid as a machine, must continue to give us the impression of a living being. The more exactly these two images, that of a person and that of a machine, fit into each other, the more striking is the comic effect, and the more consummate the art of the draughtsman. The originality of a comic artist is thus expressed in the special kind of life he imparts to a mere puppet.

We will, however, leave on one side the immediate application of the principle, and at this point insist only on the more remote consequences. The illusion of a machine working in the inside of the person is a thing that only crops up amid a host of amusing effects; but for the most part it is a fleeting glimpse, that is immediately lost in the laughter it provokes. To render it permanent, analysis and reflection must be called into play.

In a public speaker, for instance, we find that gesture vies with speech. Jealous of the latter, gesture closely dogs the speaker's thought, demanding also to act as interpreter. Well and good; but then it must pledge itself to follow thought through all the phases of its development. An idea is something that grows, buds, blossoms and ripens from the beginning to the end of a speech. It never halts, never repeats itself. It must be changing every moment, for to cease to change would be to cease to live. Then let gesture display a like animation! Let it accept the fundamental law of life, which is the complete negation of repetition! But I find that a certain movement of head or arm, a movement always the same, seems to return at regular intervals. If I notice it and it succeeds in diverting my attention, if I wait for it to occur and it occurs when I expect it, then involuntarily I laugh. Why? Because I now have before me a machine that works automatically. This is no longer life, it is automatism established in life and imitating it. It belongs to the comic.

This is also the reason why gestures, at which we never dreamt of laughing, become laughable when imitated by another individual. The most elaborate explanations have been offered for this extremely simple fact. A little reflection, however, will show that our mental state is ever changing, and that if our gestures faithfully followed these inner movements, if they were as fully alive as we, they would never repeat themselves, and so would keep imitation at bay. We begin, then, to become imitable only when we cease to be ourselves. I mean our gestures can only be imitated in their mechanical uniformity, and therefore exactly in what is alien to our living personality. To imitate any one is to bring out the element of automatism he has allowed to creep into his person. And as this is the very essence of the ludicrous, it is no wonder that imitation gives rise to laughter.

Still, if the imitation of gestures is intrinsically laughable, it will become even more so when it busies itself in deflecting them, though without altering their form, towards some mechanical occupation, such as sawing wood, striking on an anvil, or tugging away at an imaginary bell-rope. Not that vulgarity is the essence of the comic—although certainly it is to some extent an ingredient—but rather that the incriminated gesture seems more frankly mechanical when it can be connected with a simple operation, as though it were intentionally mechanical. To suggest this mechanical interpretation ought to be one of the favourite devices of parody. We have reached this result through deduction, but I imagine clowns have long had an intuition of the fact.

This seems to me the solution of the little riddle propounded by Pascal in one passage of his *Thoughts*: "Two faces that are alike, although neither of them excites laughter by itself, make us laugh when together, on account of their likeness." It might just as well be said: "The gestures of a public speaker, no one of which is laughable by itself, excite laughter by their repetition." The truth is that a really living life should never repeat itself. Wherever there is repetition or complete similarity, we always suspect some mechanism at work behind the living. Analyse the impression you get from two faces that are too much alike, and you will find that you are thinking of two copies cast in the same mould, or two impressions of the same seal, or two reproductions of the same negative,-in a word, of some manufacturing process or other. This deflection of life towards the mechanical is here the real cause of laughter.

And laughter will be more pronounced still, if we find on the stage not merely two characters, as in the example from Pascal, but several, nay, as great a number as possible, the image of one another, who come and go, dance and gesticulate together, simultaneously striking the same attitudes and tossing their arms about in the same manner. This time, we distinctly think of marionettes. Invisible threads seem to us to be joining arms to arms, legs to legs, each muscle in one face to its fellow-muscle in the other: by reason of the absolute uniformity which prevails, the very litheness of the bodies seems to stiffen as we gaze, and the actors themselves seem transformed into automata. Such, at least, appears to be the artifice underlying this somewhat obvious form of amusement. I daresay the performers have never read Pascal, but what they do is merely to realise to the full the suggestions contained in Pascal's words. If, as is undoubtedly the case, laughter is caused in the second instance by the hallucination of a mechanical effect, it must already have been so, though in more subtle fashion, in the first.

Continuing along this path, we dimly perceive the increasingly important and far-reaching consequences of the law we have just stated. We faintly catch still more fugitive glimpses of mechanical effects, glimpses suggested by man's complex actions, no longer merely by his gestures. We instinctively feel that the usual devices of comedy, the periodical repetition of a word or a scene, the systematic inversion of the parts, the geometrical development of a farcical misunderstanding, and many other stage contrivances, must derive their comic force from the same source—the art of the playwright probably consisting in setting before us an obvious clockwork arrangement of human events, while carefully preserving an outward aspect of probability and thereby retaining something of the suppleness of life. But we must not forestall results which will be duly disclosed in the course of our analysis.

V

Before going further, let us halt a moment and glance around. As we hinted at the outset of this study, it would be idle to attempt to derive every comic effect from one simple formula. The formula exists well enough in a certain sense, but its development does not follow a straightforward course. What I mean is that the process of deduction ought from time to time to stop and study certain culminating effects, and that these effects each appear as models round which new effects resembling them take their places in a circle. These latter are not deductions from the formula, but are comic through their relationship with those that are.

To quote Pascal again, I see no objection, at this stage, to defining the process by the curve which that geometrician studied under the name of roulette or cycloid—the curve traced by a point in the circumference of a wheel when the carriage is advancing in a straight line: this point turns like the wheel, though it advances like the carriage. Or else we might think of an immense avenue such as are to be seen in the forest of Fontainebleau, with crosses at intervals to indicate the cross-ways: at each of these we shall walk round the cross, explore for a while the paths that open out before us, and then return to our original course. Now, we have just reached one of these mental crossways. Something mechanical encrusted on the living, will represent a cross at which we must halt, a central image from which the imagination branches off in different directions. What are these directions? There appear to be three main ones. We will follow them one after the other, and then continue our onward course.

1. In the first place, this view of the mechanical and the living dovetailed into each other makes us incline towards the vaguer image of *some rigidity or other* applied to the mobility of life, in an awkward attempt to follow its lines and counterfeit its suppleness. Here we perceive how easy it is for a garment to become ridiculous. It might almost be said that every fashion is laughable in some respect. Only, when we are dealing with the fashion of the day, we are so accustomed to it that the garment seems, in our mind, to form one with the individual wearing it. We do not separate them in imagination. The idea no longer occurs to us to contrast the inert rigidity of the covering with the living suppleness of the object covered: consequently, the comic here remains in a latent condition.

It will only succeed in emerging when the natural incompatibility is so deep-seated between the covering and the covered that even an immemorial association fails to cement this union: a case in point is our head and top hat. Suppose, however, some eccentric individual dresses himself in the fashion of former times: our attention is immediately drawn to the clothes themselves, we absolutely distinguish them from the individual, we say that the latter *is disguising himself*—as though every article of clothing were not a disguise!—and the laughable aspect of fashion comes out of the shadow into the light.

Here we are beginning to catch a faint glimpse of the highly intricate difficulties raised by this problem of the comic. One of the reasons that must have given rise to many erroneous or unsatisfactory theories of laughter is that many things are comic de jure without being comic de facto, the continuity of custom having deadened within them the comic quality. A sudden dissolution of continuity is needed, a break with fashion, for this quality to revive. Hence the impression that this dissolution of continuity is the parent of the comic, whereas all it does is to bring it to our notice. Hence, again, the explanation of laughter by surprise, contrast, etc., definitions which would equally apply to a host of cases in which we have no inclination whatever to laugh.

The truth of the matter is far from being so simple. But to return to our idea of disguise, which, as we have just shown, has been entrusted with the special mandate of arousing laughter. It will not be out of place to investigate the uses it makes of this power.

Why do we laugh at a head of hair which has changed from dark to blond? What is there comic about a rubicund nose? And why does one laugh at a negro? The question would appear to be an embarrassing one, for it has been asked by successive psychologists such as Hecker, Kraepelin and Lipps, and all have given different replies. And yet I rather fancy the correct answer was suggested to me one day in the street by an ordinary cabby, who applied the expression "unwashed" to the negro fare he was driving. Unwashed! Does not this mean that a black face, in our imagination, is one daubed over with ink or soot? If so, then a red nose can only be one which has received a coating of vermilion. And so we see that the notion of disguise has passed on something of its comic quality to instances in which there is actually no disguise, though there might be.

In the former set of examples, although his usual dress was distinct from the individual, it appeared in our mind to form one with him, because we had become accustomed to the sight. In the latter, although the black or red colour is indeed inherent in the skin, we look upon it as artificially laid on, because it surprises us.

But here we meet with a fresh crop of difficulties in the theory of the comic. Such a proposition as the following: "My usual dress forms part of my body" is absurd in the eyes of reason. Yet imagination looks upon it as true. "A red nose is a painted nose," "A negro is a white man in disguise," are also absurd to the reason which rationalises; but they are gospel truths to pure imagination. So there is a logic of the imagination which is not the logic of reason, one which at times is even opposed to the latter—with which, however, philosophy must reckon, not only in the study of the comic, but in every other investigation of the same kind.

It is something like the logic of dreams, though of dreams that have not been left to the whim of individual fancy, being the dreams dreamt by the whole of society. In order to reconstruct this hidden logic, a special kind of effort is needed, by which the outer crust of carefully stratified judgments and firmly established ideas will be lifted, and we shall behold in the depths of our mind, like a sheet of subterranean water, the flow of an unbroken stream of images which pass from one into another.

This interpenetration of images does not come about by chance. It obeys laws, or rather habits, which hold the same relation to imagination that logic does to thought.

Let us then follow this logic of the imagination in the special case in hand. A man in disguise is comic. A man we regard as disguised is also comic. So, by analogy, any disguise is seen to become comic, not only that of a man, but that of society also, and even the disguise of nature.

Let us start with nature. You laugh at a dog that is half-clipped, at a bed of artificially coloured flowers, at a wood in which the trees are plastered over with election addresses, etc. Look for the reason, and you will see that you are once more thinking of a masquerade. Here, however, the comic element is very faint; it is too far from its source. If you wish to strengthen it, you must go back to the source itself and contrast the derived image, that of a masquerade, with the original one, which, be it remembered, was that of a mechanical tampering with life.

In "a nature that is mechanically tampered with" we possess a thoroughly comic theme, on which fancy will be able to play ever so many variations with the certainty of successfully provoking the heartiest hilarity. You may call to mind that amusing passage in *Tartarin Sur Les Alpes*, in which Bompard makes Tartarin—and therefore also the reader to some slight extent—accept the idea of a Switzerland choke-full of machinery like the basement of the opera, and run by a company which maintains a series of waterfalls, glaciers and artificial crevasses.

The same theme reappears, though transposed in quite another key, in the *Novel Notes* of the English humorist, Jerome K. Jerome. An elderly Lady Bountiful, who does not want her deeds of charity to take up too much of her time, provides homes within easy hail of her mansion for the conversion of atheists who have been specially manufactured for her, so to speak, and for a number of honest folk who have been made into drunkards so that she may cure them of their failing, etc. There are comic phrases in which this theme is audible, like a distant echo, coupled with an ingenuousness, whether sincere or affected, which acts as accompaniment. Take, as an instance, the remark made by a lady whom Cassini, the astronomer, had invited to see an eclipse of the moon. Arriving too late, she said, "M. de Cassini, I know, will have the goodness to begin it all over again, to please me." Or, take again the exclamation of one of Gondiinet's characters on arriving in a town and learning that there is an extinct volcano in the neighbourhood, "They had a volcano, and they have let it go out!"

Let us go on to society. As we are both in and of it, we cannot help treating it as a living being. Any image, then, suggestive of the notion of a society disguising itself, or of a social masquerade, so to speak, will be laughable. Now, such a notion is formed when we perceive anything inert or stereotyped, or simply ready-made, on the surface of living society. There we have rigidity over again, clashing with the inner suppleness of life. The ceremonial side of social life must, therefore, always include a latent comic element, which is only waiting for an opportunity to burst into full view.

It might be said that ceremonies are to the social body what clothing is to the individual body: they owe their seriousness to the fact that they are identified, in our minds, with the serious object with which custom associates them, and when we isolate them in imagination, they forthwith lose their seriousness. For any ceremony, then, to become comic, it is enough that our attention be fixed on the ceremonial element in it, and that we neglect its matter, as philosophers say, and think only of its form. Everyone knows how easily the comic spirit exercises its ingenuity on social actions of a stereotyped nature, from an ordinary prize-distribution to the solemn sitting of a court of justice. Any form or formula is a ready-made frame into which the comic element may be fitted.

Here, again, the comic will be emphasised by bringing it nearer to its source. From the idea of travesty, a derived one, we must go back to the original idea, that of a mechanism superposed upon life. Already, the stiff and starched formality of any ceremonial suggests to us an image of this kind. For, as soon as we forget the serious object of a solemnity or a ceremony, those taking part in it give us the impression of puppets in motion. Their mobility seems to adopt as a model the immobility of a formula. It becomes automatism.

But complete automatism is only reached in the official, for instance, who performs his duty like a mere machine, or again in the unconsciousness that marks an administrative regulation working with inexorable fatality, and setting itself up for a law of nature. Quite by chance, when reading the newspaper, I came across a specimen of the comic of this type. Twenty years ago, a large steamer was wrecked off the coast at Dieppe. With considerable difficulty some of the passengers were rescued in a boat. A few custom-house officers, who had courageously rushed to their assistance, began by asking them "if they had anything to declare."

We find something similar, though the idea is a more subtle one, in the remark of an M.P. when questioning the Home Secretary on the morrow of a terrible murder which took place in a railway carriage: "The assassin, after despatching his victim, must have got out the wrong side of the train, thereby infringing the Company's rules."

A mechanical element introduced into nature and an automatic regulation of society, such, then, are the two types of laughable effects at which we have arrived. It remains for us, in conclusion, to combine them and see what the result will be.

The result of the combination will evidently be a human regulation of affairs usurping the place of the laws of nature. We may call to mind the answer Sganarelle gave Geronte when the latter remarked that the heart was on the left side and the liver on the right: "Yes, it was so formerly, but we have altered all that; now, we practise medicine in quite a new way." We may also recall the consultation between M. de Pourceaugnac's two doctors: "The arguments you have used are so erudite and elegant that it is impossible for the patient not to be hypochondriacally melancholic; or, even if he were not, he must surely become so because of the elegance of the things you have said and the accuracy of your reasoning."

We might multiply examples, for all we need do would be to call up Moliere's doctors, one after the other. However far, moreover, comic fancy may seem to go, reality at times undertakes to improve upon it. It was suggested to a contemporary philosopher, an out-and-out arguer, that his arguments, though irreproachable in their deductions, had experience against them. He put an end to the discussion by merely remarking, "Experience is in the wrong." The truth is, this idea of regulating life as a matter of business routine is more widespread than might be imagined; it is natural in its way, although we have just obtained it by an artificial process of reconstruction. One might say that it gives us the very quintessence of pedantry, which, at bottom, is nothing else than art pretending to outdo nature.

To sum up, then, we have one and the same effect, which assumes ever subtler forms as it passes from the idea of an artificial *mechanisa-*

tion of the human body, if such an expression is permissible, to that of any substitution whatsoever of the artificial for the natural. A less and less rigorous logic, that more and more resembles the logic of dreamland, transfers the same relationship into higher and higher spheres, between increasingly immaterial terms, till in the end we find a mere administrative enactment occupying the same relation to a natural or moral law that a ready-made garment, for instance, does to the living body. We have now gone right to the end of the first of the three directions we had to follow. Let us turn to the second and see where it will lead us.

2. Our starting-point is again "something mechanical encrusted upon the living." Where did the comic come from in this case? It came from the fact that the living body became rigid, like a machine. Accordingly, it seemed to us that the living body ought to be the perfection of suppleness, the ever-alert activity of a principle always at work. But this activity would really belong to the soul rather than to the body. It would be the very flame of life, kindled within us by a higher principle and perceived through the body, as if through a glass.

When we see only gracefulness and suppleness in the living body, it is because we disregard in it the elements of weight, of resistance, and, in a word, of matter; we forget its materiality and think only of its vitality, a vitality which we regard as derived from the very principle of intellectual and moral life. Let us suppose, however, that our attention is drawn to this material side of the body; that, so far from sharing in the lightness and subtlety of the principle with which it is animated, the body is no more in our eyes than a heavy and cumbersome vesture, a kind of irksome ballast which holds down to earth a soul eager to rise aloft. Then the body will become to the soul what, as we have just seen, the garment was to the body itself-inert matter dumped down upon living energy.

The impression of the comic will be produced as soon as we have a clear apprehension of this putting the one on the other. And we shall experience it most strongly when we are shown the soul *tantalised* by the needs of the body: on the one hand, the moral personality with its intelligently varied energy, and, on the other, the stupidly monotonous body, perpetually obstructing everything with its machine-like obstinacy. The more paltry and uniformly repeated these claims of the body, the more striking will be the result. But that is only a matter of degree, and the general law of these phenomena may be formulated as follows: *Any incident is comic that calls our attention to the physical in a person when it is the moral side that is concerned.*

Why do we laugh at a public speaker who sneezes just at the most pathetic moment of his speech? Where lies the comic element in this sentence, taken from a funeral speech and quoted by a German philosopher: "He was virtuous and plump"? It lies in the fact that our attention is suddenly recalled from the soul to the body. Similar instances abound in daily life, but if you do not care to take the trouble to look for them, you have only to open at random a volume of Labiche, and you will be almost certain to light upon an effect of this kind. Now, we have a speaker whose most eloquent sentences are cut short by the twinges of a bad tooth; now, one of the characters who never begins to speak without stopping in the middle to complain of his shoes being too small, or his belt too tight, etc. *A person embarrassed by his body* is the image suggested to us in all these examples. The reason that excessive stoutness is laughable is probably because it calls up an image of the same kind. I almost think that this too is what sometime makes bashfulness somewhat ridiculous. The bashful man rather gives the impression of a person embarrassed by his body, looking round for some convenient cloak-room in which to deposit it.

This is just why the tragic poet is so careful to avoid anything calculated to attract attention to the material side of his heroes. No sooner does anxiety about the body manifest itself than the intrusion of a comic element is to be feared. On this account, the hero in a tragedy does not eat or drink or warm himself. He does not even sit down any more than can be helped. To sit down in the middle of a fine speech would imply that you remembered you had a body. Napoleon, who was a psychologist when he wished to be so, had noticed that the transition from tragedy to comedy is effected simply by sitting down. In the *Journal inedit* of Baron Gourgaud—when speaking of an interview with the Queen of Prussia after the battle of Jena—he expresses himself in the following terms: "She received me in tragic fashion like Chimene: Justice! Sire, Justice! Magdeburg! Thus she continued in a way most embarrassing to me. Finally, to make her change her style, I requested her to take a seat. This is the best method for cutting short a tragic scene, for as soon as you are seated it all becomes comedy."

Let us now give a wider scope to this image of *the body taking precedence of the soul.* We shall obtain something more general—*the manner seeking to outdo the matter, the letter aiming at ousting the spirit.* Is it not perchance this idea that comedy is trying to suggest to us when holding up a profession to ridicule? It makes the lawyer, the magistrate and the doctor speak as though health and justice were of little moment—the main point being that we should have lawyers, magistrates and doctors, and that all outward formalities pertaining to these professions should be scrupulously respected. And so we find the means substituted for the end, the manner for the matter; no longer is it the profession that is made for the public, but rather the public for the profession.

Constant attention to form and the mechanical application of rules here bring about a kind of professional automatism analogous to that imposed upon the soul by the habits of the body, and equally laughable. Numerous are the examples of this on the stage. Without entering into details of the variations executed on this theme, let us quote two or three passages in which the theme itself is set forth in all its simplicity. "You are only bound to treat people according to form," says Doctor Diafoirus in the *Malade imaginaire*. Again, says Doctor Bahis, in *L'Amour medecin*: "It is better to die through following the rules than to recover through violating them." In the same play, Desfonandres had previously said: "We must always observe the formalities of professional etiquette, whatever may happen." And the reason is given by Tomes, his colleague: "A dead man is but a dead man, but the non-observance of a formality causes a notable prejudice to the whole faculty." Brid'oison's words, though. embodying a rather different idea, are none the less significant: "F-form, mind you, f-form. A man laughs at a judge in a morning coat, and yet he would quake with dread at the mere sight of an attorney in his gown. F-form, all a matter of f-form."

Here we have the first illustration of a law which will appear with increasing distinctness as we proceed with our task. When a musician strikes a note on an instrument, other notes start up of themselves, not so loud as the first, yet connected with it by certain definite relations, which coalesce with it and determine its quality. These are what are called in physics the overtones of the fundamental note. It would seem that comic fancy, even in its most far-fetched inventions, obeys a similar law. For instance, consider this comic note: appearance seeking to triumph over reality. If our analysis is correct, this note must have as its overtones the body tantalising the mind, the body taking precedence of the mind. No sooner, then, does the comic poet strike the first note than he will add the second on to it, involuntarily and instinctively. In other words, *he will duplicate what is ridiculous professsionally with something that is ridiculous physically*.

When Brid'oison the judge comes stammering on to the stage, is he not actually preparing us, by this very stammering, to understand the phenomenon of intellectual ossification we are about to witness? What bond of secret relationship can there be between the physical defect and the moral infirmity? It is difficult to say; yet we feel that the relationship is there, though we cannot express it in words. Perhaps the situation required that this judging machine should also appear before us as a talking machine. However it may be, no other overtone could more perfectly have completed the fundamental note.

When Moliere introduces to us the two ridiculous doctors, Bahis and Macroton, in *L'Amour medecin*, he makes one of them speak very slowly, as though scanning his words syllable by syllable, whilst the other stutters. We find the same contrast between the two lawyers in *Monsieur de Pourceaugnac*. In the rhythm of speech is generally to be found the physical peculiarity that is destined to complete the element of professional ridicule. When the author has failed to suggest a defect of this kind, it is seldom the case that the actor does not instinctively invent one.

Consequently, there is a natural relationship, which we equally naturally recognise, between the two images we have been comparing with each other, the mind crystallising in certain grooves, and the body losing its elasticity through the influence of certain defects. Whether or not our attention be diverted from the matter to the manner, or from the moral to the physical, in both cases the same sort of impression is conveyed to our imagination; in both, then, the comic is of the same kind. Here, once more, it has been our aim to follow the natural trend of the movement of the imagination. This trend or direction, it may be remembered, was the second of those offered to us, starting from a central image. A third and final path remains unexplored, along which we will now proceed.

3. Let us then return, for the last time, to our central image: something mechanical encrusted on something living. Here, the living being under discussion was a human being, a person. A mechanical arrangement, on the other hand, is a thing. What, therefore, incited laughter was the momentary transformation of a person into a thing, if one considers the image from this standpoint. Let us then pass from the exact idea of a machine to the vaguer one of a thing in general. We shall have a fresh series of laughable images which will be obtained by taking a blurred impression, so to speak, of the outlines of the former

and will bring us to this new law: *We laugh every time a person gives us the impression of being a thing.*

We laugh at Sancho Panza tumbled into a bed-quilt and tossed into the air like a football. We laugh at Baron Munchausen turned into a cannon-ball and travelling through space. But certain tricks of circus clowns might afford a still more precise exemplification of the same law. True, we should have to eliminate the jokes, mere interpolations by the clown into his main theme, and keep in mind only the theme itself, that is to say, the divers attitudes, capers and movements which form the strictly "clownish" element in the clown's art.

On two occasions only have I been able to observe this style of the comic in its unadulterated state, and in both I received the same impression. The first time, the clowns came and went, collided, fell and jumped up again in a uniformly accelerated rhythm, visibly intent upon affecting a *crescendo*. And it was more and more to the jumping up again, the *rebound*, that the attention of the public was attracted. Gradually, one lost sight of the fact that they were men of flesh and blood like ourselves; one began to think of bundles of all sorts, falling and knocking against each other. Then the vision assumed a more definite aspect. The forms grew rounder, the bodies rolled together and seemed to pick themselves up like balls. Then at last appeared the image towards which the whole of this scene had doubtless been unconsciously evolving-large rubber balls hurled against one another in every direction.

The second scene, though even coarser than the first, was no less instructive. There came on the stage two men, each with an enormous head, bald as a billiard ball. In their hands they carried large sticks which each, in turn, brought down on to the other's cranium. Here, again, a certain gradation was observable. After each blow, the bodies seemed to grow heavier and more unyielding, overpowered by an increasing degree of rigidity. Then came the return blow, in each case heavier and more resounding than the last, coming, too, after a longer interval. The skulls gave forth a formidable ring throughout the silent house. At last the two bodies, each quite rigid and as straight as an arrow, slowly bent over towards each other, the sticks came crashing down for the last time on to the two heads with a thud as of enormous mallets falling upon oaken beams, and the pair lay prone upon the ground. At that instant appeared in all its vividness the suggestion that the two artists had gradually driven into the imagination of the spectators: "We are about to become . . . we have now become solid wooden dummies."

A kind of dim, vague instinct may enable even an uncultured mind to get an inkling here of the subtler results of psychological science. We know that it is possible to call up hallucinatory visions in a hypnotised subject by simple suggestion. If he be told that a bird is perched on his hand, he will see the bird and watch it fly away. The idea suggested, however, is far from being always accepted with like docility. Not infrequently, the mesmeriser only succeeds in getting an idea into his subject's head by slow degrees through a carefully graduated series of hints. He will then start with objects really perceived by the subject, and will endeavour to make the perception of these objects more and more indefinite; then, step by step, he will bring out of this state of mental chaos the precise form of the object of which he wishes to create an hallucination. Something of the kind happens to many people when dropping off to sleep; they see those coloured, fluid, shapeless masses, which occupy the field of vision, insensibly solidifying into distinct objects.

Consequently, the gradual passing from the dim and vague to the clear and distinct is the method of suggestion par excellence. I fancy it might be found to be at the root of a good many comic suggestions, especially in the coarser forms of the comic, in which the transformation of a person into a thing seems to be taking place before our eyes. But there are other and more subtle methods in use, among poets, for instance, which perhaps unconsciously lead to the same end. By a certain arrangement of rhythm, rhyme and assonance, it is possible to lull the imagination, to rock it to and fro between like and like with a regular see-saw motion, and thus prepare it submissively to accept the vision suggested. Listen to these few lines of Regnard, and see whether something like the fleeting image of a *doll* does not cross the field of your imagination: "Further, he owes to many an honest wight the sum two thousand pounds, one farthing, for having on his simple word of honour sans intermission for an entire year clothed him, conveyed him, warmed him, shod him, gloved him, fed him and shaved him, quenched his thirst and borne him."

Is not something of the same kind found in the following sally of Figaro's (though here an attempt is perhaps made to suggest the image of an animal rather than that of a thing): "What sort of man is here?—He is a handsome, stout, short, youthful old gentleman, iron-grey, an artful knave, clean shaved, clean 'used up,' who spies and pries and growls and groans all in the same breath."

Now, between these coarse scenes and these subtle suggestions there is room for a countless number of amusing effects, for all those that can be obtained by talking about persons as one would do about mere things. We will only select one or two instances from the plays of Labiche, in which they are legion.

Just as M. Perrichon is getting into the railway carriage, he makes certain of not forgetting any of his parcels: "Four, five, six, my wife seven, my daughter eight, and myself nine." In another play, a fond father is boasting of his daughter's learning in the following terms: "She will tell you, without faltering, all the kings of France that have occurred." This phrase, "that have occurred," though not exactly transforming the kings into mere things, likens them, all the same, to events of an impersonal nature.

As regards this latter example, note that it is unnecessary to complete the identification of the person with the thing in order to ensure a comic effect. It is sufficient for us to start in this direction by feigning, for instance, to confuse the person with the function he exercises. I will only quote a sentence spoken by a village mayor in one of About's novels: "The prefect, who has always shown us the same kindness, though he has been changed several times since 1847."

All these witticisms are constructed on the same model. We might make up any number of them, when once we are in possession of the recipe. But the art of the story-teller or the playwright does not merely consist in concocting jokes. The difficulty lies in giving to a joke its power of suggestion, i.e., in making it acceptable. And we only do accept it either because it seems to be the natural product of a particular state of mind or because it is in keeping with the circumstances of the case. For instance, we are aware that M. Perrichon is greatly excited on the occasion of his first railway journey. The expression "to occur" is one that must have cropped up a good many times in the lessons repeated by the girl before her father; it makes us think of such a repetition. Lastly, admiration of the governmental machine might, at a pinch, be extended to the point of making us believe that no change takes place in the prefect when he changes his name, and that the function gets carried on independently of the functionary.

We have now reached a point very far from the original cause of laughter. Many a comic form, that cannot be explained by itself, can indeed only be understood from its resemblance to another, which only makes us laugh by reason of its relationship with a third, and so on indefinitely, so that psychological analysis, however luminous and searching, will go astray unless it holds the thread along which the comic impression has travelled from one end of the series to the other. Where does this progressive continuity come from? What can be the driving force, the strange impulse which causes the comic to glide thus from image to image, farther and farther away from the starting-point, until it is broken up and lost in infinitely remote analogies? But what is that force which divides and subdivides the branches of a tree into smaller boughs and its roots into radicles?

An inexorable law dooms every living energy, during the brief interval allotted to it in time, to cover the widest possible extent in space. Now, comic fancy is indeed a living energy, a strange plant that has nourished on the stony portions of the social soil, until such time as culture should allow it to vie with the most refined products of art. True, we are far from great art in the examples of the comic we have just been reviewing. But we shall draw nearer to it, though without attaining to it completely, in the following chapter. Below art, we find artifice, and it is this zone of artifice, midway between nature and art, that we are now about to enter. We are going to deal with the comic playwright and the wit.

Chapter Two
The Comic Element in Situations and the Comic Element in Words

I

We have studied the comic element in forms, in attitudes, and in movements generally; now let us look for it in actions and in situations. We encounter, indeed, this kind of comic readily enough in everyday life. It is not here, however, that it best lends itself to analysis. Assuming that the stage is both a magnified and a simplified view of life, we shall find that comedy is capable of furnishing us with more information than real life on this particular part of our subject. Perhaps we ought even to carry simplification still farther, and, going back to our earliest recollections, try to discover, in the games that amused us as children, the first faint traces of the combinations that make us laugh as grown-up persons.

We are too apt to speak of our feelings of pleasure and of pain as though full grown at birth, as though each one of them had not a history of its own. Above all, we are too apt to ignore the childish element, so to speak, latent in most of our joyful emotions. And yet, how many of our present pleasures, were we to examine them closely, would shrink into nothing more than memories of past ones! What would there be left of many of our emotions were we to reduce them to the exact quantum of pure feeling they contain, by subtracting from them all that is merely reminiscence?

Indeed, it seems possible that, after a certain age, we become impervious to all fresh or novel forms of joy, and the sweetest pleasures of the middle-aged man are perhaps nothing more than a revival of the sensations of childhood, a balmy zephyr wafted in fainter and fainter breaths by a past that is ever receding. In any case, whatever reply we give to this broad question, one thing is certain: there can be no break in continuity between the child's delight in games and that of the grown-up person.

Now, comedy is a game, a game that imitates life. And since, in the games of the child when working its dolls and puppets, many of the movements are produced by strings, ought we not to find those same strings, somewhat frayed by wear, reappearing as the threads that knot together the situations in a comedy? Let us, then, start with the games of a child, and follow the imperceptible process by which, as he grows himself, he makes his puppets grow, inspires them with life, and finally brings them to an ambiguous state in which, without ceasing to be puppets, they have yet become human beings. We thus obtain characters of a comedy type. And upon them we can test the truth of the law of which all our preceding analyses gave an inkling, a law in accordance with which we will define all broadly comic situations in general. *Any arrangement of acts and events is comic which gives us, in a single combination, the illusion of life and the distinct impression of a mechanical arrangement.*

1. *The Jack-in-the-box.* — As children we have all played with the little man who springs out of his box. You squeeze him flat, he jumps up again. Push him lower, and he shoots up still higher. Crush him down beneath the lid, and often he will send everything flying. It is hard to tell whether or no the toy itself is very ancient, but the kind of amusement it affords belongs to all time. It is a struggle between two stubborn elements, one of which, being simply mechanical, generally ends by giving in to the other, which treats it as a plaything. A cat playing with a mouse, which from time to time she releases like a spring, only to pull it up short with a stroke of her paw, indulges in the same kind of amusement.

We will now pass on to the theatre, beginning with a Punch and Judy show. No sooner does the policeman put in an appearance on the stage than, naturally enough, he receives a blow which fells him. He springs to his feet, a second blow lays him flat. A repetition of the offence is followed by a repetition of the punishment. Up and down the constable flops and hops with the uniform rhythm of the bending and release of a spring, whilst the spectators laugh louder and louder. Now, let us think of a spring that is rather of a moral type, an idea that is first expressed, then repressed, and then expressed again; a stream of words that bursts forth, is checked, and keeps on starting afresh. Once more we have the vision of one stubborn force, counteracted by another, equally pertinacious. This vision, however, will have discarded a portion of its materiality. No longer is it Punch and Judy that we are watching, but rather a real comedy.

Many a comic scene may indeed be referred to this simple type. For instance, in the scene of the marriage forced between Sganarelle and Pancrace, the entire *vis comica* lies in the conflict set up between the idea of Sganarelle, who wishes to make the philosopher listen to him, and the obstinacy of the philosopher, a regular talking-machine working automatically. As the scene progresses, the image of the Jack-in-the-box becomes more apparent, so that at last the characters themselves adopt its movements—Sganarelle pushing Pancrace, each time he shows himself, back into the wings, Pancrace returning to the stage after each repulse to continue his patter. And when Sganarelle finally drives Pancrace back and shuts him up inside the house—inside the box, one is tempted to say—a window suddenly flies open, and the head of the philosopher again appears as though it had burst open the lid of a box.

The same by-play occurs in the *Malade Imaginaire*. Through the mouth of Monsieur Purgon the outraged medical profession pours out its vials of wrath upon Argan, threatening him with every disease that flesh is heir to. And every time Argan rises from his seat, as though to silence Purgon, the latter disappears for a moment, being, as it were, thrust back into the wings; then, as though impelled by a spring, he rebounds on to the stage with a fresh curse on his lips. The self-same exclamation: "Monsieur Purgon!" recurs at regular beats, and, as it were, marks the *tempo* of this little scene.

Let us scrutinise more closely the image of the spring which is bent, released, and bent again. Let us disentangle its central element, and we shall hit upon one of the usual processes of classic comedy—*repetition*.

Why is it there is something comic in the repetition of a word on the stage? No theory of the ludicrous seems to offer a satisfactory answer to this very simple question. Nor can an answer be found so long as we look for the explanation of an amusing word or phrase in the phrase or word itself, apart from all it suggests to us. Nowhere will the usual method prove to be so inadequate as here. With the exception, however, of a few special instances to which we shall recur later, the repetition of a word is never laughable in itself. It makes us laugh only because it symbolises a special play of moral elements, this play itself being the symbol of an altogether material diversion. It is the diversion of the cat with the mouse, the diversion of the child pushing back the Jack-in-the-box, time after time, to the bottom of his box, but in a refined and spiritualised form, transferred to the realm of feelings and ideas. Let us then state the law which, we think, defines the main comic varieties of word-repetition on the stage: *In a comic repetition of words we generally find two terms: a repressed feeling which goes off like a spring, and an idea that delights in repressing the feeling anew.*

When Dorine is telling Orgon of his wife's illness, and the latter continually interrupts him with inquiries as to the health of Tartuffe, the question: "Et tartuffe?" repeated every few moments, affords us the distinct sensation of a spring being released. This spring Dorine delights in pushing back, each time she resumes her account of Elmire's illness. And when Scapin informs old Geronte that his son has been taken prisoner on the famous galley, and that a ransom must be paid without delay, he is playing with the avarice of Geronte exactly as Dorine does with the infatuation of Orgon. The old man's avarice is no sooner repressed than up it springs again automatically, and it is this automatism that Moliere tries to indicate by the mechanical repetition of a sentence expressing regret at the money that would have to be forthcoming: "What the deuce did he want in that galley?" The same criticism is applicable to the scene in which Valere points out to Harpagon the wrong he would be doing in marrying his daughter to a man she did not love. "No dowry wanted!" interrupts the miserly Harpagon every few moments. Behind this exclamation, which recurs automatically, we faintly discern a complete repeating-machine set going by a fixed idea.

At times this mechanism is less easy to detect, and here we encounter a fresh difficulty in the theory of the comic. Sometimes the whole interest of a scene lies in one character playing a double part, the intervening speaker acting as a mere prism, so to speak, through which the dual personality is developed. We run the risk, then, of going astray if we look for the secret of the effect in what we see and hear—in the external scene played by the characters—and not in the altogether inner comedy of which this scene is no more than the outer refraction. For instance, when Alceste stubbornly repeats the words, "I don't say that!" on Oronte asking him if he thinks his poetry bad, the repetition is laughable, though evidently Oronte is not now playing with Alceste at the game we have just described. We must be careful, however, for, in reality, we have two men in Alceste: on the one hand, the "misanthropist" who has vowed henceforth to call a spade a spade, and on the other the gentleman who cannot unlearn, in a trice, the usual forms of politeness, or even, it may be, just the honest fellow who, when called upon to put his words into practice, shrinks from wounding another's self-esteem or hurting his feelings.

Accordingly, the real scene is not between Alceste and Oronte, it is between Alceste and himself. The one Alceste would fain blurt out the truth, and the other stops his mouth just as he is on the point of telling everything. Each "I don't say that!" reveals a growing effort to repress something that strives and struggles to get out. And so the tone in which the phrase is uttered gets more and more violent, Alceste becoming more and more angry—not with Oronte, as he thinks—but with himself. The tension of the spring is continually being renewed and reinforced until it at last goes off with a bang. Here, as elsewhere, we have the same identical mechanism of repetition.

For a man to make a resolution never henceforth to say what he does not think, even though he "openly defy the whole human race," is not necessarily laughable; it is only a phase of life at its highest and best. For another man, through amiability, selfishness, or disdain, to prefer to flatter people is only another phase of life; there is nothing in it to make us laugh. You may even combine these two men into one, and arrange that the individual waver between offensive frankness and delusive politeness, this duel between two opposing feelings will not even then be comic, rather it will appear the essence of seriousness if these two feelings through their very distinctness complete each other, develop side by side, and make up between them a composite mental condition, adopting, in short, a modus vivendi which merely gives us the complex impression of life. But imagine these two feelings as *inelastic* and unvarying elements in a really living man, make him oscillate from one to the other; above all, arrange that this oscillation becomes entirely mechanical by adopting the well-known form of some habitual, simple, childish contrivance: then you will get the image we have so far found in all laughable objects, *something mechanical in something living*; in fact, something comic.

We have dwelt on this first image, the Jack-in-the-box, sufficiently to show how comic fancy gradually converts a material mechanism into a moral one. Now we will consider one or two other games, confining ourselves to their most striking aspects.

2. *The dancing-jack.* — There are innumerable comedies in which one of the characters thinks he is speaking and acting freely, and, consequently, retains all the essentials of life, whereas, viewed from a certain standpoint, he appears as a mere toy in the hands of another who is playing with him. The transition is easily made, from the dancing-jack which a child works with a string, to Geronte and Argante manipulated by Scapin. Listen to Scapin himself: "The *machine* is all there"; and again: "Providence has brought them into my net," etc. Instinctively, and because one would rather be a cheat than be cheated, in imagination at all events, the spectator sides with the knaves; and for the rest of the time, like a child who has persuaded his playmate to lend him his doll, he takes hold of the strings himself and makes the marionette come and go on the stage as he pleases. But this latter condition is not indispensable; we can remain outside the pale of what is taking place if only we retain the distinct impression of a mechanical arrangement. This is what happens whenever one of the characters vacillates between two contrary opinions, each in turn appealing to him, as when Panurge asks Tom, Dick, and Harry whether or no he ought to get married. Note that, in such a case, a comic author is always careful to *personify* the two opposing decisions. For, if there is no spectator, there must at all events be actors to hold the strings.

All that is serious in life comes from our freedom. The feelings we have matured, the passions we have brooded over, the actions we have weighed, decided upon, and carried through, in short, all that comes from us and is our very own, these are the things that give life its ofttimes dramatic and generally grave aspect. What, then, is requisite to transform all this into a comedy? Merely to fancy that our seeming, freedom conceals the strings of a dancing-Jack, and that we are, as the poet says: "humble marionettes / The wires of which are pulled by Fate" (Sully-Prudhomme). So there is not a real, a serious, or even a dramatic scene that fancy cannot render comic by simply calling forth this image. Nor is there a game for which a wider field lies open.

3. *The snow-ball.* — The farther we proceed in this investigation into the methods of comedy, the more clearly we see the part played

by childhood's memories. These memories refer, perhaps, less to any special game than to the mechanical device of which that game is a particular instance. The same general device, moreover, may be met with in widely different games, just as the same operatic air is found in many different arrangements and variations. What is here of importance and is retained in the mind, what passes by imperceptible stages from the games of a child to those of a man, is the mental diagram, the skeleton outline of the combination, or, if you like, the abstract formula of which these games are particular illustrations.

Take, for instance, the rolling snow-ball, which increases in size as it moves along. We might just as well think of toy soldiers standing behind one another. Push the first and it tumbles down on the second, this latter knocks down the third, and the state of things goes from bad to worse until they all lie prone on the floor. Or again, take a house of cards that has been built up with infinite care: the first you touch seems uncertain whether to move or not, its tottering neighbour comes to a quicker decision, and the work of destruction, gathering momentum as it goes on, rushes headlong to the final collapse.

These instances are all different, but they suggest the same abstract vision, that of an effect which grows by arithmetical progression, so that the cause, insignificant at the outset, culminates by a necessary evolution in a result as important as it is unexpected. Now let us open a children's picture-book; we shall find this arrangement already on the high road to becoming comic. Here, for instance—in one of the comic chap-books picked up by chance—we have a caller rushing violently into a drawing-room; he knocks against a lady, who upsets her cup of tea over an old gentleman, who slips against a glass window which falls in the street on to the head of a constable, who sets the whole police force agog, etc.

The same arrangement reappears in many a picture intended for grownup persons. In the "stories without words" sketched by humorous artists we are often shown an object which moves from place to place, and persons who are closely connected with it, so that through a series of scenes a change in the position of the object mechanically brings about increasingly serious changes in the situation of the persons. Let us now turn to comedy. Many a droll scene, many a comedy even, may be referred to this simple type. Read the speech of Chicanneau in the *Plaideurs*: here we find lawsuits within lawsuits, and the mechanism works faster and faster—Racine produces in us this feeling of increasing acceleration by crowding his law terms ever closer together—until the lawsuit over a truss of hay costs the plaintiff the best part of his fortune.

And again the same arrangement occurs in certain scenes of *Don Quixote*; for instance, in the inn scene, where, by an extraordinary concatenation of circumstances, the mule-driver strikes Sancho, who belabours Maritornes, upon whom the innkeeper falls, etc. Finally, let us pass to the light comedy of today. Need we call to mind all the forms in which this same combination appears? There is one that is employed rather frequently. For instance, a certain thing, say a letter, happens to be of supreme importance to a certain person and must be recovered at all costs. This thing, which always vanishes just when you think you have caught it, pervades the entire play, "rolling up" increasingly serious and unexpected incidents as it proceeds. All this is far more like a child's game than appears at first blush. Once more the effect produced is that of the snowball.

It is the characteristic of a mechanical combination to be generally *reversible*. A child is delighted when he sees the ball in a game of nine-pins knocking down everything in its way and spreading havoc in all directions; he laughs louder than ever when the ball returns to its starting-point after twists and turns and waverings of every kind. In other words, the mechanism just described is laughable even when rectilinear, it is much more so on becoming circular and when every effort the player makes, by a fatal interaction of cause and effect, merely results in bringing it back to the same spot.

Now, a considerable number of light comedies revolve round this idea. An Italian straw hat has been eaten up by a horse. There is only one other hat like it in the whole of Paris; it *must* be secured regardless of cost. This hat, which always slips away at the moment its capture seems inevitable, keeps the principal character on the run, and through him all the others who hang, so to say, on to his coat tails, like a magnet which, by a successive series of attractions, draws along in its train the grains of iron filings that hang on to each other. And when at last, after all sorts of difficulties, the goal seems in sight, it is found that the hat so ardently sought is precisely the one that has been eaten. The same voyage of discovery is depicted in another equally well-known comedy of Labiche, *La Cagnotte*. The curtain rises on an old bachelor and an old maid, acquaintances of long standing, at the moment of enjoying their daily rubber. Each of them, unknown to the other, has applied to the same matrimonial agency.

Through innumerable difficulties, one mishap following on the heels of another, they hurry along, side by side, right through the play, to the interview which brings them back, purely and simply, into each other's presence. We have the same circular effect, the same return to the starting-point, in a more recent play (*Les Surprises du divorce*). A henpecked husband imagines he has escaped by divorce from the clutches of his wife and his mother-in-law. He marries again, when, lo and behold, the double combination of marriage and divorce brings back to him his former wife in the aggravated form of a second mother-in-law!

When we think how intense and how common is this type of the comic, we understand why it has fascinated the imagination of certain philosophers. To cover a good deal of ground only to come back unwittingly to the starting-point, is to make a great effort for a result that is nil. So we might be tempted to define the comic in this latter fashion. And such, indeed, seems to be the idea of Herbert Spencer: according to him, laughter is the indication of an effort which suddenly encounters a void. Kant had already said something of the kind: "Laughter is the result of an expectation, which, of a sudden, ends in nothing."

No doubt these definitions would apply to the last few examples given, although, even then, the formula needs the addition of sundry limitations, for we often make an ineffectual effort which is in no way provocative of laughter. While, however, the last few examples are illustrations of a great cause resulting in a small effect, we quoted others, immediately before, which might be defined inversely as a great effect springing from a small cause. The truth is, this second definition has scarcely more validity than the first. Lack of proportion between cause and effect, whether appearing in one or in the other, is never the direct source of laughter.

What we do laugh at is something that this lack of proportion may in certain cases disclose, namely, a particular mechanical arrangement which it reveals to us, as through a glass, at the back of the series of effects and causes. Disregard this arrangement, and you let go the only clue capable of guiding you through the labyrinth of the comic. Any hypothesis you otherwise would select, while possibly applicable to a few carefully chosen cases, is liable at any moment to be met and overthrown by the first unsuitable instance that comes along.

But why is it we laugh at this mechanical arrangement? It is doubtless strange that the history of a person or of a group should sometimes appear like a game worked by strings, or gearings, or springs; but from what source does the special character of this strangeness arise? What is it that makes it laughable? To this question, which we have already propounded in various forms, our answer must always be the same. The rigid mechanism which we occasionally detect, as a foreign body, in the living continuity of human affairs is of peculiar interest to us as being a kind of *absentmindedness* on the part of life.

Were events unceasingly mindful of their own course, there would be no coincidences, no conjunctures and no circular series; everything would evolve and progress continuously. And were all men always attentive to life, were we constantly keeping in touch with others as well as with ourselves, nothing within us would ever appear as due to the working of strings or springs. The comic is that side of a person which reveals his likeness to a thing, that aspect of human events which, through its peculiar inelasticity, conveys the impression of pure mechanism, of automatism, of movement without life. Consequently it expresses an individual or collective imperfection which calls for an immediate corrective. This corrective is laughter, a social gesture that singles out and represses a special kind of absentmindedness in men and in events.

But this in turn tempts us to make further investigations. So far, we have spent our time in rediscovering, in the diversions of the grownup man, those mechanical combinations which amused him as a child. Our methods, in fact, have been entirely empirical. Let us now attempt to frame a full and methodical theory, by seeking, as it were, at the fountainhead, the changeless and simple archetypes of the manifold and transient practices of the comic stage. Comedy, we said, combines events so as to introduce mechanism into the outer forms of life. Let us now ascertain in what essential characteristics life, when viewed from without, seems to contrast with mere mechanism. We shall only have, then, to turn to the opposite characteristics, in order to discover the abstract formula, this time a general and complete one, for every real and possible method of comedy.

Life presents itself to us as evolution in time and complexity in space. Regarded in time, it is the continuous evolution of a being ever growing older; it never goes backwards and never repeats anything. Considered in space, it exhibits certain coexisting elements so closely interdependent, so exclusively made for one another, that not one of them could, at the same time, belong to two different organisms: each living being is a closed system of phenomena, incapable of interfering with other systems. A continual change of aspect, the irreversibility of the order of phenomena, the perfect individuality of a perfectly self-contained series: such, then, are the outward characteristics—whether real or apparent is of little moment—which distinguish the living from the merely mechanical. Let us take the counterpart of each of these: we shall obtain three processes which might be called *repetition, inversion,* and *reciprocal interference of series.* Now, it is easy to see that these are also the methods of light comedy, and that no others are possible.

As a matter of fact, we could discover them, as ingredients of varying importance, in the composition of all the scenes we have just been considering, and, a fortiori, in the children's games, the mechanism of which they reproduce. The requisite analysis would, however, delay us too long, and it is more profitable to study them in their purity by taking fresh examples. Nothing could be easier, for it is in their pure state that they are found both in classic comedy and in contemporary plays.

1. *Repetition.* — Our present problem no longer deals, like the preceding one, with a word or a sentence repeated by an individual, but rather with a situation, that is, a combination of circumstances, which recurs several times in its original form and thus contrasts with the changing stream of life. Everyday experience supplies us with this type of the comic, though only in a rudimentary state. Thus, you meet a friend in the street whom you have not seen for an age; there is nothing comic in the situation. If, however, you meet, him again the same day, and then a third and a fourth time, you may laugh at the "coincidence." Now, picture to yourself a series of imaginary events which affords a tolerably fair illusion of life, and within this ever-moving series imagine one and the same scene reproduced either by the same characters or by different ones: again you will have a coincidence, though a far more extraordinary one.

Such are the repetitions produced on the stage. They are the more laughable in proportion as the scene repeated is more complex and more naturally introduced—two conditions which seem mutually exclusive, and which the play-writer must be clever enough to reconcile. Contemporary light comedy employs this method in every shape and form. One of the best-known examples consists in bringing a group of characters, act after act, into the most varied surroundings, so as to reproduce, under ever fresh circumstances, one and the same series of incidents or accidents more or less symmetrically identical.

In several of Moliere's plays we find one and the same arrangement of events repeated right through the comedy from beginning to end. Thus, the *Ecole des femmes* does nothing more than reproduce and repeat a single incident in three tempi: first tempo, Horace tells Arnolphe of the plan he has devised to deceive Agnes's guardian, who turns out to be Arnolphe himself; second tempo, Arnolphe thinks he has checkmated the move; third tempo, Agnes contrives that Horace gets all the benefit of Arnolphe's precautionary measures. There is the same symmetrical repetition in the *Ecole des marts*, in *L'Etourdi*, and above all in *George Dandin*, where the same effect in three tempi is again met with: first tempo, George Dandin discovers that his wife is unfaithful; second tempo, he summons his father- and mother-in-law to his assistance; third tempo, it is George Dandin himself, after all, who has to apologise.

At times the same scene is reproduced with groups of different characters. Then it not infrequently happens that the first group consists of masters and the second of servants. The latter repeat in another key a scene already played by the former, though the rendering is naturally less refined. A part of the *Depit amoureux* is constructed on this plan, as is also *Amphitryon*. In an amusing little comedy of Benedix, *Der Eigensinn*, the order is inverted: we have the masters reproducing a scene of stubbornness in which their servants have set the example.

But, quite irrespective of the characters who serve as pegs for the arrangement of symmetrical situations, there seems to be a wide gulf between classic comedy and the theatre of today. Both aim at introducing a certain mathematical order into events, while none the less maintaining their aspect of likelihood, that is to say, of life. But the means they employ are different. The majority of light comedies of our day seek to mesmerise directly the mind of the spectator. For, however extraordinary the coincidence, it becomes acceptable from the very fact that it is accepted; and we do accept it, if we have been gradually prepared for its reception.

Such is often the procedure adopted by contemporary authors. In Moliere's plays, on the contrary, it is the moods of the persons on the stage, not of the audience, that make repetition seem natural. Each of the characters represents a certain force applied in a certain direction, and it is because these forces, constant in direction, necessarily combine together in the same way, that the same situation is reproduced. Thus interpreted, the comedy of situation is akin to the comedy of character. It deserves to be called classic, if classic art is indeed that which does not claim to derive from the effect more than it has put into the cause.

2. *Inversion.* — This second method has so much analogy with the first that we will merely define it without insisting on illustrations. Picture to yourself certain characters in a certain situation: if you reverse the situation and invert the roles, you obtain a comic scene. The double rescue scene in *Le Voyage de M. Perrichon* belongs to this class. There is no necessity, however, for both the identical scenes to be played before us. We may be shown only one, provided the other is really in our minds. Thus, we laugh at the prisoner at the bar lecturing the magistrate; at a child presuming to teach its parents; in a word, at everything that comes under the heading of "topsyturvydom."

Not infrequently comedy sets before us a character who lays a trap in which he is the first to be caught. The plot of the villain who is the victim of his own villainy, or the cheat cheated, forms the stock-in-trade of a good many plays. We find this even in primitive farce. Lawyer Pathelin tells his client of a trick to outwit the magistrate; the client employs the self-same trick to avoid paying the lawyer. A termagant of a wife insists upon her husband doing all the housework; she has put down each separate item on a "rota." Now let her fall into a copper, her husband will refuse to drag her out, for "that is not down on his 'rota.'" In modern literature we meet with hundreds of variations on the theme of the robber robbed. In every case the root idea involves an inversion of roles, and a situation which recoils on the head of its author.

Here we apparently find the confirmation of a law, some illustrations of which we have already pointed out. When a comic scene has been reproduced a number of times, it reaches the stage of being a classical type or model. It becomes amusing in itself, quite apart from the causes which render it amusing. Henceforth, new scenes, which are not comic de jure, may become amusing de facto, on account of their partial resemblance to this model. They call up in our mind a more or less confused image which we know to be comical. They range themselves in a category representing an officially recognised type of the comic. The scene of the "robber robbed" belongs to this class. It casts over a host of other scenes a reflection of the comic element it contains. In the end it renders comic any mishap that befalls one through one's own fault, no matter what the fault or mishap may be—nay, an allusion to this mishap, a single word that recalls it, is sufficient. There would be nothing amusing in the saying, "It serves you right, George Dandin," were it not for the comic overtones that take up and re-echo it.

3. We have dwelt at considerable length on repetition and inversion; we now come to the reciprocal interference of series.[2] This is a comic effect, the precise formula of which is very difficult to disentangle, by reason of the extraordinary variety of forms in which it appears on the stage. Perhaps it might be defined as follows: A situation is invariably comic when it belongs simultaneously to two altogether independent series of events and is capable of being interpreted in two entirely different meanings at the same time.

You will at once think of an equivocal situation. And the equivocal situation is indeed one which permits of two different meanings at the same time, the one merely plausible, which is put forward by the actors, the other a real one, which is given by the public. We see the real meaning of the situation, because care has been taken to show us every aspect of it; but each of the actors knows only one of these aspects: hence the mistakes they make and the erroneous judgments they pass both on what is going on around them and on what they are doing themselves. We proceed from this erroneous judgment to the correct one, we waver between the possible meaning and the real, and it is this mental seesaw between two contrary interpretations which is at first apparent in the enjoyment we derive from an equivocal situation.

It is natural that certain philosophers should have been specially struck by this mental instability, and that some of them should regard the very essence of the ludicrous as consisting in the collision or coincidence of two judgments that contradict each other. Their definition, however, is far from meeting every case, and even when it does, it defines—not the principle of the ludicrous, but only one of its more or less distant consequences. Indeed, it is easy to see that the stage-made misunderstanding is nothing but a particular instance of a far more general phenomenon—the reciprocal interference of independent series, and that, moreover, it is not laughable in itself, but only as a sign of such an interference.

As a matter of fact, each of the characters in every stage-made misunderstanding has his setting in an appropriate series of events which he correctly interprets as far as he is concerned, and which give the key-note to his words and actions. Each of the series peculiar to the several characters develop independently, but at a certain moment

---

[2]The word "interference" has here the meaning given to it in optics, where it indicates the partial superposition and neutralisation, by each other, of two series of light-waves.

they meet under such conditions that the actions and words that belong to one might just as well belong to another. Hence arise the misunderstandings and the equivocal nature of the situation. But this latter is not laughable in itself, it is so only because it reveals the coincidence of the two independent series.

The proof of this lies in the fact that the author must be continually taxing his ingenuity to recall our attention to the double fact of independence and coincidence. This he generally succeeds in doing by constantly renewing the vain threat of dissolving partnership between the two coinciding series. Every moment the whole thing threatens to break down, but manages to get patched up again; it is this diversion that excites laughter, far more than the oscillation of the mind between two contradictory ideas. It makes us laugh because it reveals to us the reciprocal interference of two independent series, the real source of the comic effect.

And so the stage-made misunderstanding is nothing more than one particular instance, one means—perhaps the most artificial—of illustrating the reciprocal interference of series, but it is not the only one. Instead of two contemporary series, you might take one series of events belonging to the past and another belonging to the present: if the two series happen to coincide in our imagination, there will be no resulting cross-purposes, and yet the same comic effect will continue to take place. Think of Bonivard, captive in the Castle of Chillon: one series of facts. Now picture to yourself Tartarin, travelling in Switzerland, arrested and imprisoned: second series, independent of the former. Now let Tartarin be manacled to Bonivard's chain, thus making the two stories seem for a moment to coincide, and you will get a very amusing scene, one of the most amusing that Daudet's imagination has pictured [in *Tartarin sur les Alpes*].

Numerous incidents of the mock-heroic style, if analysed, would reveal the same elements. The transposition from the ancient to the modern—always a laughable one—draws its inspiration from the same idea. Labiche has made use of this method in every shape and form. Sometimes he begins by building up the series separately, and then delights in making them interfere with one another: he takes an independent group—a wedding-party, for instance—and throws them into altogether unconnected surroundings, into which certain coincidences allow of their being foisted for the time being. Sometimes he keeps one and the same set of characters right through the play, but contrives that certain of these characters have something to conceal—have, in fact, a secret understanding on the point—in short, play a smaller comedy within the principal one: at one moment, one of the two comedies is on the point of upsetting the other; the next, everything comes right and the coincidence between the two series is restored. Sometimes, even, he introduces into the actual series a purely immaterial series of events, an inconvenient past, for instance, that someone has an interest in concealing, but which is continually cropping up in the present, and on each occasion is successfully brought into line with situations with which it seemed destined to play havoc. But in every case we find the two independent series, and also their partial coincidence.

We will not carry any further this analysis of the methods of light comedy. Whether we find reciprocal interference of series, inversion, or repetition, we see that the objective is always the same—to obtain what we have called a *mechanisation* of life. You take a set of actions and relations and repeat it as it is, or turn it upside down, or transfer it bodily to another set with which it partially coincides—all these being processes that consist in looking upon life as a repeating mechanism, with reversible action and interchangeable parts.

Actual life is comedy just so far as it produces, in a natural fashion, actions of the same kind—consequently, just so far as it forgets itself, for were it always on the alert, it would be ever-changing continuity, irreversible progress, undivided unity. And so the ludicrous in events may be defined as absentmindedness in things, just as the ludicrous in an individual character always results from some fundamental absentmindedness in the person, as we have already intimated and shall prove later on. This absentmindedness in events, however, is exceptional. Its results are slight. At any rate it is incurable, so that it is useless to laugh at it. Therefore the idea would never have occurred to any one of exaggerating that absentmindedness, of converting it into a system and creating an art for it, if laughter were not always a pleasure and mankind did not pounce upon the slightest excuse for indulging in it.

This is the real explanation of light comedy, which holds the same relation to actual life as does a jointed dancing-doll to a man walking —being, as it is, an artificial exaggeration of a natural rigidity in things. The thread that binds it to actual life is a very fragile one. It is scarcely more than a game which, like all games, depends on a previously accepted convention. Comedy in character strikes far deeper roots into life. With that kind of comedy we shall deal more particularly in the final portion of our investigation. But we must first analyse a certain type of the comic, in many respects similar to that of light comedy: the comic in words.

II

There may be something artificial in making a special category for the comic in words, since most of the varieties of the comic that we have examined so far were produced through the medium of language. We must make a distinction, however, between the comic *expressed* and the comic *created* by language. The former could, if necessary, be translated from one language into another, though at the cost of losing the greater portion of its significance when introduced into a fresh society different in manners, in literature, and above all in association of ideas. But it is generally impossible to translate the latter. It owes its entire being to the structure of the sentence or to the choice of the words. It does not set forth, by means of language, special cases of absentmindedness in man or in events. It lays stress on lapses of attention in language itself. In this case, it is language itself that becomes comic.

Comic sayings, however, are not a matter of spontaneous generation; if we laugh at them, we are equally entitled to laugh at their author. This latter condition, however, is not indispensable, since the saying or expression has a comic virtue of its own. This is proved by the fact that we find it very difficult, in the majority of these cases, to say whom we are laughing at, although at times we have a dim, vague feeling that there is someone in the background.

Moreover, the person implicated is not always the speaker. Here it seems as though we should draw an important distinction between the *witty* (*spirituel*) and the *comic*. A word is said to be comic when it makes us laugh at the person who utters it, and witty when it makes us laugh either at a third party or at ourselves. But in most cases we can hardly make up our minds whether the word is comic or witty. All that we can say is that it is laughable.

Before proceeding, it might be well to examine more closely what is meant by *esprit*. A witty saying makes us at least smile; consequently, no investigation into laughter would be complete did it not get to the bottom of the nature of wit and throw light on the underlying idea. It is to be feared, however, that this extremely subtle essence is one that evaporates when exposed to the light.

Let us first make a distinction between the two meanings of the word wit *esprit*, the broader one and the more restricted. In the broader meaning of the word, it would seem that what is called wit is a certain *dramatic* way of thinking. Instead of treating his ideas as mere symbols, the wit sees them, he hears them and, above all, makes them converse with one another like persons. He puts them on the stage, and himself, to some extent, into the bargain. A witty nation is, of necessity, a nation enamoured of the theatre. In every wit there is something of a poet—just as in every good reader there is the making of an actor. This comparison is made purposely, because a proportion might easily be established between the four terms. In order to read well we need only the intellectual side of the actor's art; but in order to act well one must be an actor in all one's soul and body.

In just the same way, poetic creation calls for some degree of self-forgetfulness, whilst the wit does not usually err in this respect. We always get a glimpse of the latter behind what he says and does. He is not wholly engrossed in the business, because he only brings his intelligence into play. So any poet may reveal himself as a wit when he pleases. To do this there will be no need for him to acquire anything; it seems rather as though he would have to give up something. He would simply have to let his ideas hold converse with one another "for nothing, for the mere joy of the thing!" (Victor Hugo, *Marion Delorme*). He would only have to unfasten the double bond which keeps his ideas in touch with his feelings and his soul in touch with life. In short, he would turn into a wit by simply resolving to be no longer a poet in feeling, but only in intelligence.

But if wit consists, for the most part, in seeing things *sub specie theatri* [from the perspective of theater], it is evidently capable of being specially directed to one variety of dramatic art, namely, comedy. Here we have a more restricted meaning of the term, and, moreover, the only one that interests us from the point of view of the theory of laughter. What is here called *wit* is a gift for dashing off comic scenes in a few strokes—dashing them off, however, so subtly, delicately and rapidly, that all is over as soon as we begin to notice them.

Who are the actors in these scenes? With whom has the wit to deal? First of all, with his interlocutors themselves, when his witticism is a direct retort to one of them. Often with an absent person whom he supposes to have spoken and to whom he is replying. Still oftener, with the whole world—in the ordinary meaning of the term—which he takes to task, twisting a current idea into a paradox, or making use of a hackneyed phrase, or parodying some quotation or proverb. If we compare these scenes in miniature with one another, we find they are almost always variations of a comic theme with which we are well acquainted, that of the "robber robbed." You take up a metaphor, a phrase, an argument, and turn it against the man who is, or might be, its author, so that he is made to say what he did not mean to say and lets himself be caught, to some extent, in the toils of language. But the theme of the "robber robbed" is not the only possible one. We have gone over many varieties of the comic, and there is not one of them that is incapable of being volatilised into a witticism.

Every witty remark, then, lends itself to an analysis, whose chemical formula, so to say, we are now in a position to state. It runs as follows: Take the remark, first enlarge it into a regular scene, then find out the category of the comic to which the scene evidently belongs: by this means you reduce the witty remark to its simplest elements and obtain a full explanation of it.

Let us apply this method to a classic example. "Your chest hurts me" (*j'ai mal a votre poitrine*) wrote Mme. de Sevigne to her ailing daughter—clearly a witty saying. If our theory is correct, we need only lay stress upon the saying, enlarge and magnify it, and we shall see it expand into a comic scene. Now, we find this very scene, readymade, in the *Amour Medecin* of Moliere. The sham doctor, Clitandre, who has been summoned to attend Sganarelle's daughter, contents himself with feeling Sganarelle's own pulse, whereupon, relying on the sympathy there must be between father and daughter, he unhesitatingly concludes: "Your daughter is very ill!"

Here we have the transition from the witty to the comical. To complete our analysis, then, all we have to do is to discover what there is comical in the idea of giving a diagnosis of the child after sounding the father or the mother. Well, we know that one essential form of comic fancy lies in picturing to ourselves a living person as a kind of jointed dancing-doll, and that frequently, with the object of inducing us to form this mental picture, we are shown two or more persons speaking and acting as though attached to one another by invisible strings. Is not this the idea here suggested when we are led to materialise, so to speak, the sympathy we postulate as existing between father and daughter?

We now see how it is that writers on wit have perforce confined themselves to commenting on the extraordinary complexity of the things denoted by the term without ever succeeding in defining it. There are many ways of being witty, almost as many as there are of being the reverse. How can we detect what they have in common with one another, unless we first determine the general relationship between the witty and the comic? Once, however, this relationship is cleared up, everything is plain sailing. We then find the same connection between the comic and the witty as exists between a regular scene and the fugitive suggestion of a possible one.

Hence, however numerous the forms assumed by the comic, wit will possess an equal number of corresponding varieties. So that the comic, in all its forms, is what should be defined first, by discovering (a task which is already quite difficult enough) the clue that leads from one form to the other. By that very operation wit will have been analysed, and will then appear as nothing more than the comic in a highly volatile state. To follow the opposite plan, however, and attempt directly to evolve a formula for wit, would be courting certain failure. What should we think of a chemist who, having ever so many jars of a certain substance in his laboratory, would prefer getting that substance from the atmosphere, in which merely infinitesimal traces of its vapour are to be found?

But this comparison between the witty and the comic is also indicative of the line we must take in studying the comic in words. On the one hand, indeed, we find there is no essential difference between a word that is comic and one that is witty; on the other hand, the latter, although connected with a figure of speech, invariably calls up the image, dim or distinct, of a comic scene. This amounts to saying that the comic in speech should correspond, point by point, with the comic in actions and in situations, and is nothing more, if one may so express oneself, than their projection on to the plane of words. So let us return to the comic in actions and in situations, consider the chief methods by which it is obtained, and apply them to the choice of words and the building up of sentences. We shall thus have every possible form of the comic in words as well as every variety of wit.

1. Inadvertently to say or do what we have no intention of saying or doing, as a result of inelasticity or momentum, is, as we are aware, one of the main sources of the comic. Thus, absentmindedness is essentially laughable, and so we laugh at anything rigid, ready-made, mechanical in gesture, attitude and even facial expression. Do we find this kind of rigidity in language also? No doubt we do, since language contains ready-made formulas and stereotyped phrases. The man who always expressed himself in such terms would invariably be comic. But if an isolated phrase is to be comic in itself, when once separated from the person who utters it, it must be something more than ready-made, it

must bear within itself some sign which tells us, beyond the possibility of doubt, that it was uttered automatically. This can only happen when the phrase embodies some evident absurdity, either a palpable error or a contradiction in terms. Hence the following general rule: *A comic meaning is invariably obtained when an absurd idea is fitted into a well-established phrase-form.*

"*Ce sabre est le plus beau jour de ma vie,*" said M. Prudhomme. Translate the phrase into English or German and it becomes purely absurd, though it is comic enough in French. The reason is that "*le plus beau jour de ma vie*" is one of those ready-made phrase-endings to which a Frenchman's ear is accustomed. To make it comic, then, we need only clearly indicate the automatism of the person who utters it. This is what we get when we introduce an absurdity into the phrase. Here the absurdity is by no means the source of the comic, it is only a very simple and effective means of making it obvious.

We have quoted only one saying of M. Prudhomme, but the majority of those attributed to him belong to the same class. M. Prudhomme is a man of ready-made phrases. And as there are ready-made phrases in all languages, M. Prudhomme is always capable of being transposed, though seldom of being translated. At times the commonplace phrase, under cover of which the absurdity slips in, is not so readily noticeable. "I don't like working between meals," said a lazy lout. There would be nothing amusing in the saying did there not exist that salutary precept in the realm of hygiene: "One should not eat between meals."

Sometimes, too, the effect is a complicated one. Instead of one commonplace phrase-form, there are two or three which are dovetailed into each other. Take, for instance, the remark of one of the characters in a play by Labiche, "Only God has the right to kill His fellow-creature." It would seem that advantage is here taken of two separate familiar sayings; "It is God who disposes of the lives of men," and, "It is criminal for a man to kill his fellow-creature." But the two sayings are combined so as to deceive the ear and leave the impression of being one of those hackneyed sentences that are accepted as a matter of course. Hence our attention nods, until we are suddenly aroused by the absurdity of the meaning. These examples suffice to show how one of the most important types of the comic can be projected—in a simplified form—on the plane of speech. We will now proceed to a form which is not so general.

2. "We laugh if our attention is diverted to the physical in a person when it is the moral that is in question," is a law we laid down in the first part of this work. Let us apply it to language. Most words might be said to have a *physical* and a *moral* meaning, according as they are interpreted literally or figuratively. Every word, indeed, begins by denoting a concrete object or a material action; but by degrees the meaning of the word is refined into an abstract relation or a pure idea. If, then, the above law holds good here, it should be stated as follows: "A comic effect is obtained whenever we pretend to take literally an expression which was used figuratively"; or, "Once our attention is fixed on the material aspect of a metaphor, the idea expressed becomes comic."

In the phrase, *Tous les arts sont freres* (all the arts are brothers), the word *frere* (brother) is used metaphorically to indicate a more or less striking resemblance. The word is so often used in this way, that when we hear it we do not think of the concrete, the material connection implied in every relationship. We should notice it more if we were told that *Tous les arts sont cousins*, for the word "cousin" is not so often employed in a figurative sense; that is why the word here already assumes a slight tinge of the comic. But let us go further still, and suppose that our attention is attracted to the material side of the metaphor by the choice of a relationship which is incompatible with the gender of the two words composing the metaphorical expression: we get a laughable result.

Such is the well-known saying, also attributed to M. Prudhomme, *Tous les arts* (masculine) *sont soeurs* (feminine). "He is always running after a joke," was said in Boufflers' presence regarding a very conceited fellow. Had Boufflers replied, "He won't catch it," that would have been the beginning of a witty saying, though nothing more than the beginning, for the word "catch" is interpreted figureatively almost as often as the word "run"; nor does it compel us more strongly than the latter to materialise the image of two runners, the one at the heels of the other. In order that the rejoinder may appear to be a thoroughly witty one, we must borrow from the language of sport an expression so vivid and concrete that we cannot refrain from witnessing the race in good earnest. This is what Boufflers does when he retorts, "I'll back the joke!"

We said that wit often consists in extending the idea of one's interlocutor to the point of making him express the opposite of what he thinks and getting him, so to say, entrapped by his own words. We must now add that this trap is almost always some metaphor or comparison the concrete aspect of which is turned against him. You may remember the dialogue between a mother and her son in the *Faux Bonshommes*: "My dear boy, gambling on chance is very risky. You win one day and lose the next." — "Well, then, I will gamble only every other day." In the same play too we find the following edifying conversation between two company-promoters: "Is this a very honourable thing we are doing? These unfortunate shareholders, you see, we are taking the money out of their very pockets" — "Well, out of what do you expect us to take it?"

An amusing result is likewise obtainable whenever a symbol or an emblem is expanded on its concrete side, and a pretense is made of retaining the same symbolical value for this expansion as for the emblem itself. In a very lively comedy we are introduced to a Monte Carlo official, whose uniform is covered with medals, although he has only received a single decoration. "You see, I staked my medal on a number at roulette," he said, "and as the number turned up, I was entitled to thirty-six times my stake." This reasoning is very similar to that offered by Giboyer in the *Effrontes*. Criticism is made of a bride of forty summers who is wearing orange-blossoms with her wedding costume: "Why, she was entitled to oranges, let alone orange-blossoms!" remarked Giboyer.

But we should never cease were we to take one by one all the laws we have stated, and try to prove them on what we have called the plane of language. We had better confine ourselves to the three general propositions of the preceding section. We have shown that "series of events" may become comic either by repetition, by inversion, or by reciprocal interference. Now we shall see that this is also the case with series of words.

To take series of events and repeat them in another key or another environment, or to invert them whilst still leaving them a certain meaning, or mix them up so that their respective meanings jostle one another, is invariably comic, as we have already said, for it is getting life to submit to be treated as a machine. But thought, too, is a living thing. And language, the translation of thought, should be just as living. We may thus surmise that a phrase is likely to become comic if, though reversed, it still makes sense, or if it expresses equally well two quite independent sets of ideas, or, finally, if it has been obtained by transposing an idea into some key other than its own. Such, indeed, are the three fundamental laws of what might be called *the comic transformation of sentences*, as we shall show by a few examples.

Let it first be said that these three laws are far from being of equal importance as regards the theory of the ludicrous. *Inversion* is the least interesting of the three. It must be easy of application, however, for it is noticeable that, no sooner do professional wits hear a sentence spoken than they experiment to see if a meaning cannot be obtained by reversing it—by putting, for instance, the subject in place of the object, and the object in place of the subject. It is not unusual for this device to be employed for refuting an idea in more or less humorous terms. One of the characters in a comedy of Labiche shouts out to his neighbour on the floor above, who is in the habit of dirtying his balcony, "What do you mean by emptying your pipe on to my terrace?" The neighbour retorts, "What do you mean by putting your terrace under my pipe?"

There is no necessity to dwell upon this kind of wit, instances of which could easily be multiplied. The *reciprocal interference* of two sets of ideas in the same sentence is an inexhaustible source of amusing varieties. There are many ways of bringing about this interference, I mean of bracketing in the same expression two independent meanings that apparently tally. The least reputable of these ways is the pun. In the pun, the same sentence appears to offer two independent meanings, but it is only an appearance; in reality there are two different sentences made up of different words, but claiming to be one and the same because both have the same sound.

We pass from the pun, by imperceptible stages, to the true play upon words. Here there is really one and the same sentence through which two different sets of ideas are expressed, and we are confronted with only one series of words; but advantage is taken of the different meanings a word may have, especially when used figuratively instead of literally. So that in fact there is often only a slight difference between the play upon words on the one hand, and a poetic metaphor or an illuminating comparison on the other.

Whereas an illuminating comparison and a striking image always seem to reveal the close harmony that exists between language and nature, regarded as two parallel forms of life, the play upon words makes us think somehow of a negligence on the part of language, which, for the time being, seems to have forgotten its real function and now claims to accommodate things to itself instead of accommodating itself to things. And so the play upon words always betrays a momentary *lapse of attention* in language, and it is precisely on that account that it is amusing. *Inversion* and *reciprocal interference*, after all, are only a certain playfulness of the mind which ends at playing upon words. The comic in *transposition* is much more far-reaching. Indeed, transposition is to ordinary language what repetition is to comedy.

We said that repetition is the favourite method of classic comedy. It consists in so arranging events that a scene is reproduced either between the same characters under fresh circumstances or between fresh characters under the same circumstances. Thus we have, repeated by lackeys in less dignified language, a scene already played by their masters. Now, imagine ideas expressed in suitable style and thus placed in the setting of their natural environment. If you think of some arrangement whereby they are transferred to fresh surroundings, while maintaining their mutual relations, or, in other words, if you can induce them to express themselves in an altogether different style and to transpose themselves into another key, you will have language itself playing a comedy—language itself made comic.

There will be no need, moreover, actually to set before us both expressions of the same ideas, the transposed expression and the natural one. For we are acquainted with the natural one—the one which we should have chosen instinctively. So it will be enough if the effort of comic invention bears on the other, and on the other alone. No sooner is the second set before us than we spontaneously supply the first. Hence the following general rule: *A comic effect is always obtainable by transposing the nature expression of an idea into another key.*

The means of transposition are so many and varied, language affords so rich a continuity of themes and the comic is here capable of passing through so great a number of stages, from the most insipid buffoonery up to the loftiest forms of humour and irony, that we shall forego the attempt to make out a complete list. Having stated the rule, we will simply, here and there, verify its main applications.

In the first place, we may distinguish two keys at the extreme ends of the scale, the solemn and the familiar. The most obvious effects are obtained by merely transposing the one into the other, which thus provides us with two opposite currents of comic fancy. Transpose the solemn into the familiar and the result is parody. The effect of parody, thus defined, extends to instances in which the idea expressed in familiar terms is one that, if only in deference to custom, ought to be pitched in another key. Take as an example the following description of the dawn, quoted by Jean Paul Richter: "The sky was beginning to change from black to red, like a lobster being boiled." Note that the expression of old-world matters in terms of modern life produces the same effect, by reason of the halo of poetry which surrounds classical antiquity.

It is doubtless the comic in parody that has suggested to some philosophers, and in particular to Alexander Bain, the idea of defining the comic, in general, as a species of *degradation*. They describe the laughable as causing something to appear mean that was formerly dignified. But if our analysis is correct, degradation is only one form of transposition, and transposition itself only one of the means of obtaining laughter. There is a host of others, and the source of laughter must be sought for much further back. Moreover, without going so far, we see that while the transposition from solemn to trivial, from better to worse, is comic, the inverse transposition may be even more so.

It is met with as often as the other, and, apparently, we may distinguish two main forms of it, according as it refers to the *physical dimensions* of an object or to its *moral value*.

To speak of small things as though they were large is, in a general way, *to exaggerate*. Exaggeration is always comic when prolonged, and especially when systematic; then, indeed, it appears as one method of transposition. It excites so much laughter that some writers have been led to define the comic as exaggeration, just as others have defined it as degradation. As a matter of fact, exaggeration, like degradation, is only one form of one kind of the comic. Still, it is a very striking form. It has given birth to the mock-heroic poem, a rather old-fashioned device, I admit, though traces of it are still to be found in persons inclined to exaggerate methodically. It might often be said of braggadocio that it is its mock-heroic aspect which makes us laugh.

Far more artificial, but also far more refined, is the transposition upwards from below when applied to the moral value of things, not to their physical dimensions. To express in reputable language some disreputable idea, to take some scandalous situation, some low-class calling or disgraceful behaviour, and describe them in terms of the utmost "*respectability*," is generally comic.

The English word is here purposely employed, as the practice itself is characteristically English. Many instances of it may be found in Dickens and Thackeray, and in English literature generally. Let us remark, in passing, that the intensity of the effect does not here depend on its length. A word is sometimes sufficient, provided it gives us a glimpse of an entire system of transposition accepted in certain social circles and reveals, as it were, a moral organisation of immorality. Take the following remark made by an official to one of his subordinates in a novel of Gogol's, "Your peculations [embezzlings] are too extensive for an official of your rank."

Summing up the foregoing, then, there are two extreme terms of comparison, the very large and the very small, the best and the worst, between which transposition may be effected in one direction or the other. Now, if the interval be gradually narrowed, the contrast between the terms obtained will be less and less violent, and the varieties of comic transposition more and more subtle.

The most common of these contrasts is perhaps that between the real and the ideal, between what is and what ought to be. Here again transposition may take place in either direction. Sometimes we state what ought to be done, and pretend to believe that this is just what is actually being done; then we have *irony*. Sometimes, on the contrary, we describe with scrupulous minuteness what is being done, and pretend to believe that this is just what ought to be done; such is often the method of *humour*. Humour, thus denned, is the counterpart of irony. Both are forms of satire, but irony is oratorical in its nature, whilst humour partakes of the scientific.

Irony is emphasised the higher we allow ourselves to be uplifted by the idea of the good that ought to be: thus irony may grow so hot within us that it becomes a kind of high-pressure eloquence. On the other hand, humour is the more emphasised the deeper we go down into an evil that actually is, in order t o set down its details in the most cold-blooded indifference. Several authors, Jean Paul amongst them, have noticed that humour delights in concrete terms, technical details, definite facts. If our analysis is correct, this is not an accidental trait of humour, it is its very essence. A humorist is a moralist disguised as a scientist, something like an anatomist who practises dissection with the sole object of filling us with disgust; so that humour, in the restricted sense in which we are here regarding the word, is really a transposition from the moral to the scientific.

By still further curtailing the interval between the terms transposed, we may now obtain more and more specialised types of comic transpositions. Thus, certain professions have a technical vocabulary: what a wealth of laughable results have been obtained by transposing the ideas of everyday life into this professional jargon! Equally comic is the extension of business phraseology to the social relations of life—for instance, the phrase of one of Labiche's characters in allusion to an invitation he has received, "Your kindness of the third ult.," thus transposing the commercial formula, "Your favour of the third instant." This class of the comic, moreover, may attain a special profundity of its own when it discloses not merely a professional practice, but a fault in character. Recall to mind the scenes in the *Faux Bonshommes* and the *Famille Benoiton*, where marriage is dealt with as a business affair, and matters of sentiment are set down in strictly commercial language.

Here, however, we reach the point at which peculiarities of language really express peculiarities of character, a closer investigation of which we must hold over to the next chapter. Thus, as might have been expected and may be seen from the foregoing, the comic in words follows closely on the comic in situation and is finally merged, along with the latter, in the comic in character.

Language only attains laughable results because it is a human product, modelled as exactly as possible on the forms of the human mind. We feel it contains some living element of our own life; and if this life of language were complete and perfect, if there were nothing stereotype in it, if, in short, language were an absolutely unified organism incapable of being split up into independent organisms, it would evade the comic as would a soul whose life was one harmonious whole, unruffled as the calm surface of a peaceful lake. There is no pool, however, which has not some dead leaves floating on its surface, no human soul upon which there do not settle habits that make it rigid against itself by making it rigid against others, no language, in short, so subtle and instinct with life, so fully alert in each of its parts as to eliminate the ready-made and oppose the mechanical operations of inversion, transposition, etc., which one would fain perform upon it as on some lifeless thing.

The rigid, the ready—made, the mechanical, in contrast with the supple, the ever-changing and the living, absentmindedness in contrast with attention, in a word, automatism in contrast with free activity, such are the defects that laughter singles out and would fain correct. We appealed to this idea to give us light at the outset, when starting upon the analysis of the ludicrous. We have seen it shining at every decisive turning in our road. With its help, we shall now enter upon a more important investigation, one that will, we hope, be more instructive. We purpose, in short, studying comic characters, or rather determining the essential conditions of comedy in character, while endeavouring to bring it about that this study may contribute to a better understanding of the real nature of art and the general relation between art and life.

Chapter Three
The Comic in Character

I

We have followed the comic along many of its winding channels in an endeavour to discover how it percolates into a form, an attitude, or a gesture; a situation, an action, or an expression. The analysis of comic *characters* has now brought us to the most important part of our task. It would also be the most difficult, had we yielded to the temptation of defining the laughable by a few striking—and consequently obvious—examples; for then, in proportion as we advanced towards the loftiest manifestations of the comic, we should have found the facts slipping between the over-wide meshes of the definition intended to retain them.

But, as a matter of fact, we have followed the opposite plan, by throwing light on the subject from above. Convinced that laughter has a social meaning and import, that the comic expresses, above all else, a special lack of adaptability to society, and that, in short, there is nothing comic apart from man, we have made man and character generally our main objective. Our chief difficulty, therefore, has lain in explaining how we come to laugh at anything else than character, and by what subtle processes of fertilisation, combination or amalgamation, the comic can worm its way into a mere movement, an impersonal situation, or an independent phrase. This is what we have done so far. We started with the pure metal, and all our endeavours have been directed solely towards reconstructing the ore. It is the metal itself we are now about to study. Nothing could be easier, for this time we have a simple element to deal with. Let us examine it closely and see how it reacts upon everything else.

There are moods, we said, which move us as soon us as soon as we perceive them, joys and sorrows with which we sympathise, passions and vices which call forth painful astonishment, terror or pity, in the beholder; in short, sentiments that are prolonged in sentimental overtones from mind to mind. All this concerns the essentials of life. All this is serious, at times even tragic. Comedy can only begin at the point where our neighbour's personality ceases to affect us. It begins, in fact, with what might be called a growing callousness to social life.

Any individual is comic who automatically goes his own way without troubling himself about getting into touch with the rest of his fellow-beings. It is the part of laughter to reprove his absentmindedness and wake him out of his dream. If it is permissible to compare important things with trivial ones, we would call to mind what happens when a youth enters one of our military academies. After getting through the dreaded ordeal of the examination, he finds he has other ordeals to face, which his seniors have arranged with the object of fitting him for the new life he is entering upon, or, as they say, of "breaking him into harness." Every small society that forms within the larger is thus impelled, by a vague kind of instinct, to devise some method of discipline or "breaking in," so as to deal with the rigidity of habits that have been formed elsewhere and have now to undergo a partial modification.

Society, properly so-called, proceeds in exactly the same way. Each member must be ever attentive to his social surroundings; he must model himself on his environment; in short, he must avoid shutting himself up in his own peculiar character as a philosopher in his ivory tower. Therefore society holds suspended over each individual member, if not the threat of correction, at all events the prospect of a snubbing, which, although it is slight, is none the less dreaded. Such must be the function of laughter. Always rather humiliating for the one against whom it is directed, laughter is, really and truly, a kind of social "ragging."

Hence the equivocal nature of the comic. It belongs neither altogether to art nor altogether to life. On the one hand, characters in real life would never make us laugh were we not capable of watching their vagaries in the same way as we look down at a play from our seat in a box; they are only comic in our eyes because they perform a kind of comedy before us. But, on the other hand, the pleasure caused by laughter, even on the stage, is not an unadulterated enjoyment; it is not a pleasure that is exclusively esthetic or altogether disinterested. It always implies a secret or unconscious intent, if not of each one of us, at all events of society as a whole.

In laughter we always find an unavowed intention to humiliate, and consequently to correct our neighbour, if not in his will, at least in his deed. This is the reason a comedy is far more like real life than a drama is. The more sublime the drama, the more profound the analysis to which the poet has had to subject the raw materials of daily life in order to obtain the tragic element in its unadulterated form. On the contrary, it is only in its lower aspects, in light comedy and farce, that comedy is in striking contrast to reality: the higher it rises, the more it approximates to life; in fact, there are scenes in real life so closely bordering on high-class comedy that the stage might adopt them without changing a single word.

Hence it follows that the elements of comic character on the stage and in actual life will be the same. What are these elements? We shall find no difficulty in deducing them. It has often been said that it is the *trifling* faults of our fellow-men that make us laugh. Evidently there is a considerable amount of truth in this opinion; still, it cannot be regarded as altogether correct. First, as regards faults, it is no easy matter to draw the line between the trifling and the serious; maybe it is not because a fault is trifling that it makes us laugh, but rather because it makes us laugh that we regard it as trifling, for there is nothing disarms us like laughter.

But we may go even farther, and maintain that there are faults at which we laugh, even though fully aware that they are serious—Harpagon's avarice, for instance. And then, we may as well confess—though somewhat reluctantly—that we laugh not only at the faults of our fellow-men, but also, at times, at their good qualities. We laugh at Alceste. The objection may be urged that it is not the earnestness of Alceste that is ludicrous, but rather the special aspect which earnestness assumes in his case, and, in short, a certain eccentricity that mars it in our eyes. Agreed; but it is none the less true that this eccentricity in Alceste, at which we laugh, *makes his earnestness laughable,* and that is the main point. So we may conclude that the ludicrous is not always an indication of a fault, in the moral meaning of the word, and if critics insist on seeing a fault, even though a trifling one, in the ludicrous, they must point out what it is here that exactly distinguishes the trifling from the serious.

The truth is, the comic character may, strictly speaking, be quite in accord with stern morality. All it has to do is to bring itself into accord with society. The character of Alceste is that of a thoroughly honest man. But then he is unsociable, and, on that very account, ludicrous. A flexible vice may not be so easy to ridicule as a rigid virtue. It is rigidity that society eyes with suspicion. Consequently, it is the rigidity of Alceste that makes us laugh, though here rigidity stands for honesty. The man who withdraws into himself is liable to ridicule, because the comic is largely made up of this very withdrawal. This accounts for the comic being so frequently dependent on the manners or ideas, or, to put it bluntly, on the prejudices, of a society.

It must be acknowledged, however, to the credit of mankind, that there is no essential difference between the social ideal and the rule, that it is the faults of others that make us laugh, provided we add that they make us laugh by reason of their *unsociability* rather than of their *immorality*. What, then, are the faults capable of becoming ludicrous, and in what circumstances do we regard them as being too serious to be laughed at?

We have already given an implicit answer to this question. The comic, we said, appeals to the intelligence, pure and simple; laughter is incompatible with emotion. Depict some fault, however trifling, in such a way as to arouse sympathy, fear, or pity; the mischief is done, it is impossible for us to laugh. On the other hand, take a downright vice —even one that is, generally speaking, of an odious nature—you may make it ludicrous if, by some suitable contrivance, you arrange so that it leaves our emotions unaffected. Not that the vice must then be ludicrous, but it *may*, from that time forth, become so. *It must not arouse our feelings*; that is the sole condition really necessary, though assuredly it is not sufficient.

But, then, how will the comic poet set to work to prevent our feelings being moved? The question is an embarrassing one. To clear it up thoroughly, we should have to enter upon a rather novel line of investigation, to analyse the artificial sympathy which we bring with us to the theatre, and determine upon the circumstances in which we accept and those in which we refuse to share imaginary joys and sorrows. There is an art of lulling sensibility to sleep and providing it with dreams, as happens in the case of a mesmerised person. And there is also an art of throwing a wet blanket upon sympathy at the very moment it might arise, the result being that the situation, though a serious one, is not taken seriously. This latter art would appear to be governed by two methods, which are applied more or less unconsciously by the comic poet.

The first consists in *isolating*, within the soul of the character, the feeling attributed to him, and making it a parasitic organism, so to speak, endowed with an independent existence. As a general rule, an intense feeling successively encroaches upon all other mental states and colours them with its own peculiar hue; if, then, we are made to witness this gradual impregnation, we finally become impregnated ourselves with a corresponding emotion.

To employ a different image, an emotion may be said to be dramatic and contagious when all the harmonics in it are heard along with the fundamental note. It is because the actor thus thrills throughout his whole being that the spectators themselves feel the thrill. On the contrary, in the case of emotion that leaves us indifferent and that is about to become comic, there is always present a certain rigidity which prevents it from establishing a connection with the rest of the soul in which it has taken up its abode. This rigidity may be manifestted, when the time comes, by puppet-like movements, and then it will provoke laughter; but, before that, it had already alienated our sympathy: how can we put ourselves in tune with a soul which is not in tune with itself?

In Moliere's *L'Avare* we have a scene bordering upon drama. It is the one in which the borrower and the usurer, who have never seen each other, meet face to face and find that they are son and father. Here we should be in the thick of a drama, if only greed and fatherly affection, conflicting with each other in the soul of Harpagon, had effected a more or less original combination. But such is not the case. No sooner has the interview come to an end than the father forgets everything. On meeting his son again he barely alludes to the scene, serious though it has been: "You, my son, whom I am good enough to forgive your recent escapade, etc."

Greed has thus passed close to all other feelings *absentmindedly*, without either touching them or being touched. Although it has taken up its abode in the soul and become master of the house, none the less it remains a stranger. Far different would be avarice of a tragic sort. We should find it attracting and absorbing, transforming and assimilating the divers energies of the man: feelings and affections, likes and dislikes, vices and virtues, would all become something into which avarice would breathe a new kind of life. Such seems to be the first essential difference between high-class comedy and drama.

There is a second, which is far more obvious and arises out of the first. When a mental state is depicted to us with the object of making it dramatic, or even merely of inducing us to take it seriously, it gradually crystallises into *actions* which provide the real measure of its greatness. Thus, the miser orders his whole life with a view to acquiring wealth, and the pious hypocrite, though pretending to have his eyes fixed upon heaven, steers most skillfully his course here below.

Most certainly, comedy does not shut out calculations of this kind; we need only take as an example the very machinations of Tartuffe. But that is what comedy has in common with drama; and in order to keep distinct from it, to prevent our taking a serious action seriously, in short, in order to prepare us for laughter, comedy utilises a method, the formula of which may be given as follows: *Instead of concentrating our attention on actions, comedy directs it rather to gestures.*

By *gestures* we here mean the attitudes, the movements and even the language by which a mental state expresses itself outwardly without any aim or profit, from no other cause than a kind of inner itching. Gesture, thus defined, is profoundly different from action. Action is intentional or, at any rate, conscious; gesture slips out unawares, it is automatic. In action, the entire person is engaged; in gesture, an isolated part of the person is expressed, unknown to, or at least apart from, the whole of the personality.

Lastly—and here is the essential point—action is in exact proportion to the feeling that inspires it: the one gradually passes into the other, so that we may allow our sympathy or our aversion to glide along the line running from feeling to action and become increasingly interested. About gesture, however, there is something explosive, which awakes our sensibility when on the point of being lulled to sleep and, by thus rousing us up, prevents our taking matters seriously.

Thus, as soon as our attention is fixed on gesture and not on action, we are in the realm of comedy. Did we merely take his actions into account, Tartuffe would belong to drama: it is only when we take his gestures into consideration that we find him comic. You may remember how he comes on to the stage with the words: "Laurent, lock up my hair-shirt and my scourge." He knows Dorine is listening to him, but doubtless he would say the same if she were not there. He enters so thoroughly into the role of a hypocrite that he plays it almost sincerely. In this way, and this way only, can he become comic. Were it not for this material sincerity, were it not for the language and attitudes that his long-standing experience as a hypocrite has transformed into natural gestures, Tartuffe would be simply odious, because we should only think of what is meant and willed in his conduct.

And so we see why action is essential in drama, but only accessory in comedy. In a comedy, we feel any other situation might equally well have been chosen for the purpose of introducing the character; he would still have been the same man though the situation were different. But we do not get this impression in a drama. Here characters and situations are welded together, or rather, events form part and parcel with the persons, so that were the drama to tell us a different story, even though the actors kept the same names, we should in reality be dealing with other persons.

To sum up, whether a character is good or bad is of little moment: granted he is unsociable, he is capable of becoming comic. We now see that the seriousness of the case is of no importance either: whether serious or trifling, it is still capable of making us laugh, provided that care be taken not to arouse our emotions. Unsociability in the performer and insensibility in the spectator—such, in a word, are the two essential conditions. There is a third, implicit in the other two, which so far it has been the aim of our analysis to bring out.

This third condition is automatism. We have pointed it out from the outset of this work, continually drawing attention to the following point: what is essentially laughable is what is done automatically. In a vice, even in a virtue, the comic is that element by which the person unwittingly betrays himself—the involuntary gesture or the unconscious remark. Absentmindedness is always comical. Indeed, the deeper the absentmindedness the higher the comedy. Systematic absentmindedness, like that of Don Quixote, is the most comical thing imaginable: it is the comic itself, drawn as nearly as possible from its very source. Take any other comic character: however unconscious he may be of what he says or does, he cannot be comical unless there be some aspect of his person of which he is unaware, one side of his nature which he overlooks; on that account alone does he make us laugh.[3]

Profoundly comic sayings are those artless ones in which some vice reveals itself in all its nakedness: how could it thus expose itself were it capable of seeing itself as it is? It is not uncommon for a comic character to condemn in general terms a certain line of conduct and immediately afterwards afford an example of it himself: for instance, M. Jourdain's teacher of philosophy flying into a passion after inveighing against anger; Vadius taking a poem from his pocket after heaping ridicule on readers of poetry, etc. What is the object of such contradictions except to help us to put our finger on the obliviousness of the characters to their own actions?

Inattention to self, and consequently to others, is what we invariably find. And if we look at the matter closely, we see that inattention is here equivalent to what we have called unsociability. The chief cause of rigidity is the neglect to look around—and more especially within oneself: how can a man fashion his personality after that of another if he does not first study others as well as himself? Rigidity, automatism, absent-mindedness and unsociability are all inextricably entwined; and all serve as ingredients to the making up of the comic in character.

In a word, if we leave on one side, when dealing with human personality, that portion which interests our sensibility or appeals to our feeling, all the rest is capable of becoming comic, and the comic

---

[3] When the humorist laughs at himself, he is really acting a double part; the self who laughs is indeed conscious, but not the self who is laughed at.

will be proportioned to the rigidity. We formulated this idea at the outset of this work. We have verified it in its main results, and have just applied it to the definition of comedy. Now we must get to closer quarters, and show how it enables us to delimitate the exact position comedy occupies among all the other arts.

In one sense it might be said that all character is comic, provided we mean by character the ready-made element in our personality, that mechanical element which resembles a piece of clockwork wound up once for all and capable of working automatically. It is, if you will, that which causes us to imitate ourselves. And it is also, for that very reason, that which enables others to imitate us. Every comic character is a type. Inversely, every resemblance to a type has something comic in it. Though we may long have associated with an individual without discovering anything about him to laugh at, still, if advantage is taken of some accidental analogy to dub him with the name of a famous hero of romance or drama, he will in our eyes border upon the ridiculous, if only for a moment. And yet this hero of romance may not be a comic character at all. But then it is comic to be like him. It is comic to wander out of one's own self. It is comic to fall into a readymade category. And what is most comic of all is to become a category oneself into which others will fall, as into a ready-made frame; it is to crystallise into a stock character.

Thus, to depict characters, that is to say, general types, is the object of high-class comedy. This has often been said. But it is as well to repeat it, since there could be no better definition of comedy. Not only are we entitled to say that comedy gives us general types, but we might add that it is the *only* one of all the arts that aims at the general; so that once this objective has been attributed to it, we have said all that it is and all that the rest cannot be.

To prove that such is really the essence of comedy, and that it is in this respect opposed to tragedy, drama and the other forms of art, we should begin by defining art in its higher forms: then, gradually coming down to comic poetry, we should find that this latter is situated on the border-line between art and life, and that, by the generality of its subject-matter, it contrasts with the rest of the arts. We cannot here plunge into so vast a subject of investigation; but we needs must sketch its main outlines, lest we overlook what, to our mind, is essential on the comic stage.

What is the object of art? Could reality come into direct contact with sense and consciousness, could we enter into immediate communion with things and with ourselves, probably art would be useless, or rather we should all be artists, for then our soul would continually vibrate in perfect accord with nature. Our eyes, aided by memory, would carve out in space and fix in time the most inimitable of pictures. Hewn in the living marble of the human form, fragments of statues, beautiful as the relics of antique statuary, would strike the passing glance. Deep in our souls we should hear the strains of our inner life's unbroken melody—a music that is ofttimes gay, but more frequently plaintive and always original.

All this is around and within us, and yet no whit of it do we distinctly perceive. Between nature and ourselves, nay, between ourselves and our own consciousness a veil is interposed: a veil that is dense and opaque for the common herd—thin, almost transparent, for the artist and the poet. What fairy wove that veil? Was it done in malice or in friendliness? We had to live, and life demands that we grasp things in their relations to our own needs. Life is action. Life implies the acceptance only of the *utilitarian* side of things in order to respond to them by appropriate reactions: all other impressions must be dimmed or else reach us vague and blurred.

I look and I think I see, I listen and I think I hear, I examine myself and I think I am reading the very depths of my heart. But what I see and hear of the outer world is purely and simply a selection made by my senses to serve as a light to my conduct; what I know of myself is what comes to the surface, what participates in my actions. My senses and my consciousness, therefore, give me no more than a practical simplification of reality. In the vision they furnish me of myself and of things, the differences that are useless to man are obliterated, the resemblances that are useful to him are emphasised; ways are traced out for me in advance, along which my activity is to travel. These ways are the ways which all mankind has trod before me.

Things have been classified with a view to the use I can derive from them. And it is this classification I perceive, far more clearly than the colour and the shape of things. Doubtless man is vastly superior to the lower animals in this respect. It is not very likely that the eye of a wolf makes any distinction between a kid and a lamb; both appear to the wolf as the same identical quarry, alike easy to pounce upon, alike good to devour. We, for our part, make a distinction between a goat and a sheep; but can we tell one goat from another, one sheep from another? The *individuality* of things or of beings escapes us, unless it is materially to our advantage to perceive it. Even when we do take note of it—as when we distinguish one man from another—it is not the individuality itself that the eye grasps, i.e., an entirely original harmony of forms and colours, but only one or two features that will make practical recognition easier.

In short, we do not see the actual things themselves; in most cases we confine ourselves to reading the labels affixed to them. This tendency, the result of need, has become even more pronounced under the influence of speech; for words—with the exception of proper nouns—all denote genera. The word, which only takes note of the most ordinary function and commonplace aspect of the thing, intervenes between it and ourselves, and would conceal its form from our eyes, were that form not already masked beneath the necessities that brought the word into existence.

Not only external objects, but even our own mental states, are screened from us in their inmost, their personal aspect, in the original life they possess. When we feel love or hatred, when we are gay or sad, is it really the feeling itself that reaches our consciousness with those innumerable fleeting shades of meaning and deep resounding echoes that make it something altogether our own? We should all, were it so, be novelists or poets or musicians. Mostly, however, we perceive nothing but the outward display of our mental state. We catch only the impersonal aspect of our feelings, that aspect which speech has set down once for all because it is almost the same, in the same conditions, for all men.

Thus, even in our own individual, individuality escapes our ken. We move amidst generalities and symbols, as within a tilt-yard in which our force is effectively pitted against other forces; and fascinated by action, tempted by it, for our own good, on to the field it has selected, we live in a zone midway between things and ourselves, externally to things, externally also to ourselves. From time to time, however, in a fit of absentmindedness, nature raises up souls that are more detached from life. Not with that intentional, logical, systematical detachment—the result of reflection and philosophy—but rather with natural detachment, one innate in the structure of sense or consciousness, which at once reveals itself by a virginal manner, so to speak, of seeing, hearing or thinking.

Were this detachment complete, did the soul no longer cleave to action by any of its perceptions, it would be the soul of an artist such as the world has never yet seen. It would excel alike in every art at the same time; or rather, it would fuse them all into one. It would perceive all things in their native purity: the forms, colours, sounds of the physical world as well as the subtlest movements of the inner life. But this is asking too much of nature. Even for such of us as she has made artists, it is by accident, and on one side only, that she has lifted the veil. In one direction only has she forgotten to rivet the perception to the need. And since each direction corresponds to what we call a *sense*—through one of his senses, and through that sense alone, is the artist usually wedded to art.

Hence, originally, the diversity of arts. Hence also the speciality of predispositions. This one applies himself to colours and forms, and since he loves colour for colour and form for form, since he perceives them for their sake and not for his own, it is the inner life of things that he sees appearing through their forms and colours. Little by little he insinuates it into our own perception, baffled though we may be at the outset. For a few moments at least, he diverts us from the prejudices of form and colour that come between ourselves and reality. And thus he realises the loftiest ambition of art, which here consists in revealing to us nature.

Others, again, retire within themselves. Beneath the thousand rudimentary actions which are the outward and visible signs of an emotion, behind the commonplace, conventional expression that both reveals and conceals an individual mental state, it is the emotion, the original mood, to which they attain in its undefiled essence. And then, to induce us to make the same effort ourselves, they contrive to make us see something of what they have seen: by rhythmical arrangement of words, which thus become organised and animated with a life of their own, they tell us—or rather suggest—things that speech was not calculated to express.

Others delve yet deeper still. Beneath these joys and sorrows which can, at a pinch, be translated into language, they grasp something that has nothing in common with language, certain rhythms of life and breath that. are closer to man than his inmost feelings, being the living law—varying with each individual—of his enthusiasm and despair, his hopes and regrets. By setting free and emphasising this music, they force it upon our attention; they compel us, willy-nilly, to fall in with it, like passers-by who join in a dance. And thus they impel us to set in motion, in the depths of our being, some secret chord which was only waiting to thrill.

So art, whether it be painting or sculpture, poetry or music, has no other object than to brush aside the utilitarian symbols, the conventional and socially accepted generalities, in short, everything that veils reality from us, in order to bring us face to face with reality itself. It is from a misunderstanding on this point that the dispute between realism and idealism in art has arisen. Art is certainly only a more direct vision of reality. But this purity of perception implies a break with utilitarian convention, an innate and specially localised disinterestedness of sense or consciousness, in short, a certain immateriality of life, which is what has always been called idealism. So that we might say, without in any way playing upon the meaning of the words, that realism is in the work when idealism is in the soul, and that it is only through ideality that we can resume contact with reality.

Dramatic art forms no exception to this law. What drama goes forth to discover and brings to light, is a deep-seated reality that is veiled from us, often in our own interests, by the necessities of life. What is this reality? What are these necessities? Poetry always expresses inward states. But amongst these states some arise mainly from contact with our fellow-men. They are the most intense as well as the most violent. As contrary electricities attract each other and accumulate between the two plates of the condenser from which the spark will presently flash, so, by simply bringing people together, strong attractions and repulsions take place, followed by an utter loss of balance, in a word, by that electrification of the soul known as passion.

Were man to give way to the impulse of his natural feelings, were there neither social nor moral law, these outbursts of violent feeling would be the ordinary rule in life. But utility demands that these outbursts should be foreseen and averted. Man must live in society, and consequently submit to rules. And what interest advises, reason commands: duty calls, and we have to obey the summons. Under this dual influence has perforce been formed an outward layer of feelings and ideas which make for permanence, aim at becoming common to all men, and cover, when they are not strong enough to extinguish it, the inner fire of individual passions.

The slow progress of mankind in the direction of an increasingly peaceful social life has gradually consolidated this layer, just as the life of our planet itself has been one long effort to cover over with a cool and solid crust the fiery mass of seething metals. But volcanic eruptions occur. And if the earth were a living being, as mythology has feigned, most likely when in repose it would take delight in dreaming of these sudden explosions, whereby it suddenly resumes possession of its innermost nature. Such is just the kind of pleasure that is provided for us by drama.

Beneath the quiet humdrum life that reason and society have fashioned for us, it stirs something within us which luckily does not explode, but which it makes us feel in its inner tension. It offers nature her revenge upon society. Sometimes it makes straight for the goal, summoning up to the surface, from the depths below, passions that produce a general upheaval. Sometimes it effects a flank movement, as is often the case in contemporary drama; with a skill that is frequently sophistical, it shows up the inconsistencies of society; it exaggerates the shams and shibboleths of the social law; and so indirectly, by merely dissolving or corroding the outer crust, it again brings us back to the inner core. But, in both cases, whether it weakens society or strengthens nature, it has the same end in view: that of laying bare a secret portion of ourselves—what might be called the tragic element in our character.

This is indeed the impression we get after seeing a stirring drama. What has just interested us is not so much what we have been told about others as the glimpse we have caught of ourselves—a whole host of ghostly feelings, emotions and events that would fain have come into real existence, but, fortunately for us, did not. It also seems as if an appeal had been made within us to certain ancestral memories belonging to a far-away past—memories so deep-seated and so foreign to our present life that this latter, for a moment, seems something unreal and conventional, for which we shall have to serve a fresh apprenticeship. So it is indeed a deeper reality that drama draws up from beneath our superficial and utilitarian attainments, and this art has the same end in view as all the others.

Hence it follows that art always aims at what is *individual*. What the artist fixes on his canvas is something he has seen at a certain spot, on a certain day, at a certain hour, with a colouring that will never be seen again. What the poet sings of is a certain mood which was his, and his alone, and which will never return. What the dramatist unfolds before us is the life-history of a soul, a living tissue of feelings and events—something, in short, which has once happened and can never be repeated. We may, indeed, give general names to these feelings, but they cannot be the same thing in another soul. They are *individualised*. Thereby, and thereby only, do they belong to art; for generalities, symbols or even types, form the current coin of our daily perception. How, then, does a misunderstanding on this point arise?

The reason lies in the fact that two very different things have been mistaken for each other: the generality of things and that of the opinions we come to regarding them. Because a feeling is generally recognised as true, it does not follow that it is a general feeling. Nothing could be more unique than the character of Hamlet. Though he may resemble other men in some respects, it is clearly not on that account that he interests us most. But he is universally accepted and regarded as a living character. In this sense only is he universally true.

The same holds good of all the other products of art. Each of them is unique, and yet, if it bear the stamp of genius, it will come to be accepted by everybody. Why will it be accepted? And if it is unique of its kind, by what sign do we know it to be genuine? Evidently, by the very effort it forces us to make against our predispositions in order to see sincerely. Sincerity is contagious. What the artist has seen we shall probably never see again, or at least never see in exactly the same way; but if he has actually seen it, the attempt he has made to lift the veil compels our imitation. His work is an example which we take as a lesson. And the efficacy of the lesson is the exact standard of the genuineness of the work.

Consequently, truth bears within itself a power of conviction, nay, of conversion, which is the sign that enables us to recognise it. The greater the work and the more profound the dimly apprehended truth, the longer may the effect be in coming, but, on the other hand, the more universal will that effect tend to become. So the universality here lies in the effect produced, and not in the cause.

Altogether different is the object of comedy. Here it is in the work itself that the generality lies. Comedy depicts characters we have already come across and shall meet with again. It takes note of similarities. It aims at placing types before our eyes. It even creates new types, if necessary. In this respect it forms a contrast to all the other arts.

The very titles of certain classical comedies are significant in themselves. Le Misanthrope, l'Avare, le Joueur, le Distrait, etc., are names of whole classes of people; and even when a character comedy has a proper noun as its title, this proper noun is speedily swept away, by the very weight of its contents, into the stream of common nouns. We say "a Tartuffe," but we should never say "a Phedre" or "a Polyeucte."

Above all, a tragic poet will never think of grouping around the chief character in his play secondary characters to serve as simplified copies, so to speak, of the former. The hero of a tragedy represents an individuality unique of its kind. It may be possible to imitate him, but then we shall be passing, whether consciously or not, from the tragic to the comic. No one is like him, because he is like no one. But a remarkable instinct, on the contrary, impels the comic poet, once he has elaborated his central character, to cause other characters, displaying the same general traits, to revolve as satellites round him.

Many comedies have either a plural noun or some collective term as their title. *Les Femmes savantes, Les Precieuses ridicules, Le Monde ou l'on s'ennuie*, etc., represent so many rallying points on the stage adopted by different groups of characters, all belonging to one identical type. It would be interesting to analyse this tendency in comedy.

Maybe dramatists have caught a glimpse of a fact recently brought forward by mental pathology, viz., that cranks of the same kind are drawn, by a secret attraction, to seek each other's company. Without precisely coming within the province of medicine, the comic individual, as we have shown, is in some way absentminded, and the transition from absentmindedness to crankiness is continuous. But there is also another reason. If the comic poet's object is to offer us types, that is to say, characters capable of self-repetition, how can he set about it better than by showing us, in each instance, several different copies of the same model? That is just what the naturalist does in order to define a species. He enumerates and describes its main varieties.

This essential difference between tragedy and comedy, the former being concerned with individuals and the latter with classes, is revealed in yet another way. It appears in the first draft of the work. From the outset it is manifested by two radically different methods of observation.

Though the assertion may seem paradoxical, a study of other men is probably not necessary to the tragic poet. We find some of the great poets have lived a retiring, homely sort of life, without having a chance of witnessing around them an outburst of the passions they have so faithfully depicted. But, supposing even they had witnessed such a spectacle, it is doubtful whether they would have found it of much use. For what interests us in the work of the poet is the glimpse we get of certain profound moods or inner struggles. Now, this glimpse cannot be obtained from without. Our souls are impenetrable to one another.

Certain signs of passion are all that we ever apperceive externally. These we interpret—though always, by the way, defectively—only by analogy with what we have ourselves experienced. So what we experience is the main point, and we cannot become thoroughly acquainted with anything but our own heart—supposing we ever get so far. Does this mean that the poet has experienced what he depicts, that he has gone through the various situations he makes his characters traverse, and lived the whole of their inner life?

Here, too, the biographies of poets would contradict such a supposition. How, indeed, could the same man have been Macbeth, Hamlet, Othello, King Lear, and many others? But then a distinction should perhaps here be made between the personality *we have* and all those we might have had. Our character is the result of a choice that is continually being renewed. There are points—at all events there seem to be—all along the way, where we may branch off, and we perceive many possible directions though we are unable to take more than one. To retrace one's steps, and follow to the end the faintly distinguishable directions, appears to be the essential element in poetic imagination.

Of course, Shakespeare was neither Macbeth, nor Hamlet, nor Othello; still, he *might have been* these several characters if the circumstances of the case on the one hand, and the consent of his will on the other, had caused to break out into explosive action what was nothing more than an inner prompting. We are strangely mistaken as to the part played by poetic imagination, if we think it pieces together its heroes out of fragments filched from right and left, as though it were patching together a harlequin's motley. Nothing living would result from that. Life cannot be recomposed; it can only be looked at and reproduced.

Poetic imagination is but a fuller view of reality. If the characters created by a poet give us the impression of life, it is only because they are the poet himself—multiplication or division of the poet—the poet plumbing the depths of his own nature in so powerful an effort of inner observation that he lays hold of the potential in the real, and takes up what nature has left as a mere outline or sketch in his soul in order to make of it a finished work of art.

Altogether different is the kind of observation from which comedy springs. It is directed outwards. However interested a dramatist may be in the comic features of human nature, he will hardly go, I imagine, to the extent of trying to discover his own. Besides, he would not find them, for we are never ridiculous except in some point that remains hidden from our own consciousness. It is on others, then, that such observation must perforce be practised. But it will, for this very reason, assume a character of generality that it cannot have when we apply it to ourselves. Settling on the surface, it will not be more than skin-deep, dealing with persons at the point at which they come into contact and become capable of resembling one another. It will go no farther. Even if it could, it would not desire to do so, for it would have nothing to gain in the process.

To penetrate too far into the personality, to couple the outer effect with causes that are too deep-seated, would mean to endanger and in the end to sacrifice all that was laughable in the effect. In order that we may be tempted to laugh at it, we must localise its cause in some intermediate region of the soul. Consequently, the effect must appear to us as an average effect, as expressing an average of mankind. And, like all averages, this one is obtained by bringing together scattered data, by comparing analogous cases and extracting their essence, in short by a process of abstraction and generalisation similar to that which the physicist brings to bear upon facts with the object of grouping them under laws. In a word, method and object are here of the same nature as in the inductive sciences, in that observation is always external and the result always general.

And so we come back, by a roundabout way, to the double conclusion we reached in the course of our investigations. On the one hand, a person is never ridiculous except through some mental attribute resembling absent-mindedness, through something that lives upon him without forming part of his organism, after the fashion of a parasite; that is the reason this state of mind is observable from without and capable of being corrected. But, on the other hand, just because laughter aims at correcting, it is expedient that the correction should reach as great a number of persons as possible.

This is the reason comic observation instinctively proceeds to what is general. It chooses such peculiarities as admit of being reproduced and consequently are not indissolubly bound up with the individuality of a single person—a possibly common sort of uncommonness, so to say—peculiarities that are held in common. By transferring them to the stage, it creates works which doubtless belong to art in that their only visible aim is to please, but which will be found to contrast with other works of art by reason of their generality and also of their scarcely confessed or scarcely conscious intention to correct and instruct.

So we were probably right in saying that comedy lies midway between art and life. It is not disinterested as genuine art is. By organising laughter, comedy accepts social life as a natural environment, it even obeys an impulse of social life. And in this respect it turns its back upon art, which is a breaking away from society and a return to pure nature.

II

Now let us see, in the light of what has gone before, the line to take for creating an ideally comic type of character, comic in itself, in its origin, and in all its manifestations. It must be deep-rooted, so as to supply comedy with inexhaustible matter, and yet superficial, in order that it may remain within the scope of comedy; invisible to its actual owner, for the comic ever partakes of the unconscious, but visible to everybody else, so that it may call forth general laughter, extremely considerate to its own self, so that it may be displayed without scruple, but troublesome to others, so that they may repress it without pity; immediately repressible, so that our laughter may not have been wasted, but sure of reappearing under fresh aspects, so that laughter may always find something to do; inseparable from social life, although insufferable to society; capable—in order that it may assume the greatest imaginable variety of forms—of being tacked on to all the vices and even to a good many virtues.

Truly a goodly number of elements to fuse together! But a chemist of the soul, entrusted with this elaborate preparation, would be somewhat disappointed when pouring out the contents of his retort. He would find he had taken a vast deal of trouble to compound a mixture which may be found ready-made and free of expense, for it is as widespread throughout mankind as air throughout nature.

This mixture is vanity. Probably there is not a single failing that is more superficial or more deep-rooted. The wounds it receives are never very serious, and yet they are seldom healed. The services rendered to it are the most unreal of all services, and yet they are the very ones that meet with lasting gratitude. It is scarcely a vice, and yet all the vices are drawn into its orbit and, in proportion as they become more refined and artificial, tend to be nothing more than a means of satisfying it.

The outcome of social life, since it is an admiration of ourselves based on the admiration we think we are inspiring in others, it is even more natural, more universally innate than egoism; for egoism may be conquered by nature, whereas only by reflection do we get the better of vanity. It does not seem, indeed, as if men were ever born modest, unless we dub with the name of modesty a sort of purely physical bashfulness, which is nearer to pride than is generally supposed. True modesty can be nothing but a meditation on vanity. It springs from the sight of others' mistakes and the dread of being similarly deceived. It is a sort of scientific cautiousness with respect to what we shall say and think of ourselves. It is made up of improvements and after-touches. In short, it is an acquired virtue.

It is no easy matter to define the point at which the anxiety to become modest may be distinguished from the dread of becoming ridiculous. But surely, at the outset, this dread and this anxiety are one and the same thing. A complete investigation into the illusions of vanity, and into the ridicule that clings to them, would cast a strange light upon the whole theory of laughter. We should find laughter performing, with mathematical regularity, one of its main functions—that of bringing back to complete self-consciousness a certain self-admiration which is almost automatic, and thus obtaining the greatest possible sociability of characters. We should see that vanity, though it is a natural product of social life, is an inconvenience to society, just as certain slight poisons, continually secreted by the human organism, would destroy it in the long run, if they were not neutralised by other secretions. Laughter is unceasingly doing work of this kind. In this respect, it might be said that the specific remedy for vanity is laughter, and that the one failing that is essentially laughable is vanity.

While dealing with the comic in form and movement, we showed how any simple image, laughable in itself, is capable of worming its way into other images of a more complex nature and instilling into them something of its comic essence; thus, the highest forms of the comic can sometimes be explained by the lowest. The inverse process, however, is perhaps even more common, and many coarse comic effects are the direct result of a drop from some very subtle comic element. For instance, vanity, that higher form of the comic, is an element we are prone to look for, minutely though unconsciously, in every manifestation of human activity. We look for it if only to laugh at it. Indeed, our imagination often locates it where it has no business to be.

Perhaps we must attribute to this source the altogether coarse comic element in certain effects which psychologists have very inadequately explained by contrast: a short man bowing his head to pass beneath a large door; two individuals, one very tall the other a mere dwarf, gravely walking along arm-in-arm, etc. By scanning narrowly this latter image, we shall probably find that the shorter of the two persons seems as though he were trying *to raise himself* to the height of the taller, like the frog that wanted to make itself as large as the ox.

III

It would be quite impossible to go through all the peculiarities of character that either coalesce or compete with vanity in order to force themselves upon the attention of the comic poet. We have shown that all failings may become laughable, and even, occasionally, many a good quality. Even though a list of all the peculiarities that have ever been found ridiculous were drawn up, comedy would manage to add to them, not indeed by creating artificial ones, but by discovering lines of comic development that had hitherto gone unnoticed; thus does imagination isolate ever fresh figures in the intricate design of one and the same piece of tapestry. The essential condition, as we know, is that the peculiarity observed should straightway appear as a kind of *category* into which a number of individuals can step.

Now, there are ready-made categories established by society itself, and necessary to it because it is based on the division of labour. We mean the various trades, public services and professions. Each particular profession impresses on its corporate members certain habits of mind and peculiarities of character in which they resemble each other and also distinguish themselves from the rest. Small societies are thus formed within the bosom of society at large. Doubtless they arise from the very organisation of society as a whole. And yet, if they held too much aloof, there would be a risk of their proving harmful to sociability.

Now, it is the business of laughter to repress any separatist tendency. Its function is to convert rigidity into plasticity, to readapt the individual to the whole, in short, to round off the corners wherever they are met with. Accordingly, we here find a species of the comic whose varieties might be calculated beforehand. This we shall call the *professional comic*.

Instead of taking up these varieties in detail, we prefer to lay stress upon what they have in common. In the forefront we find professional vanity. Each one of M. Jourdain's teachers exalts his own art above all the rest. In a play of Labiche there is a character who cannot understand how it is possible to be anything else than a timber merchant. Naturally he is a timber merchant himself. Note that vanity here tends to merge into *solemnity*, in proportion to the degree of quackery there is in the profession under consideration.

For it is a remarkable fact that the more questionable an art, science or occupation is, the more those who practise it are inclined to regard themselves as invested with a kind of priesthood and to claim that all should bow before its mysteries. Useful professions are clearly meant for the public, but those whose utility is more dubious can only justify their existence by assuming that the public is meant for them: now, this is just the illusion that lies at the root of solemnity. Almost everything comic in Moliere's doctors comes from this source. They treat the patient as though he had been made for the doctors, and nature herself as an appendage to medicine.

Another form of this comic rigidity is what may be called *professsional callousness*. The comic character is so tightly jammed into the rigid frame of his functions that he has no room to move or to be moved like other men. Only call to mind the answer Isabelle receives from Perrin Dandin, the judge, when she asks him how he can bear to look on when the poor wretches are being tortured: "Bah! it always helps to while away an hour or two." Does not Tartuffe also manifest a sort of professional callousness when he says—it is true, by the mouth of Orgon: "Let brother, children, mother and wife all die, what should I care!"

The device most in use, however, for making a profession ludicrous is to confine it, so to say, within the four corners of its own particular jargon. Judge, doctor and soldier are made to apply the language of law, medicine and strategy to the everyday affairs of life, as though they had become incapable of talking like ordinary people. As a rule, this kind of the ludicrous is rather coarse. It becomes more refined, however, as we have already said, if it reveals some peculiarity of character in addition to a professional habit.

We will instance only Regnard's Joueur, who expresses himself with the utmost originality in terms borrowed from gambling, giving his valet the name of Hector, and calling his betrothed Pallas, "from the well-known name of the Queen of Spades." Or Moliere's *Femmes savantes*, where the comic element evidently consists largely in the translation of ideas of a scientific nature into terms of feminine sensibility: "Epicurus is charming," "I dote on vortices," etc. You have only to read the third act to find that Armande, Philaminte and Belise almost invariably express themselves in this style.

Proceeding further in the same direction, we discover that there is also such a thing as a professional logic, i.e., certain ways of reasoning that are customary in certain circles, which are valid for these circles, but untrue for the rest of the public. Now, the contrast between these two kinds of logic—one particular, the other universal—produces comic effects of a special nature, on which we may advantageously dwell at greater length. Here we touch upon a point of some consequence in the theory of laughter. We propose, therefore, to give the question a wider scope and consider it in its most general aspect.

IV

Eager as we have been to discover the deep-seated cause of the comic, we have so far had to neglect one of its most striking phenomena. We refer to the logic peculiar to the comic character and the comic group, a strange kind of logic, which, in some cases, may include a good deal of absurdity.

Theophile Gautier said that the comic in its extreme form was the logic of the absurd. More than one philosophy of laughter revolves round a like idea. Every comic effect, it is said, implies contradiction in some of its aspects. What makes us laugh is alleged to be the absurd realised in concrete shape, a "palpable absurdity"; or, again, an apparent absurdity, which we swallow for the moment only to rectify it immediately afterwards; or, better still, something absurd from one point of view though capable of a natural explanation from another, etc.

All these theories may contain some portion of the truth; but, in the first place, they apply only to certain rather obvious comic effects, and then, even where they do apply, they evidently take no account of the characteristic element of the laughable, that is, the *particular kind* of absurdity the comic contains when it does contain something absurd. Is an immediate proof of this desired? You have only to choose one of these definitions and make up effects in accordance with the formula: twice out of every three times there will be nothing laughable in the effect obtained.

So we see that absurdity, when met with in the comic, is not absurdity *in general*. It is an absurdity of a definite kind. It does not create the comic; rather, we might say that the comic infuses into it its own particular essence. It is not a cause, but an effect—an effect of a very special kind, which reflects the special nature of its cause. Now, this cause is known to us; consequently we shall have no trouble in understanding the nature of the effect.

Assume, when out for a country walk, that you notice on the top of a hill something that bears a faint resemblance to a large motionless body with revolving arms. So far you do not know what it is, but you begin to search amongst your *ideas*—that is to say, in the present instance, amongst the recollections at your disposal—for that recollection which will best fit in with what you see. Almost immediately the image of a windmill comes into your mind: the object before you is a windmill. No matter if, before leaving the house, you have just been reading fairy-tales telling of giants with enormous arms; for although common sense consists mainly in being able to remember, it consists even more in being able to forget.

Common sense represents the endeavour of a mind continually adapting itself anew and changing ideas when it changes objects. It is the mobility of the intelligence conforming exactly to the mobility of things. It is the moving continuity of our attention to life. But now, let us take Don Quixote setting out for the wars. The romances he has been reading all tell of knights encountering, on the way, giant adversaries. He therefore must needs encounter a giant. This idea of a giant is a privileged recollection which has taken its abode in his mind and lies there in wait, motionless, watching for an opportunity to sally forth and become embodied in a thing. It *is bent* on entering the material world, and so the very first object he sees bearing the faintest resemblance to a giant is invested with the form of one. Thus Don Quixote sees giants where we see windmills. This is comical; it is also absurd. But is it a mere absurdity—an absurdity of an indefinite kind?

It is a very special inversion of common sense. It consists in seeking to mould things on an idea of one's own, instead of moulding one's ideas on things—in seeing before us what we are thinking of, instead of thinking of what we see. Good sense would have us leave all our memories in their proper rank and file; then the appropriate memory will every time answer the summons of the situation of the moment and serve only to interpret it. But in Don Quixote, on the contrary, there is one group of memories in command of all the rest and dominating the character itself: thus it is reality that now has to bow to imagination, its only function being to supply fancy with a body. Once the illusion has been created, Don Quixote develops it logically enough in all its consequences; he proceeds with the certainty and precision of a somnambulist who is acting his dream. Such, then, is the origin of his delusions, and such the particular logic which controls this particular absurdity. Now, is this logic peculiar to Don Quixote?

We have shown that the comic character always errs through obstinacy of mind or of disposition, through absentmindedness, in short, through automatism. At the root of the comic there is a sort of rigidity which compels its victims to keep strictly to one path, to follow it straight along, to shut their ears and refuse to listen. In Moliere's plays how many comic scenes can be reduced to this simple type: *A character following up his one idea,* and continually recurring to it in spite of incessant interruptions! The transition seems to take place imperceptibly from the man who will listen to nothing to the one who will see nothing, and from this latter to the one who sees only what he wants to see. A stubborn spirit ends by adjusting things to its own way of thinking, instead of accommodating its thoughts to the things. So every comic character is on the highroad to the above-mentioned illusion, and Don Quixote furnishes us with the general type of comic absurdity.

Is there a name for this inversion of common sense? Doubtless it may be found, in either an acute or a chronic form, in certain types of insanity. In many of its aspects it resembles a fixed idea. But neither insanity in general, nor fixed ideas in particular, are provocative of laughter: they are diseases, and arouse our pity.

Laughter, as we have seen, is incompatible with emotion. If there exists a madness that is laughable, it can only be one compatible with the general health of the mind—a sane type of madness, one might say. Now, there is a sane state of the mind that resembles madness in every respect, in which we find the same associations of ideas as we do in lunacy, the same peculiar logic as in a fixed idea. This state is that of dreams. So either our analysis is incorrect, or it must be capable of being stated in the following theorem: Comic absurdity is of the same nature as that of dreams.

The behaviour of the intellect in a dream is exactly what we have just been describing. The mind, enamoured of itself, now seeks in the outer world nothing more than a pretext for realising its imaginations. A confused murmur of sounds still reaches the ear, colours enter the field of vision, the senses are not completely shut in. But the dreamer, instead of appealing to the whole of his recollections for the interprettation of what his senses perceive, makes use of what he perceives to give substance to the particular recollection he favours: thus, according to the mood of the dreamer and the idea that fills his imagination at the time, a gust of wind blowing down the chimney becomes the howl of a wild beast or a tuneful melody. Such is the ordinary mechanism of illusion in dreams.

Now, if comic illusion is similar to dream illusion, if the logic of the comic is the logic of dreams, we may expect to discover in the logic of the laughable all the peculiarities of dream logic. Here, again, we shall find an illustration of the law with which we are well acquainted: given one form of the laughable, other forms that are lacking in the same comic essence become laughable from their outward resemblance to the first. Indeed, it is not difficult to see that any *play of ideas* may afford us amusement if only it bring back to mind, more or less distinctly, the play of dreamland.

We shall first call attention to a certain general relaxation of the rules of reasoning. The reasonings at which we laugh are those we know to be false, but which we might accept as true were we to hear them in a dream. They counterfeit true reasoning just sufficiently to deceive a mind dropping off to sleep. There is still an element of logic in them, if you will, but it is a logic lacking in tension and, for that very reason, affording us relief from intellectual effort. Many "witticisms" are reasonings of this kind, considerably abridged reasonings, of which we are given only the beginning and the end. Such play upon ideas evolves in the direction of a play upon words in proportion as the relations set up between the ideas become more superficial: gradually we come to take no account of the meaning of the words we hear, but only of their sound.

It might be instructive to compare with dreams certain comic scenes in which one of the characters systematically repeats in a nonsensical fashion what another character whispers in his ear. If you fall asleep with people talking round you, you sometimes find that what they say gradually becomes devoid of meaning, that the sounds get distorted, as it were, and recombine in a haphazard fashion to form in your mind the strangest of meanings, and that you are reproducing between yourself and the different speakers the scene between Petit-Jean and The Prompter (in Racine's *Les Plaideurs*).

There are also *comic obsessions* that seem to bear a great resemblance to dream obsessions. Who has not had the experience of seeing the same image appear in several successive dreams, assuming a plausible meaning in each of them, whereas these dreams had no other point in common. Effects of repetition sometimes present this special form on the stage or in fiction: some of them, in fact, sound as though they belonged to a dream. It may be the same with the burden of many a song: it persistently recurs, always unchanged, at the end of every verse, each time with a different meaning.

Not infrequently do we notice in dreams a particular *crescendo*, a weird effect that grows more pronounced as we proceed. The first concession extorted from reason introduces a second; and this one, another of a more serious nature; and so on till the crowning absurdity is reached. Now, this progress towards the absurd produces on the dreamer a very peculiar sensation. Such is probably the experience of the tippler when he feels himself pleasantly drifting into a state of blankness in which neither reason nor propriety has any meaning for him.

Now, consider whether some of Moliere's plays would not produce the same sensation: for instance, *Monsieur de Pourceaugnac*, which, after beginning almost reasonably, develops into a sequence of all sorts of absurdities. Consider also the *Bourgeois gentilhomme,* where the different characters seem to allow themselves to be caught up in a very whirlwind of madness as the play proceeds. "If it is possible to find a man more completely mad, I will go and publish it in Rome." This sentence, which warns us that the play is over, rouses us from the increasingly extravagant dream into which, along with M. Jourdain, we have been sinking.

But, above all, there is a special madness that is peculiar to dreams. There are certain special contradictions so natural to the imagination of a dreamer, and so absurd to the reason of a man wide-awake, that it would be impossible to give a full and correct idea of their nature to anyone who had not experienced them. We allude to the strange fusion that a dream often effects between two persons who henceforth form only one and yet remain distinct. Generally one of these is the dreamer himself. He feels he has not ceased to be what he is; yet he has become someone else. He is himself, and not himself. He hears himself speak and sees himself act, but he feels that some other "he" has borrowed his body and stolen his voice. Or perhaps he is conscious of speaking and acting as usual, but he speaks of himself as a stranger with whom he has nothing in common; he has stepped out of his own self.

Does it not seem as though we found this same extraordinary confusion in many a comic scene? I am not speaking of *Amphitryon,* in which play the confusion is perhaps suggested to the mind of the spectator, though the bulk of the comic effect proceeds rather from what we have already called a "reciprocal interference of two series." I am speaking of the extravagant and comic reasonings in which we really meet with this confusion in its pure form, though it requires some looking into to pick it out. For instance, listen to Mark Twain's replies to the reporter who called to interview him:

QUESTION. Isn't that a brother of yours?
ANSWER. Oh! yes, yes, yes! Now you remind me of it, that *was* a brother of mine. That's William—Bill we called him. Poor old Bill!
Q. Why? Is he dead, then?

A. Ah! well, I suppose so. We never could tell. There was a great mystery about it.

Q. That is sad, very sad. He disappeared, then?

A. Well, yes, in a sort of general way. We buried him.

Q. *Buried* him! *Buried* him, without knowing whether he was dead or not?

A. Oh no! Not that. He was dead enough.

Q. Well, I confess that I can't understand this. If you buried him, and you knew he was dead . . . .

A. No! no! We only thought he was.

Q. Oh, I see! He came to life again?

A. I bet he didn't.

Q. Well, I never heard anything like this. *Somebody* was dead. *Somebody* was buried. Now, where was the mystery?

A. Ah! that's just it! That's it exactly. You see, we were twins—defunct and I—and we got mixed in the bath-tub when we were only two weeks old, and one of us was drowned. But we didn't know which. Some think it was Bill. Some think it was me.

Q. Well, that is remarkable. What do *you* think?

A. Goodness knows! I would give whole worlds to know. This solemn, this awful tragedy has cast a gloom over my whole life. But I will tell you a secret now, which I have never revealed to any creature before. One of us had a peculiar mark—a large mole on the back of his left hand: that was *me. That child was the one that was drowned!*

A close examination will show us that the absurdity of this dialogue is by no means an absurdity of an ordinary type. It would disappear were not the speaker himself one of the twins in the story. It results entirely from the fact that Mark Twain asserts he is one of these twins, whilst all the time he talks as though he were a third person who tells the tale. In many of our dreams we adopt exactly the same method.

V

Regarded from this latter point of view, the comic seems to show itself in a form somewhat different from the one we lately attributed to it. Up to this point, we have regarded laughter as first and foremost a means of correction. If you take the series of comic varieties and isolate the predominant types at long intervals, you will find that all the intervening varieties borrow their comic quality from their resemblance to these types, and that the types themselves are so many models of impertinence with regard to society. To these impertinences society retorts by laughter, an even greater impertinence. So evidently there is nothing very benevolent in laughter. It seems rather inclined to return evil for evil.

But this is not what we are immediately struck by in our first impression of the laughable. The comic character is often one with whom, to begin with, our mind, or rather our body, sympathises. By this is meant that we put ourselves for a very short time in his place, adopt his gestures, words, arid actions, and, if amused by anything laughable in him, invite him, in imagination, to share his amusement with us; in fact, we treat him first as a playmate. So, in the laugher we find a "hail-fellow-well-met" spirit—as far, at least, as appearances go —which it would be wrong of us not to take into consideration. In particular, there is in laughter a movement of relaxation which has often been noticed, and the reason of which we must try to discover. Nowhere is this impression more noticeable than in the last few examples. In them, indeed, we shall find its explanation.

When the comic character automatically follows up his idea, he ultimately thinks, speaks and acts as though he were dreaming. Now, a dream is a relaxation. To remain in touch with things and men, to see nothing but what is existent and think nothing but what is consistent, demands a continuous effort of intellectual tension. This effort is common sense. And to remain sensible is, indeed, to remain at work. But to detach oneself from things and yet continue to perceive images, to break away from logic and yet continue to string together ideas, is to indulge in play or, if you prefer, *in dolce far niente* [sweet doing nothing, sweet idleness].

So, comic absurdity gives us from the outset the impression of playing with ideas. Our first impulse is to join in the game. That relieves us from the strain of thinking. Now, the same might be said of the other forms of the laughable. Deep-rooted in the comic, there is always a tendency, we said, to take the line of least resistance, generally that of habit. The comic character no longer tries to be ceaselessly adapting and readapting himself to the society of which he is a member. He slackens in the attention that is due to life. He more or less resembles the absentminded. Maybe his will is here even more concerned than his intellect, and there is not so much a want of attention as a lack of tension; still, in some way or another, he is absent, away from his work, taking it easy. He abandons social convention, as indeed—in the case we have just been considering—he abandoned logic. Here, too, our first impulse is to accept the invitation to take it easy. For a short time, at all events, we join in the game. And that relieves us from the strain of living.

But we rest only for a short time. The sympathy that is capable of entering into the impression of the comic is a very fleeting one. It also comes from a lapse in attention. Thus, a stern father may at times forget himself and join in some prank his child is playing, only to check himself at once in order to correct it.

Laughter is, above all, a corrective. Being intended to humiliate, it must make a painful impression on the person against whom it is directed. By laughter, society avenges itself for the liberties taken with it. It would fail in its object if it bore the stamp of sympathy or kindness.

Shall we be told that the motive, at all events; may be a good one, that we often punish because we love, and that laughter, by checking the outer manifestations of certain failings, thus causes the person laughed at to correct these failings and thereby improve himself inwardly?

Much might be said on this point. As a general rule, and speaking roughly, laughter doubtless exercises a useful function. Indeed, the whole of our analysis points to this fact. But it does not therefore follow that laughter always hits the mark or is invariably inspired by sentiments of kindness or even of justice.

To be certain of always hitting the mark, it would have to proceed from an act of reflection. Now, laughter is simply the result of a mechanism set up in us by nature or, what is almost the same thing, by our long acquaintance with social life. It goes off spontaneously and returns tit for tat. It has no time to look where it hits. Laughter punishes certain failing's somewhat as disease punishes certain forms of excess, striking down some who are innocent and sparing some who are guilty, aiming at a general result and incapable of dealing separately with each individual case. And so it is with everything that comes to pass by natural means instead of happening by conscious reflection. An average of justice may show itself in the total result, though the details, taken separately, often point to anything but justice.

In this sense, laughter cannot be absolutely just. Nor should it be kind-hearted either. Its function is to intimidate by humiliating. Now, it would not succeed in doing this, had not nature implanted for that very purpose, even in the best of men, a spark of spitefulness or, at all events, of mischief. Perhaps we had better not investigate this point too closely, for we should not find anything very flattering to ourselves. We should see that this movement of relaxation or expansion is nothing but a prelude to laughter, that the laugher immediately retires within himself, more self-assertive and conceited than ever, and is evidently disposed to look upon another's personality as a marionette of which he pulls the strings. In this presumptuousness we speedily discern a degree of egoism and, behind this latter, something less spontaneous and more bitter, the beginnings of a curious pessimism which becomes the more pronounced as the laugher more closely analyses his laughter.

Here, as elsewhere, nature has utilised evil with a view to good. It is more especially the good that has engaged our attention throughout this work. We have seen that the more society improves, the more plastic is the adaptability it obtains from its members; while the greater the tendency towards increasing stability below, the more does it force to the surface the disturbing elements inseparable from so vast a bulk; and thus laughter performs a useful function by emphasising the form of these significant undulations.

Such is also the truceless warfare of the waves on the surface of the sea, whilst profound peace reigns in the depths below. The billows clash and collide with each other, as they strive to find their level. A fringe of snow-white foam, feathery and frolicsome, follows their changing outlines. From time to time, the receding wave leaves behind a remnant of foam on the sandy beach. The child, who plays hard by, picks up a handful, and, the next moment, is astonished to find that nothing remains in his grasp but a few drops of water, water that is far more brackish, far more bitter than that of the wave which brought it.

Laughter comes into being in the self-same fashion. It indicates a slight revolt on the surface of social life. It instantly adopts the changing forms of the disturbance. It, also, is afroth with a saline base. Like froth, it sparkles. It is gaiety itself. But the philosopher who gathers a handful to taste may find that the substance is scanty, and the aftertaste bitter.

MICHEL FOUCAULT
THIS IS NOT A PIPE

TWO PIPES

The first version, that of 1926 I believe: a carefully drawn pipe, and underneath it (handwritten in a steady, painstaking, artificial scrip! a script from the convent, like that found heading the notebooks of schoolboys or on a blackboard after an object lesson), this note: "This is not a pipe."

The other version—the last, I assume—can be found in *Aube à l'antipode*. The same pipe, same statement same handwriting. But instead of being juxtaposed in a neutral, limitless, unspecified space, the text and the figure are set within a frame. The frame itself is placed upon an easel, and the latter in turn upon the clearly visible slats of the floors. Above everything, a pipe exactly like the one in the picture, but much larger. The first version disconcerts us by its very simplicity. The second multiplies intentional ambiguities before our eyes. standing upright against the easel and resting on wooden pegs, the frame indicates that this is an artist's painting: a finished work, exhibited and bearing for an eventual viewer the statement that comments on or explains it. And yet this naive handwriting, neither precisely the work's title nor one of its pictorial elements; the absence of any other trace of the artist's presence; the roughness of the ensemble; the wide slats of the floor—everything suggests a blackboard in a classroom. Perhaps a swipe of the rag will soon erase the drawing and the text. Perhaps it will erase only one or

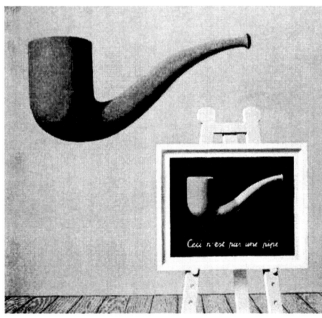

267

the other, in order to correct the "error" (drawing something that will truly not be a pipe, or else writing a sentence affirming that this indeed is a pipe). A temporary slip (a "miswriting" suggesting a misunderstanding) that one gesture will dissipate in white dust?

But this is still only the least of the ambiguities; here are some others. There are two pipes. Or rather must we not say, two drawings of the same pipe? Or yet a pipe and the drawing of that pipe, or yet again two drawings each representing a different pipe? Or two drawings, one representing a pipe and the other not, or two more drawings yet, of which neither the one nor the other are or represent pipes? And so I am surprised to find myself confusing *being* and *representing* as if they were equivalent, as if a sketch were what it represents; and I see well that were I to have to—and I must—dissociate carefully (as the Port Royal *Logic* has asked me to do for more than three centuries) a representation from what it represents, I should have to take up all the hypotheses I just proposed again, and multiply them by two. But it still strikes me that the pipe represented in the drawing—blackboard or canvas, little matter—this "lower" pipe is wedged solidly in a space of visible reference points: width (the written text the upper and lower borders of the frame) and depth (the grooves of the floor). A stable prison.

On the other hand, the higher pipe lacks coordinates. Its enormous proportions render uncertain its location (an opposite effect to that found in *Tombeau des lutteurs* [*The Wrestler's Tomb*], where the gigantic is caught inside the most precise space). Is the disproportionate pipe drawn in front of the painting, which itself rests far in back? Or, indeed, is it suspended just above the easel like an emanation, a mist just detaching itself from the painting-pipe smoke taking the form and roundness of a pipe, thus opposing and resembling the pipe (according to the same play of analogy and contrast found between the vaporous and the solid in the series *La Bataille de l'Argonne* [*The Battle of the Argonne*])? Or might we not suppose, in the end, that the pipe floats behind the painting and the easel, more gigantic than it appears? In that case, would it be its up- rooted depth, the inner dimension rupturing the canvas (or panel) and slowly, in a space henceforth without reference point, expanding to infinity?

About even this ambiguity, however, I am ambiguous. Or, rather, what appears to me very dubious is the simple opposition between the higher pipe's dislocated buoyancy and the stability of the lower one. Looking a bit more closely, we easily discern that the feet of the easel, supporting the frame where the canvas is held and where the drawing is lodged—these feet resting upon a floor made certain and visible by its own coarseness, are in fact beveled. They touch only by three tiny points, robbing the ensemble, itself somewhat ponderous, of all stability. An impending fall? The collapse of easel, frame, canvas or panel, drawing, text? Splintered wood, fragmented shapes, letters scattered one from another until words can perhaps no longer be reconstituted? All this litter on the ground, while above, the large pipe without measure or reference point will linger in its inaccessible, balloon-like immobility?

THE UNRAVELED CALLIGRAM

Magritte's drawing (for the moment I speak only of the first version) is as simple as a page borrowed from a botanical manual: a figure and the text that names it. Nothing is easier to recognize than a pipe, drawn thus; nothing is easier to say—our language knows it well in our place—than the "name of a pipe." Now, what lends the figure its strangeness is not the "contradiction" between the image and the text. For a good reason: contradiction could exist only between two statements, or within one and the same statement. Here there is clearly but one, and it cannot be contradictory because the subject of the proposition is a simple demonstrative. False, then? But who would seriously contend that the collection of intersecting lines above the text is a pipe? Must we say: My God, how simpleminded! What misleads us is the inevitability of connecting the text to the drawing (as the demonstrative pronoun, the meaning of the word pipe, and the likeness of the image all invite us to do here)—and the impossibility of defining a perspective that would let us say that the assertion is true, false, or contradictory.

I cannot dismiss the notion that the sorcery here lies in an operation rendered invisible by the simplicity of its result but which alone can explain the vague uneasiness provoked. The operation is a calligram that Magritte has secretly constructed, then carefully unraveled. Each element of the figure, their reciprocal position, and their relationship derive from this process, annulled as soon as it has been accomplished.

In its time-honored tradition, the calligram has a triple role: to augment the alphabet, to repeat something without the aid of rhetoric, to trap things in a double cipher. First it brings a text and a shape as close together as possible. It is composed of lines delimiting the form of an object while also arranging the sequence of letters. It lodges statements in the space of a shape, and makes the text say what the drawing represents. On the one hand, it alphabetizes the ideogram, populates it with discontinuous letters, and thus interrogates the silence of uninterrupted lines. But on the other hand, it distributes writing in a space no longer possessing the neutrality, openness, and inert blankness of paper. It forces the ideogram to arrange itself accordingly to the laws of a simultaneous form. For the blink of an eye, it reduces phoneticism to a mere gray murmur completing the con tours of the shape; but it renders outline as a thin skin that must be pierced in order to follow, word for word, the outpouring of its internal text.

The calligram is thus tautological—but in opposition to rhetoric. The latter toys with the fullness of language. It uses the possibility of repeating the same thing in different words, and profits from the extra richness of language that allows us to say different things with a single word. The essence of rhetoric is in allegory. The calligram uses that capacity of letters to signify both as linear elements that can be arranged in space and as signs that must unroll according to a unique chain of sound. As a sign, the letter permits us to fix words; as line, it lets us give shape to things. Thus the calligram aspires playfully to efface the oldest oppositions of our alphabetical civilization: to show and to name; to shape and to say; to reproduce and to articulate; to imitate and to signify; to look and to read.

Pursuing its quarry by two paths, the calligram sets the most perfect trap. By its double function, it guarantees capture, as neither discourse alone nor a pure drawing could do. It banishes the invincible absence that defeats words, imposing on them, by the ruses of a writing at play in space, the visible form of their reference. Cleverly arranged on a sheet of paper, signs invoke the very thing of which they speak—from outside, by the margin they outline, by the emergence of their mass on the blank space of the page. And in return, visible form is excavated, furrowed by words that work at it from within, and which, dismissing the immobile, ambiguous, nameless presence, spin forth the web of significations that christen it, determine it, fix it in the universe of discourse. A double trap, unavoidable snare: How, henceforth, would the flight of birds, the transitory form of flowers, the falling rain escape?

And now Magritte's drawing. It seems to be created from the fragments of an unraveled calligram. Under the guise of reverting to a previous arrangement, it recovers its three functions—but in order to pervert them, thereby disturbing all the traditional bonds of language and the image.

After having invaded the figure in order to reconstitute the old ideogram, the text has now resumed its place. It has returned to its natural site-below the image, where it serves to support it insert it in the series of texts and in the pages of the book. Once more it becomes a "legend." Form itself reascends to the ethereal realm from which the complicity of letters with space had forced it for an instant to descend. Free from all discursive attachment it can float anew in its natural silence. We return to the page, and to its old principle of distribution—but only apparently. Because the words we now can read underneath the drawing are themselves drawn-images of words the painter has set apart from the pipe, but within the general (yet still undefinable) perimeter of the picture. From the calligraphic pas! which I am quite obliged to extend to them, the words have conserved their logical relationship to the drawing, and their state as something drawn.

Consequently, I must read them superimposed upon themselves. At the surface of the image, they form the reflection of a sentence saying that this is not a pipe. The image of a text. But conversely, the represented pipe is drawn by the same hand and with the same pen as the letters of the text: it extends the writing more than it illustrates it or fills its void. We might imagine it brimming with small, chaotic letters, graphic signs reduced to fragments and dispersed over the entire surface of the image. A figure in the shape of writing. The invisible, preliminary calligraphic operation intertwined the writing and the drawing—and when Magritte restored things to their own places, he took care that the shape remain written, and that the text never be anything more than the drawn representation of itself.

The same for tautology. From calligraphic doubling, Magritte seemingly returns to the simple correspondence of the image with its legend. Without saying anything, a mute and adequately recognizable figure displays the object in its essence; from the image, a name written below receives its "meaning" or rule for usage. Now, compared to the traditional function of the legend, Magritte's text is doubly paradoxical. It sets out to name something that evidently does not need to be named (the form is too well known, the label too familiar). And at the moment when he should reveal the name, Magritte does so by denying that the object is what it is. Whence comes this strange game, if not from the calligram?

From the calligram that says things twice (when once would doubtless do); from the calligram that, without seeming to do so, introduced a negative relationship between what it shows and what it represents. For, in sketching out a bouquet, a bird, or a downpour by a scattering of letters, the calligram never says of those hypocritically spontaneous forms that "this is a dove, a flower, a crashing downpour"; it avoids naming what the disposition of letters sketches. Show what happens through words, in the half silence of letters; do not say what these lines are which, at the borders of the text limit it and carve it up. Once Magritte makes the text fall outside the image, it is up to the statement, for its own part, to recapture that negative relation, and to make I! in the syntax that belongs to it a negation. The "not to say" that animates the calligram silently from inside is now said from the outside, in the verbal form of "not." But the text that runs beneath the pipe must simultaneously be able to say several things to the calligram that is hidden behind it.

"This" (the drawing, whose form you doubtless recognize and whose calligraphic heritage I have just traced) "is not" (is not substantially bound to . . . , is not constituted by . . . , does not cover the same material as . . .) "a pipe" (that is, this word from your language, made up of pronounceable sounds that translate the letters you are reading). But at the same time, the text states an entirely different thing: "This" (the statement arranging itself beneath your eyes in a line of discontinuous elements, of which this is both the signifier and the first word) "is not" (could neither equal nor substitute for . . . , could not adequately represent . . .) "a pipe" (one of the objects whose possible rendering can be seen above the text, interchangeable, anonymous, inaccessible to any name).

Now, on the whole, it easily seems that Magritte's statement is negated by the immediate and reciprocal dependency between the drawing of the pipe and the text by which the pipe can be named.

Designation and design do not overlap one another, save in the calligraphic play hovering in the ensemble's background and conjured away simultaneously by the text, the drawing, and their current separation. Hence the third function of the statement: "This" (this ensemble constituted by a written pipe and a drawn text) "is not" (is incompatible with) "a pipe" (this mixed element springing at once from discourse and the image, whose ambiguous being the verbal and visual play of the calligram wants to evoke).

 A third perturbation: Magritte reopened the trap the calligram had sprung on the thing it described. But in the act the object itself escaped. On the page of an illustrated book, we seldom pay attention to the small space running above the words and below the drawings, forever serving them as a common frontier for ceaseless crossings. It is there, on these few millimeters of white, the calm sand of the page, that are established all the relations of designation, nomination, description, classification. The calligram absorbed that interstice; but once opened, it does not restore it The trap shattered on emptiness: image and text fall each to its own side, of their own weight. No longer do they have a common ground nor a place where they can meet where words are capable of taking shape and images of entering into lexical order. The slender, colorless, neutral strip, which in Magritte's drawing separates the text and the figure, must be seen as a crevasse—an uncertain, foggy region now dividing the pipe floating in its imagistic heaven from the mundane tramp of words marching in their successive line.

 Still, it is too much to claim that there is a blank or lacuna: instead, it is an absence of space, an effacement of the "common place" between the signs of writing and the lines of the image. The "pipe" that was at one with both the statement naming it and the drawing representing it—this shadow pipe knitting the lineaments of form with the fiber of words—has utterly vanished. A disappearance that from the other side of this chasm the text confirms sadly: This is not a pipe. In vain the now-solitary drawing imitates as closely as possible the shape ordinarily designated by the word *pipe*, in vain the text unfurls below the drawing with all the attentive fidelity of a label in a scholarly book. No longer can anything pass between them save the decree of divorce, the statement at once contesting the name of the drawing and the reference of the text.

On this basis, we can understand Magritte's second version of *This Is Not a Pipe*. In placing the drawing of the pipe and the statement serving as its legend on the very clearly defined surface of a picture (insofar as it is a painting, the letters are but the image of letters; insofar as it is a blackboard, the figure is only the didactic continuation of a discourse), in placing the picture on a thick, solid wood tri- pod, Magritte does everything necessary to reconstruct (either by the permanence of a work of art or else by the truth of an object lesson) the space common to language and the image. But this surface is contested at once: for the pipe that Magritte had, with so many precautions, brought near the text that he had enclosed with the text in the institutional rectangle of the printing, has indeed taken flight. It is above, floating without reference, leaving between the text and the shape that one might have said to be at once the tie and the point of convergence to the horizon only a small empty space, the narrow furrow of its absence as the unsignaled mark of its escape. So, on its beveled and visibly unstable mounts, the easel had any longer but to tilt, the frame to loosen, the picture and the pipe to roll on the ground, the letters to be scattered. The commonplace—banal *oeuvre* or mundane lesson—has disappeared.

KLEE, KANDINSKY, MAGRITTE

Two principles, I believe, ruled western painting from the fifteenth to the twentieth century. The first asserts the separation between plastic representation (which implies resemblance) and linguistic reference (which excludes it). This distinction is typically made in such a way that it allows for one or the other of two forms of subordination. Either the text is ruled by the image (as in those paintings where a book, an inscription, a letter, or the name of a person are represented); or else the image is ruled by the text (as in books where a drawing completes, as if it were merely taking a short cut the message that words are charged to represent). True, the subordination remains stable only very rarely. What happens to the text of the book is that it becomes merely a commentary on the image, and the linear channel, through words, of its simultaneous forms; and what happens to the picture is that it is dominated by a text, all of whose significations it figuratively illustrates.

But no matter the meaning of the subordination or the manner in which it prolongs, multiplies, and reverses itself. What is essential is that verbal signs and visual representations are never given at once. An order always hierarchizes them. This is the principle whose sovereignty Klee abolished, by showing the juxtaposition of shapes and the syntax of signs in an uncertain, reversible, floating space (simultaneously page and canvas, plane and volume, notebook graph and ground survey, map and chronicle). He produced both systems of representation in the interweaving of just one fabric. In so doing (in contrast to the calligraphers, who reinforced the play of reciprocal subordinations even while multiplying it), he overturned their common space and undertook to build a new one.

The second principle posits an equivalence between the fact of resemblance and the affirmation of a representative bond. Let a figure resemble an object (or some other figure), let there be a relation of analogy between them, and that alone is enough for there to slip into the pure play of the painting a statement— obvious, banal, repeated a thousand times yet almost always silent. (It is like an infinite murmur—haunting, enclosing the silence of figures, investing it, mastering it extricating the silence from itself, and finally reversing it within the domain of things that can be named.) "What you see is *that.*" No matter, again, in what sense the representative relation is posed—whether the painting is referred to the visible world around it, or whether it independently establishes an invisible world that resembles itself. The essential point is that resemblance and affirmation cannot be dissociated. The rupture of this principle can be ascribed to Kandinsky: not because he had dissociated the terms but because he gave leave simultaneously to resemblance and the representation function.

No one, apparently, is further from Klee and Kandinsky than Magritte. More than any other his painting seems wedded to exact resemblances, to the point where they willfully multiply as if to assert themselves. It is not enough that the drawing of the pipe so closely resembles a pipe which in turn . . . and so on. A painting more committed than any other to the careful and cruel separation of graphic and plastic elements. If they happen to be superimposed within the painting like a legend and its image, it is on condition that the statement contest the obvious identity of the figure, and the name we are prepared to give it. And yet Magritte's art is not foreign to the enterprise of Klee and Kandinsky. Rather it constitutes, on the basis of a system common to them all, a figure at once opposed and complementary.

THE MUFFLED WORK OF WORDS

The exteriority of written and figurative elements, so obvious in Magritte, is symbolized by the nonrelation—or in any case by the very complex and problematic relation—between the painting and its title. This gulf, which prevents us from being both the reader and the viewer at the same time, brings the image into abrupt relief above the horizontal line of words. "The titles are chosen in such a way as to keep anyone from assigning my paintings to the familiar region that habitual thought appeals to in order to escape perplexity." A little like the anonymous hand that designated the pipe by the statement, "This is not a pipe," Magritte names his paintings in order to focus attention upon the very act of naming. And yet in this split and drifting space, strange bonds are knit, there occur intrusions, brusque and destructive invasions, avalanches of images into the milieu of words, and verbal lightning flashes that streak and shatter the drawings. Patiently, Klee constructed a space without name or geometry, tangling the chain of signs with the fiber of figures. Magritte secretly mines a space he seems to maintain in the old arrangement. But he excavates it with words: and the old pyramid of perspective is no more than a molehill about to cave in.

In any reasonable drawing a subscript such as "This is not a pipe" is enough immediately to divorce the figure from itself, to isolate it from its space, and to set it floating—whether near or apart from itself, whether similar to or unlike itself, no one knows. Against *Ceci n'est pas une pipe* there is *L'Art de la conversation* [*The Art of Conversation*]: in a landscape of battling giants or of the beginning of the world, two tiny persons are speaking—an inaudible discourse, a murmur instantly reabsorbed into the silence of the stones, into the silence of a wall whose enormous blocks overhang the two garrulous mutes. Jumbled together, the blocks form at their base a group of letters where it is easy to make out the word: REVE [*dream*]—as if all these airy fragile words had been given the power to organize the chaos of stones. Or as if, on the contrary, behind the alert but immediately lost chatter of men, things could in their silence and sleep compose a word—a permanent word no one could efface; yet this word now designates the most fleeting of images.

But this is not all: because it is in dream that men, at last reduced to silence, commune with the signification of things and allow themselves to be touched by enigmatic, insistent words that come from elsewhere. *Ceci n'est pas une pipe* exemplifies the penetration of discourse into the form of things; it reveals discourse's ambiguous power to deny and to redouble. *L'Art de la conversation* marks the anonymous attraction of things that form their own words in the face of men's indifference, insinuating themselves, without men even being aware of it into their daily chatter.

Between the two extremes, Magritte's work deploys the play of words and images. The countenance of an absolutely serious man, unsmiling, unblinking, "breaks up" with a laughter that comes from nowhere. The "might that falls" cannot fall without shattering a windowpane whose fragments (still retaining, on their sharp edges and glass shards, the sun's reflections) are scattered on the floor and sin. Referring to the sun's disappearance as a "fall," the words have swept along, with the image they evoke, not only the windowpane but the other sun, the twin sun perfectly outlined on the smooth and transparent glass. Like a clapper in a bell, the key stands vertically "in the keyhole": it rings forth the familiar expression until it becomes absurd.

Moreover, listen to Magritte: "Between words and objects one can create new relations and specify characteristics of language and objects generally ignored in everyday life." Or again: "Sometimes the name of an object takes the place of an image. A word can take the place of an object in reality. An image can take the place of a word in a proposition." And the following statement, conveying no contradicttion but referring to the inextricable tangle of words and images and to the absence of a common ground to sustain them: "In a painting, words are of the same cloth as images. Rather one sees images and words differently in a painting."

Make no mistake—in a space where every element seems to obey the sole principle of resemblance and plastic representation, linguistic signs (which had an excluded aura, which prowled far around the image, which the title's arbitrariness seemed to have banished forever) have surreptitiously reapproached. Into the solidity of the image, into its meticulous resemblance, they have introduced a disorder—an order pertaining to the eyes alone. They have routed the object revealing its filmy thinness.

In order to deploy his plastic signs, Klee wove a new space. Magritte allows the old space of representation to rule, but only at the surface, no more than a polished stone, bearing words and shapes: beneath, nothing. It is a gravestone: the incisions that drew figures and those that marked letters communicate only by void, the nonplace hidden beneath marble solidity. I win note that this absence reascends to the surface and impinges upon the painting itself. When Magritte offers his version of *Madame Recamier* or *La Balcon* [*The Balcony*], he replaces the traditional paintings' characters with coffins. Invisibly contained between waxen oak planks, emptiness un does the space composed by the volume of living bodies, the arrangement of clothing, the direction of the gaze and all the faces that are about to speak. The "non-place" emerges "in person"—in place of persons and where no one is present any longer.

SEVEN SEALS OF AFFIRMATION

With a sovereign and unique gesture, Kandinsky dismissed the old equivalence between resemblance and affirmation, freeing painting from both. Magritte proceeds by dissociating the two: disrupting their bonds, establishing their inequality, bringing one into play without the other, maintaining that which stems from painting, and excluding that which is closest to discourse-pursuing as closely as possible the indefinite continuation of the similar, but excising from it any affirmation that would attempt to say what is resembled. An art of the "Same," liberated from the "as if." We are farthest from *trompe l'oeil*. The latter seeks to support the weightiest burden of affirmation by the ruse of a convincing resemblance: "What you see on the wall's surface is not an aggregate of lines and colors. It is depth, sky, clouds that have shaded your house, a real column around which you could walk, a stairway that continues the steps you have begun to climb (already you start toward it despite yourself), a stone balustrade over which lean the attentive faces of ladies and courtiers, wearing clothes identical to your own, to the very ribbons, smiling at your astonishment and your own smiles, gesturing to you in a fashion that is mysterious because they have answered you without even waiting for your own gestures to them."

Magritte's text which speaks right next to that pipe most like a pipe, stands opposed to such affirmations, resting upon such analogies. But who speaks in their singular text in which the most elementary of affirmations is conjured?

First the pipe itself: "What you see here, the lines I form or that form me, is not a pipe as you doubtless believe; but only a drawing, while the real pipe, reposing in its essence quite beyond every artificial gesture, floating in the element of its ideal truth, is above—look, just above the painting where I am, a simple and solitary similitude." To which the higher pipe responds in the same statement: "What you see floating before your eyes, beyond space and without fixed foundation, this mist that settles neither on canvas nor on a page, how could it really be a pipe? Don't be misled: I am mere similarity —not something similar to a pipe, but the cloudy similitude that, referring to nothing, traverses texts and makes texts such as the one you can read and drawings such as the one below communicate." But the statement, already articulated twice by different voices, in turn comes forward to speak for itself. "The letters that form me and that you see—the moment you try to read them as naming the pipe, how can they say that they are a pipe, these things so divorced from what they name? This is a graphism that resembles only itself, and that could never replace what it describes." But there is more. Two by two the voices mingle to say a third element is not a pipe.

Bound together by the frame of the painting enclosing them, the text and the rower pipe enter into complicity: The designating power of words and the illustrative power of drawing denounce the higher pipe, and refuse the abstract apparition the right to call itself a pipe, because its unanchored existence renders it mute and invisible. Bound together by their reciprocal similitude, the two pipes contest the written statement's right to call itself a pipe, for it is composed of signs with no resemblance to the thing they designate. Bound together by the fact that they each come from elsewhere, that one is a discourse capable of conveying truth while the other is like the ghost of a thing-in-itself, the text and the higher pipe join to assert that the pipe in the painting is not a pipe.

And perhaps it must be supposed that beside these three elements, a siteless voice speaks in this statement, and that a formless hand wrote it; it would be in speaking at once of the painting's pipe, of the pipe that rises up above, and of the text that is writing, that this anonym would say: "None of these is a pipe, but rather a text that simulates a pipe; a drawing of a pipe that simulates a drawing of a pipe; a pipe (drawn other than as a drawing) that resembles a pipe (drawn after a pipe that itself would be other than a drawing)." Seven discourses in a single statement—more than enough to demolish the fortress where similitude was the prisoner of the assertion of resemblance.

Henceforth similitude is restored to itself—unfolding from itself and folding back upon itself. It is no longer the finger perpendicularly crossing the surface of the canvas in order to refer to something else. It inaugurates a play of analogies that run, proliferate, propagate, and correspond within the layout of the painting, affirming and representing nothing. Thus in Magritte's art we find infinite games of purified similitude that never overflow the painting. They establish metamorphoses—but in what sense? Is it the plant whose leaves take flight and become birds, or the birds that drown and slowly botanize themselves, sinking into the ground with a final quiver of greenery (*Les Grâces naturelles* [*The Natural Graces*], *La Saveur des larmes* [*The Flavor of Tears*])? Is it a woman who "takes to the bottle" or the bottle that feminizes itself by becoming a "nude-study" (here composing a disturbance of plastic elements because of the latent insertion of verbal signs and the play of an analogy that affirming nothing, is doubly activated by the playfulness or the statement)? Instead of blending identities, it happens that similitude also has the power to destroy them: a woman's torso is sectioned into three parts (increasingly large as we move from top to bottom). While holding back all affirmation of identity, the shared proportions guarantee analogy: three segments lacking a fourth in just the same fashion, though the fourth element is incalculable. The head (final element = x) is missing: *Folie des grandeurs* [*Delusions of Grandeur*], says the title.

Another way analogy is freed from its old complicity with representative affirmation; perfidiously mixing (and by a ruse that seems to indicate just the opposite of what means) the painting and what it is supposed to represent. Evidently this is a way of affirming that the painting is indeed its own model. But, in fact, such an affirmation would imply an interior distance, a divergence, a disjuncture between the canvas and what it is supposed to mimic. For Magritte, on the contrary, there exists from the painting to the model of a perfect continuity of scene, a linearity, a continuous overflowing of one into the other. Either by gliding from left to right (as in *La Condition humaine* [*The Human Condition*]), where the sea's horizon follows the horizon on the canvas without a break); or by the inversion of distances (as in *La Cascade* [*The Waterfall*]), where the model invades the canvas, envelops it on all sides, and gives it the appearance of being behind what ought to be on its far side).

Opposed to this analogy that denies representation by erasing duality and distance, there—is the contrary one that evades or mocks it by means of the snare of doubling. In L*e soir qui tombe* [*Night Fall*] the windowpane bears a red sun analogous to the one hung in the sky (against Descartes and the way in which he resolved the two suns of appearance within the unity of representation). This is the converse of *La Lunette d'approche* [*Telescope*]: through the transparence of a window can be seen the passing of clouds and the sparkle of a blue sea; but the window opens into black void, showing this to be a reflection of nothing.

TO PAINT IS NOT TO AFFIRM

Rigorous separation between linguistic signs and plastic elements: equivalence of resemblance and affirmation. These two principles constituted the tension in classical painting, because the second reintroduced discourse (affirmation exists only where there is speech) into an art from which the linguistic element was rigorously excluded. Hence the fact that classical painting spoke—and spoke constantly—while constituting itself entirely outside language; hence the fact that it rested silently in a discursive space; hence the fact that it provided, beneath itself, a kind of common ground where it could restore the bonds of signs and the image.

Magritte knits verbal signs and plastic elements together, but without referring them to a prior isotopism. He skirts the base of affirmative discourse on which resemblance calmly reposes, and he brings pure similitudes and nonaffirmative verbal statements into play within the instability of a disoriented volume and an unmapped space. A process whose formulation is, in some sense, given by *Ceci n'est pas une pipe*.

1. To employ a calligram where are all found, simultaneously present and visible, image, text, resemblance, affirmation, and their common ground.

2. Then suddenly to open it up, so that the calligram immediately decomposes and disappears, leaving as a trace only its own absence.

3. To allow discourse to collapse of its own weight and to acquire the visible shape of letters. Letters which, insofar as they are drawn, enter into an uncertain, indefinite relation, confused with the drawing itself—but minus any area to serve as a common ground.

4. To allow similitudes, on the other hand, to multiply of themselves, to be born from their own vapor and to rise endlessly into an ether where they refer to nothing other than themselves.

5. To verify clearly, at the end of the operation, that the precipitate has changed color, that it has gone from black to white, that the "This is a pipe" has become "This is not a pipe." In short, that painting has stopped affirming.

SOURCES

Plato, *Symposium*
Translated by Benjamin Jowett, *Dialogues of Plato*, 3rd ed. (1891)
Reproduced under Creative Commons licence from
http://ebooks.adelaide.edu.au/p/plato/

Plato, *Republic*
Translated by Benjamin Jowett, *Dialogues of Plato*, 3rd ed. (1891)
Reproduced under Creative Commons licence from
http://ebooks.adelaide.edu.au/p/plato/

Aristotle, *Poetics*
Translated by S. H. Butcher
Reproduced under Creative Commons licence from
http://ebooks.adelaide.edu.au/a/aristotle/

Plotinus, *Concerning the Beautiful* (*Enneads* 1.6)
Translated by Thomas Taylor
Reproduced under Creative Commons licence from Project Gutenberg
EBook #29510
http://www.gutenberg.org/2/9/5/1/29510/

David Hume, *Of the Standard of Taste*
Copyright Jonathon Bennett
By permission of www.earlymoderntexts.com

Immanuel Kant, *Critique of Judgment*
Translated by James Creed Meredith
Licenced under Creative Commons Licence from
http://ebooks.adelaide.edu.au/k/kant/immanuel/k16j/

G.W.F. Hegel, *The Philosophy of Fine Art*
Translated by J. Loewenberg
Licenced under Creative Commons Licence from Project Gutenberg
EBook #12351
http://www.gutenberg.org/cache/epub/12351/pg12351.html

Arthur Schopenhauer, *The Metaphysics of Fine Art*
From *Religion: A Dialogue and Other Essays* by Arthur Schopenhauer, trans. T. Bailey Saunders, 3rd edition (London: Swan Sonnenschein & Co., 1891)

http://www.thule-italia.net/sitoinglese/Arthur%20Schopenhauer%20-%20Religion%20And%20Other%20Essays.pdf

Friedrich Nietzsche, *The Birth of Tragedy*
Translated by Ian Johnson
http://records.viu.ca/~johnstoi/Nietzsche/tragedy_all.htm#n28

Henri Bergson, Laughter: An Essay on the Meaning of the Comic (1911)
Project Gutenberg EBook #4352 (2003)

Michel Foucault, *This is Not a Pipe*
from *Aesthetics, Method, and Epistemology, Essential Works of Foucault*, ed. James D. Faubion, vol. 2 (New York: New Press, 1998), 187-202.